THE
ANCIENT AND RIGHTFUL
CUSTOMS

Geoffrey Chaucer, Controller of Customs, London Port, 1374-86. Sixteenth century painting on wood hanging in the Board Room, King's Beam House.

THE
ANCIENT AND RIGHTFUL
CUSTOMS

A HISTORY OF THE ENGLISH CUSTOMS SERVICE

EDWARD CARSON

FOREWORD BY
A. W. TAYLOR, C.B.

ARCHON BOOKS
1972

First published in 1972 by
Faber & Faber Limited

First published in the United States of America by
Archon Books
The Shoe String Press, Inc.
995 Sherman Avenue, Hamden,
Connecticut, 06514

ISBN 0–208–01271–0 All rights reserved

Printed in Great Britain

TO MY WIFE

CONTENTS

ACKNOWLEDGEMENTS
AND AUTHOR'S NOTE

I should like to thank Her Majesty's Commissioners of Customs and Excise and Her Majesty's Stationery Office for their assistance and permission to consult their Departmental records. The frontispiece is reproduced by kind permission of the Department of the Environment.

I should also point out that *The Ancient and Rightful Customs* is not an official publication and that the responsibility for the contents of this book lies with the author entirely

FOREWORD

There have been previous histories of both the Customs and the Excise but the time is ripe for another. Mr. Carson is eminently qualified to produce it. As the Department's Librarian and the keeper of its archives he has been responsible in recent years for assembling and collating many hundreds of volumes of the Department's historical records which were previously inaccessible, and he has drawn extensively on this new material.

It is a fascinating story that he has to tell. There were financial and economic problems in past centuries as now; but then as now decisions taken to resolve them would have had little significance without an organization to put them into effect. In the times of which Mr. Carson writes this responsibility fell mainly to the Customs Service, which was later paralleled by, and ultimately amalgamated with, the Excise Service.

No doubt, in an inarticulate way, the object of the Revenue Services has always been to collect the money required by the Government of the day (and to enforce such other measures as quarantine), with a minimum of disturbance to legitimate trade: to deter and prevent – rather than detect – evasion. Most of the work of the Department is thus concerned with matters of efficiency and economy, quiet progress and ready adaptability, rather than excitement and drama. But interesting happenings still abound and our past records are full of them.

The work has always spanned the scale from relations with the most illustrious to the most ordinary (or eccentric) of citizens; from important public affairs to homely and individual matters; from thrilling and entertaining incidents to the more sordid aspects of commercial life. By weaving into the historic tapestry a well-chosen selection of such anecdotes Mr. Carson has provided a graphic and informative account of the growth and development of a Department which goes back further than any other

9

into the origins of Government administration. He thus throws
fresh light on one area of our national history which does not always attract the attention it deserves.

A. W. TAYLOR   BOARD ROOM, H.M. CUSTOMS AND EXCISE, 1969

INTRODUCTION

This book is primarily intended to provide an insight into the history of the Customs and Excise Department from the time when a permanent administration was set up in 1671. It has been thought desirable, however, to include a brief survey of the earlier history.

It is hoped that the work will be of some assistance to scholars and students and an attempt has been made in the course of the text to convey the type of information which is contained in the records of the Department, which is by no means restricted to purely revenue matters.

It would be neither practicable nor desirable to attempt to cover the whole history of the Customs and Excise in these pages. Quite a number of books and articles have already been written on particular aspects of the Service and its administration and details of these are given in the bibliography. There is a great deal of scope for many more such works and there is no doubt that much more will be written.

In carrying out this task I have been particularly fortunate, inasmuch as the Outport Records of the Department have now been centralized as a result of the Public Records Act 1958, and are at present in the custody of the Commissioners of Customs and Excise together with the Headquarters' Records. Details of these records and the periods they cover are given in Appendix A.

I must acknowledge my great indebtedness to my predecessors in the Customs and Excise Library, to Henry Atton who, with H. H. Holland, produced the two volumes of *The King's Customs* and also did a great deal of pioneer work on the records of the Department; to Bertram R. Leftwich who also carried out much painstaking work on the records and produced a great deal of unpublished material and, above all, to Rupert C. Jarvis with whom I was privileged to work and who by his great enthusiasm and scholarly examination of many aspects of Customs and Excise history imbued me with my interest in the subject.

I have attempted to describe the general pattern of development without going into too much detail about any particular facet. To many people the history of Customs and Excise is the story of smuggling, but this is far from true. Even in the eighteenth century when smuggling was at its height, the Customs Service, apart from dealing with the large amount of cargo imported and exported legitimately, was also carrying out the numerous duties imposed on the Service for administrative convenience because there was no other official means of doing the work.

One has only to think of the difficult and often dangerous task of putting the Quarantine Laws into operation, of the vast amount of time spent in applying the Navigation Laws and the resultant system of Ships' Registry. There was also the difficult assignment of salving wrecks and trying to save lives while being hampered by hostile crowds intent on looting, the great amount of investigation and correspondence in connection with the ownership of wreck, the attempts to prevent the emigration of skilled tradesmen in the eighteenth century and the control of immigrants in the nineteenth century. The compiling of trade statistics, the defence of shipping against marauding privateers, the collection of Light Dues, the arresting of ships, acting as Shipping Masters, were some of the tasks which occupied the time of the Revenue Officers. Many of these duties are still performed by the Customs Service of today and now as then, take up a great deal of time, but they are carried out cheerfully in the knowledge that they represent a service to the community.

Although fighting smuggling was not the only preoccupation of the Service, it must be admitted that 'illicit trading' has always loomed large in Customs history, and is indeed the 'raison d'être' of a large part of the Service.

My information has been for the greater part derived from the records which are in my care, and I have in many cases been able to make use of the verbatim accounts of officers who were engaged in the war against illicit traders, to tell the story from their point of view.

Unfortunately there are many gaps in the records, the greatest of all being in the Headquarters' records of which very few survived the disastrous fire at the London Custom House in 1814. Another great loss was the total destruction by enemy action in the last war of all the Liverpool records apart from the Ships' Registers. During the Reform Law Riots of 1831 the Bristol Custom House was burnt down and all the Customs records of this ancient port went up in smoke. There were other losses which cannot be accounted for, but the Outport records 'in toto' form a most wonderful archive which is rich in material and will provide a happy hunting ground for researchers for many a long day.

In order to maintain a reasonable chronological sequence I have found it necessary to move from one area of the country to another, and to avoid undue interruption to the flow of the narrative I have attempted to deal with some of the more technical aspects of the work of the Service in the Appendices.

Finally, I should like to express my gratitude to Mr. Alan Card and Mr. Maurice Nockles for reading through the manuscript and making useful suggestions.

Chapter 1

EARLY CUSTOMS TOLLS

It is not known when the word 'Customs' was first applied to import and export duties, but it may be presumed that the expression antedated the Magna Carta in view of the reference therein to the 'rectae et antiquae consuetudinae'. It is probable that the earliest of such imposts were 'tolls in kind', particularly during the Roman occupation of Britain. According to Tacitus, the Britons had to provide corn, fodder and so on, for the Roman army of occupation, and it seems likely enough that imported goods were taxed. But up to the present there is no actual evidence of this.

The first written record of such taxation which has come to light is contained in a charter of *c.* 742 by Aethelbald, King of Mercia, to the Abbey of Worcester. Here it was stated, 'I have allowed them all the dues of the two ships which shall be there demanded by the Collectors in the Hithe of London Town.' Three years later a similar charter to the Bishop of London runs as follows: 'I grant to thee, Ingwald, Bishop of London, in perpetuity, the toll and tribute of one ship which formerly accrued to me of right . . .'

Over two hundred years later, in the reign of Ethelred the Unready, another document in the form of a law reputed to have been made by the King at a Witanagemot at Wantage relates to taxes at Billingsgate. It is interesting to note that men from Flanders, Pontoise, Normandy and France were to be free of tax.

It seems certain that after the Norman Conquest some particular taxes had taken root, such as the prisage of wine which had apparently begun as a means of providing wine for the sovereign;

no doubt a great deal of this commodity was imported for the Norman court. It is also likely that there was a tax on the export of wool, woolfells and hides in addition to numerous local taxes such as town tolls and those which the lord of the manor had the right to collect. The local tolls or dues became numerous and included anchorage, ballastage, busselage, keelage, lastage (lestage), prisage, towage, moreage, terrage, cranage, wharfage or keyage, housellage, tronage, pesage and measureage.

The first real attempt to set up a centralized system was made by King John at the Winchester assize in 1203. This imposed a duty of one-fifteenth on the imports and exports (the *quindecima*) and provided for officials to be appointed to deal with it. In each port of England 'six or seven or more of the wiser and more learned men of substance of the port and one knight and one clerk were to be chosen and also a further official, who should not himself receive any money but should keep rolls against the bailiffs who receive the *quindecima*'.

It is interesting to read the account of the yield of this tax which was imposed from July 1203 to November 1205. The ports concerned are Newcastle, Yarm, Cotun (now submerged), Whitby, Scarborough, Hedon, Hull, York, Selby, Lincoln, Barton, Immingham, Grimsby, St. Botolph (Boston), Lynn, Yarmouth, Norwich, Dunwich, Orford, Ipswich, Colchester, Sandwich, Dover, Rye, Winchelsea, Pevensey, Seaford, Shoreham, Chichester, Southampton, Exmouth, Dartmouth, Saltash, Fowey and London. The yield from London was £1,336 12s. 10d. and the next greatest amount was from Boston with £780 15s. 3d., followed by Southampton with £712 3s. 8d. and Lincoln with £656 12s. 2d.

The reference in the Magna Carta to the 'ancient and rightful customs' probably included the prisage of wine and the export duties on wool, woolfells and hides and possibly the recognized local tolls as well. A reference in 1209 that a Bernard Achard paid 40 marks and two tuns of wine in order to avoid prise or customs on two shiploads of wine implies that prisage was being partially commuted for monetary payment.

In 1275 Edward I imposed what was afterwards called the

'ancient custom' but was referred to at the time as the 'new custom'. This again was an export duty on wool, woolfells and hides and may only have been an affirmation of existing duties. The rates imposed were half a mark (6s. 8d.) for each sack of wool (28 stone), half a mark (6s. 8d.) for every 300 fells and one mark (13s. 4d.) for every last of leather (240 hides).

THE FARMING OF THE CUSTOMS

The farm of the New Customs for England was allocated to the merchants of Lucca under the system of farming which was the normal method of revenue collection during this period. The farmers would make a fixed payment to the king for the rent of the farm of the Customs duties and the collectors and controllers were required to keep an account of the goods. It was customary for the 'farmers' to appoint their own officials in the ports, and two local officials were also elected to represent the king. The collector held one half of a seal known as the 'cocket' and the king's official, later known as the controller, held the other half. This seal was used to seal the licence to export wool etc.

The controller also kept an account as a check on the collector's account. This account was made on a counter roll (*contrarotula*), hence the title *contrarotulator* which, in course of time, became corrupted to comptroller or controller. In connection with this an order was issued by Edward I on the 27th May 1275 to the Lord Mayor and Sheriffs of London 'to go in person to the said City and elect by the oath of good and lawful men thereof two men of the City who shall keep one part of the seal provided for the New Custom, and shall seal letters of licence to take wool out of the City, together with the attorneys of Luke de Luk and his fellows, Merchants of Lucca, deputed to collect the Custom to whom the King has committed the other half of the Seal so that such letters be sealed by view of same and to certify their names to the Treasurer and Barons of the Exchequer and cause them to be enrolled.' The collection of the New Custom in Ireland was assigned to the merchants of Florence.

An indication of the antiquity of the Customs is given in a Charter of 1278 whereby Edward I granted the barons of the Cinque Ports exemption from the prisage of wine. As this Charter is a confirmation of liberties and freedoms which they and their ancestors had had since the time of Edward the Confessor, it is possible that the system of prisage went back to Saxon times.

A further tax was imposed by Edward I in 1297 of 40s. per sack of wool exported. This was levied without the sanction of Parliament and was known as the 'Maletote'. There was so much opposition to this tax that it was eventually abandoned and the king renounced the right to levy such a tax without the consent of Parliament.

TRIANGULAR SYSTEM OF CONTROL

Customers were set up in the ports in 1297. It appears that at first they were required to receive the monies transmitted to them by the Collectors and to make payments as directed by the Exchequer, but in some ports the Collector would also be the Customer (*custodies*). Two years later the office of Searcher was established. At first the Searcher was required to assist the bailiffs in arresting persons bringing in false money. Later his duty included the examination of goods and the preparation and the returning of accounts. Thus the triangular system of control evolved, a system which worked so well that it has continued with some modification until the present day in the United Kingdom, was retained in the United States of America after the declaration of Independence, and has been adopted by Commonwealth and other countries. The basis of this system is the separation of the processes of the examination of goods, the collection of the duties and the checking of the accounts.

A most important milestone in the history of the Customs service was the Carta Mercatoria of 1303. This was, in effect, a charter of liberties to foreign merchants who were now, inter alia, freed from the necessity of paying prisage and paid instead a monetary tax which was later called 'butlerage', a name deriving from the title of the official who was required to collect the tax, the butler or King's butler. This name appears to be derived in turn from the French *bouteilleur*.

An interesting list of ports to which Collectors were appointed is given in this and other enactments of the next few years. They include Ipswich, Yarmouth, Lynn, Boston, Hull, Newcastle, Berwick (including Stirling), Sandwich, Winchelsea, Chichester, Weymouth, Plymouth, Chester, Haverford, Barnstaple, Exeter, Topsham and Lyme. We sometimes find this tax introduced by the Carta Mercatoria referred to as the New Custom or Petty Custom, presumably to differentiate it from the earlier imposts, which were sometimes called the Great Custom or the Ancient and Rightful Customs. The farm of the Customs of England had been assigned to the Frescobaldi, merchants of Florence, but arrangements were also made for payments to be made to the wine merchants of Bayonne. The king would also assign the farm of certain ports to other persons to whom he owed money. Edward II seems to have needed even more money than his father, for in 1316 he ordered the Collectors of wool, woolfells and hides to bring all money collected by them direct to the Exchequer, notwithstanding any orders of the King for payments elsewhere, and temporarily increased the export duty on wool of aliens.

At this time all wool sent to the Continent had to be shipped to a Staple port – in the early days the staple was at Bruges, and later oscillated between St. Omer, Antwerp and Bruges. By the end of the fourteenth century Calais had become the headquarters of the Company of the Staple. The difficulty was to ensure that the wool was in fact exported to the Staple port and not to other ports; and so orders were sent in 1320 to the Collectors in various ports enjoining them to be 'very strict in the swearing of the exporters'.

A list of ports in 1323 includes a number not previously mentioned, such as Scarborough, Whitby, Ravenscar, Barton-on-Humber, Grimsby, Donewell, Conway, Beaumaris and Carnarvon. The Staple was temporarily abolished in 1328 and the Confirmation of Charters was issued laying down the regulations regarding foreign merchants. In general, they could sell merchandise whole-sale only and could export all goods except wine, provided they paid the usual customs. They were required to pay extra taxes for these and some other privileges.

Further information is given about the duties of the Controller at this time by a record ordering the Collector at Ipswich not to take any Customs 'without the view and testimony of the Con-troller'. A few years later a Charter laid down that 'ships laden with wool, woolfells or hides', on which Great Customs was due, should clear out only from that port where the King's Seal was kept and where the Cocket Seal was held (*ubi thronus noster et sigillium noster quod dicitus Coket existunt, et non alibi carcentur*). King Edward III, in his efforts to raise money for his wars, was able to persuade parliament to agree to the prisage of 50,000 sacks of wool as a temporary measure although the prise of wool was abolished soon after in 1344. The king also levies the Cloth Cus-tom in 1347 against the wishes of Parliament, and in answer to a petition against this imposition maintained that it was just and proper to tax cloth as well as wool, on account of the proportion of wool it contained.

Of importance to the trade of the country was the Statute of the Staple which was introduced in 1353. As a result, certain places in England and Wales were designated as staple towns or ports and had the monopoly of the dealings in wool, woolfells, hides and lead for export. In England the towns were Newcastle, York, Lincoln, Norwich, Westminster, Canterbury, Chichester, Win-chester, Exeter and Bristol and in Wales, Carmarthen. Where these towns were not ports, ports were allocated to them, viz. Hull to York, Boston to Lincoln, London to Westminster, Sand-wich to Canterbury and Southampton to Winchester. Ireland had four ports, Dublin, Waterford, Cork and Drogheda.

Towards the end of the reign of Edward III, Geoffrey Chaucer was appointed Controller of the Customs and Subsidy of Wools, Hides and Woolfells and of the Petty Customs of Wine etc. in the Port of London, on the condition that he made the entries with his own hand.

SUBSIDIES, PROHIBITIONS AND PROTECTION

Early in the next reign we find references to the London Custom House built by John Churchman on his quay called 'le Wolle-Wharf', and to the appointment of one Richard Baret to the office of the custody of the house appertaining to the Great Custom upon 'le Woolekey' London – the earliest mention of a known Custom House and housekeeper.

At about this time an Act was passed ordering the king's subjects to employ only 'ships of the King's allegiance'. This was intended to encourage the growth of the English mercantile marine. Some years later orders to the Customs service stipulated 'that no Customer or Comptroller have any ships of their own, nor meddle with the freight of ships, and that to eschew as well the damage of the Lord the King of his Customs, as the loss of the merchants repairing to the Port, as well aliens to denizens. And that no Customer, Comptroller, Searcher, Weigher or Finder (Tronour) have any such office for term of life, but only as long as shall please the King, notwithstanding any patent or grant made to any of the contrary.' In the first year of Henry IV it was further stipulated that 'Customers and Controllers in every port of England should be resident at their Custom Houses personally and should not act by deputy', and in the fourth year of the same reign it was ordered that Searchers should not let their offices to farm, should take no money except fees allowed by the King, nor be host to any merchant or mariner, on penalty of forfeiture of office and ransom to be paid to the King.

The next King, Henry V, issued an order in 1414 to the Collectors of Customs that no gunpowder should be exported on any pretext whatever without Royal Assent. Some revenue statistics have been handed down for this period, and in 1400 returns for London show:

Ancient Customs & Subsidy	£15,615 18s. 7½d.
New Custom	£1,371 8s. 2d.

A return of Customs Revenue for 1421 gives the following details:

Wool exported	£3,976 1s. 2d.
Petty Customs	£2,438 18s. 1¾d.
1s. per £ on ad valorem goods	£8,237 10s. 9¼d.

It would appear that there were malpractices by Customs officials since it was found necessary in 1424 to impose penalties on Customers, Collectors or Controllers who 'should be attainted or convicted of falsely concealing the King's Customs or Subsidies, entered or paid'. Customers and Comptrollers were later required to write and deliver to the merchants sufficient warrants, sealed with their seal of office, for 'all and every of their merchandises every time by them to the Customers and Controulers duly shewed'. A defaulting official could be sued by the aggrieved merchant. In spite of earlier regulations governing their conduct it would seem that Customs officials were becoming slack in their observance of the rules, for it was stated in 1442 that:

'of late divers Customers, Controllers and also Searchers have divers persons to be their clerks, deputies and ministers, some have ships of their own and some of them meddle with the freighting of ships and also buy and sell divers merchandises and thereof occupy to their own use divers wharfs and keys, being by the water's side where common discharge of divers merchandises is had in ports of this Realm, by which the great deceit and damages daily do grow to the King of his Customs and Subsidies . . . Also many hold hostelries and taverns and also keep wharfs and they and their servants be factors and attornies for merchants, denizens and aliens by which great damage and loss doth grow to the King . . . by favour that such clerks, deputies and ministers holding such hostelries, taverns and wharfs do to the merchants and to other their guests.'

A penalty of £40 was laid down for any of these offences.

Early in the reign of Edward IV, in response to a petition from artisans, an Act was passed prohibiting the importation of a wide range of articles including wool, metal, dice, tennis balls, playing cards, daggers, knives, shears and scissors. The following year another statute limited the vessels in which wool and woolfells could be shipped to galleys and carracks, thus anticipating later anti-smuggling regulations governing the minimum size of vessels allowed to import merchandise. Again in 1472 an Act ordained that cloths imported should be sealed and countersealed by the Collector and Comptroller in the port of delivery before being exposed for sale, on penalty of forfeiture.

Chapter 2

THE TUDOR PERIOD

It has been said that the Tudors' lack of a standing army was matched by their lack of a civil service, that they had to rely almost exclusively upon the part-time services of amateur administrators, that all competent citizens were expected to help in the numerous branches of the service, but that by the end of their century of rule a professional governing class had emerged. The Customs service was not immune from this amateurism, and it became usual practice to choose collectors, comptrollers and searchers from local men of standing and substance who were frequently members of the merchant class. From time to time orders were issued forbidding such officers to engage in certain trade and it may therefore be assumed that there was a tendency for the more enterprising among them to take advantage of the opportunities which the growth of shipping and commerce offered. In any case, at that time there does not appear to have been any absolute ban on officials engaging in trade or other occupations.

The administration of justice was organized (sic) on the same lines as the other public services, and justices of the peace, appointed on a local basis, were consequently subject to local influences when revenue offences were being dealt with. As Professor S. T. Bindoff has pointed out, this system had the advantage of costing practically nothing to operate.

It must be borne in mind that Customs officials were, of necessity, drawn from the relatively small literate class. It is little wonder, then, that in making the arrangements for their revenue, the

Tudor monarchs and their advisers continued to adopt the easier but not very efficient course of renting the Customs revenue to enterprising merchants. Towards the end of the Tudor period, however, men like Thomas Smythe showed how much profit there was to be made by running the revenue services in a more methodical way, and, by the same token, drew attention to the amount of revenue lost to the Crown under the farming system. As a result, consideration was given to the possibility of direct collection by permanent officials.

In later years, the King frequently gave orders to collectors to make payments to certain people for services rendered, and one of the earliest recorded examples of payments made in this way is contained in the Customs Rolls of the Port of Bristol for 1496 to 1499. These payments were made by the Collector and Customers of the port to John Cabot, and as the name of one of the two Collectors at the time was Richard A'Merryke, it has been suggested that Cabot named the land he had discovered America after the Customs collector. The theory that the continent was named after Amerigo Vespucci rests on no firmer basis and failed to convince Humboldt. The great discoveries during this period, and the consequent growth in trade, had their effect on the Customs service.

The Venetians had greatly increased their share of the trade with Britain, largely at the expense of the other Italian trading cities such as Genoa, Lucca, Pisa and Leghorn, and in 1490 an act provided that 'Every butt of Malmsey shall contain CXXVI gallons and every Merchant Stranger shall pay for Customs XVIIIs. a butt, besides the Old Custom, and no butt shall be sold for above £IV., which new imposition shall be until the Venetians abate their new imposition of IV Ducats at Candy', thus showing that the government of the day did not intend to accept foreign taxes on their goods without retaliation.

A few years later another act was directed against those aliens who acquired English nationality and then used the resultant privilege of being able to import or export at lower rates of tax to trade in goods on behalf of their erstwhile fellow nationals. The new act ordained that naturalized aliens should continue to pay duty at aliens' rates.

Although mercantilist policies were continued by the Tudors, some attempts were made to come to commercial agreements with other trading countries during this period of European expansion.

In 1496 Henry VII signed a treaty of commerce with the Netherlands which included an article providing that 'the officers of either country, appointed for searching for contraband goods, shall perform it civilly, without spoiling them or breaking the chests, barrels, packs or sacks, under pain of a month's imprisonment. And when the searchers shall have opened them, they shall assist in the shutting and mending of them, etc., nor shall they compel the owners to sell or dispose of the same against their own inclinations.'

An interesting example of the way in which the Customs revenue was used is shown by the Act of 1504 which allocated the whole of the Great Custom on wool, woolfells and hides to the mayor, constables and fellowship of the Staple at Calais 'so that they pay yearly to the Treasurer of Calais £10,022 4s. 8d. for maintaining of the garrison there, if the charges thereof amount to so much'. Provision was also made inter alia, for the payment of £100 annually to the Customers of the Great Custom at London.

The treaty of commerce Henry VII made with Philip of Castile in 1506 was important as far as the Customs was concerned since article III provided that the taxes payable on merchandise should be made public, as follows: 'For the prevention of all impositions for the future, a table of all the duties, subsidies, tolls and other payments, which may be legally demanded in either country, shall be affixed on the doors of the Custom Houses in London, Bruges, Antwerp, Berg (Mons), and Middleburg.'

THE FIRST BOOK OF RATES

The following year the first official 'rate book' was published. The 'rate book' was the forerunner of the present-day 'tariff', but instead of laying down the actual rates of duty, the official values of the goods were shown. Although no copy of the original publication has survived, there is a manuscript copy in the possession of the British Museum.

The preface of the book states that it is 'A Rate made of the prysys of all maner of warys by the Kings Counsell and by the advyce surveyors and cowntrowlers and costomers off the Porte of London and the merchants adventerers of the same with other, the XVdaye of July in the XXII yere of the reyne of ower Soverayne Lorde Kyng Hary the VIIth, the same to induer and to continew for ever duryng the Kyngs pleasure.' After the list of rates has been given, instructions are laid down for the Customs officials:

'The kynges grase wyll(s) that yow take thys rate in affect and after the summa ther in contayned to charge every marchantt for the kyng and all the Marchants Adventerers in London be all agred the same for as mythe as be contayned thys booke of rattes anno 1532. Manuscript here foloweth howith that every gawger showllde marke hys playne gawge, and yf it lacke d(emi) a sestornne marke yt as thus, and yf ytt lacke an hole sestorne marke yt as thus . . .

Ih's

'He that ys gawner owght to understonde there ys in a tunne lx systerns and every systerne ys iiii galons be yt wyne or oylle.

'Allso ytt ys to be understond that xxiiii farthen' delles of Renyche wyne off Andwarpe aubyage makethe ainn ammbe and xxiiii ambys makethe a rode of Andwarpe mess(ure).

'Allso yt ys to be knowen that a farthen delle of that mezur ys but a gallon and a hallfe . . . (ms. torn) shalle have any amme of Andwarpe butt xxxvi gallons for ix sesternes ys an ambether.'

The first rate book was confirmed by Henry VIII in 1532, and early in his reign an act was passed with the intention of stiffening a previous Act of Henry VII which prevented naturalized merchants from entering the goods of aliens as their own. The new act also applied the penalties against English-born merchants indulging in the same practices. In the same year a proclamation enjoined all the king's officers to deal justly notwithstanding any

command to the contrary by any of his council. It was also pro-
claimed that merchants, clothiers and artificers should continue
their occupations without fear of untrue informations by customers, controllers or searchers.

There is an odd reference in an act of 1543 to the exporting of
beer in barrels. A cooper was permitted to receive tenpence for each
beer barrel 'by him sold' and sixpence for every kilderkin, and any
person carrying beer beyond the sea had to bring back sufficient
clap-board (stave timber) to make up for the casks exported. No
one was allowed to use a larger vessel than the standard beer barrel,
under penalty of a fine of 6s. 8d. for each such vessel.

During the reign of Edward VI an act was passed to prohibit
the sale of public offices by preventing the purchaser of an office
from holding it for ever. The same year a Royal Commission
ordered that the 'under Officers named *Vigilatores ad Ripam* commonly called Waiters in their proper persons and by no deputys do
diligently serve watch and look as well by day as by night both
by Water and by Land according as they ought to do, that no
goods Wares and Merchandizes be taken up before that the Kings
Majestie be answered for his Customs and Subsidies therefore, but
they seize and arrest the same to the Kings Majesties use.' The
Commission also stipulated that coast-bonds had to remain in the
Custom House in the joint custody of the Comptroller and Surveyor and had to be kept available for examination by the King's
Attorney and Solicitor.

An event recorded in the diary of Henry Machyn at this time
illustrated the dangers to which Customs officials were subject.
The diarist tells the following story:

'The Xiiij day of Marche [1551] was hangyd in Smythfield on
John Mosbe and ys syster, for the death of a gentylman of Fayver-
sham, one M. Arden, the Customer, and ys owne wyff was decaul
. . . (hanged?) and she was burnyd at Canturbury and her servant
hangyd there, and ij at Feyversham and on at Hospryng, and
nodur in he way to Canturbury, for the death of M. Arden of
Feyversham. And at Flushyng was bernyd Blake Tome (Black
Tom) for the sam deth of M. Arden.'

Steps were frequently taken to restrict or prohibit the export of certain goods, and in 1554 an act was passed 'to restrain the carrying of corn, victuals and wood oversea', although provision was made for goods carried as ship's stores. Also during the reign of Mary a new rate-book was produced. Commissioners were appointed to assess the rates and an ingenious method was adopted for controlling imports. This consisted of under-rating the most necessary commodities 'to draw them hither and to over-rate the superfluous commodities inward, to drive them away'.

In 1558 the Marquess of Winchester, Lord Treasurer of England, wrote to the Queen telling her that he 'will forward the building of the new Custom House and Wharfs'.

After the death of Mary in November 1558 an order to the Customs of London showed that arrangements were being made for the coronation of Elizabeth. The customers were enjoined 'to staye all sylkes of the colour of crymosyn as shall arrive within that Porte untyll the Quenes Majestie shall first have her choyse towards the furnyture of her coronacion and to give warning if any suche shall arryve there to the Lordes of the Counsell, and *to kepe this matter secrete*'.

The first session of parliament in 1559 included many provisions of importance to the Customs service. In the first place it was now laid down when and where vessels could load and discharge; in the summer between sunrise and sunset, and in the winter between 7 a.m. and 4 p.m., upon 'some such open place, key or wharf, places, keys or wharfs as your Highness, your heirs or successors shall on this side the said first day of September therefore assign and appoint by virtue of your Highness's Commission or Commissions within your Grace's ports of London, Southampton, Bristol, West Chester [Chester], Newcastle and the suburbs of the same and every of them, and in some open place, key or wharf, places, keys or wharfs in all other ports creeks havens or roads (Hull only excepted) where a Customer, Controller and Searcher of such ports, havens, creeks or roads and every of them or the servants of any of them, have by the space of ten years last past been accustomable resident or hereafter shall be resident.' Section

IV ordered that no ship could load for export before the master had given notice of his intention to load and his place of destination. Before his actual departure he was required to give full particulars of the merchandise carried, the name of the merchant owners of the cargo and answer any other questions put to him by the Customs Officers in respect of the cargo.

Later in the same year the Exchequer Commission made its report and designated the 'legal quays' where foreign goods might be landed and also other quays for specific goods. The Steel-yard, commonly called 'Guildhalla Theutonicorum', was limited to merchants of the Hanse and, with that exception, no stranger or alien was allowed any building on the wharves. 'The landing of foreign goods at Gravesend, Woolwich, Barking, Greenwich, Deptford, Blackwall, Limehouse, Ratcliffe, Wapping, St. Katherines, Tower Hill, Rotherhithe, Southwark and London Bridge (the several Keys, Wharfes, stayers, and places before limited and appointed only excepted) shall be from henceforth no more used as landing or discharging places for merchandizes, but be utterly debarred and abolished from the same for ever.'

Also in 1559 orders were sent to the customers, comptrollers and searchers at Southampton, Poole, Bristol, Plymouth and Dartmouth 'to have special care that nowe upon the publishing of peax [peace], no bullion or money be suffered by them to be transported out of the realm'.

A foretaste of mercantilist measures taken in the next century under Cromwell is to be found in an act of 1562 which ordered that:

'it shall not be lawful to any person or persons to cause to be laden and carried in any bottom or bottoms, whereof any stranger or strangers born, then be owners, shipmasters or part-owners, any kind of fish, victual, wares or things of what kind or nature soever, the same shall be, from one port or creek of this realm to another port or creek of the same realm upon pain to everyone that shall offend . . . to forfeit all the goods so laden or carried or the value thereof.'

During the reign of Elizabeth the farming of the Customs had perhaps reached its greatest extent, and the most famous of all the farmers was probably Sir Thomas Smythe who appears to have been the Collector of Tonnage and Poundage in London from 1559. In 1572 the farm of Chichester, Sandwich, Southampton and Ipswich was added to London.

In 1564 an attempt was made once again to prevent the importation of certain goods from the Low Countries such as ling, cod, hops, bricks, barrel hoops, onions and woad and in 1565 an Act was passed to prevent the exportation of rams, lambs or sheep. The penalties for non-compliance were extremely severe. Section II of the act runs:

'And further, every such offender shall suffer imprisonment by the space of one whole year without bail or mainprize, and at the year's end shall in some open market town, in the fulness of the market, on the market day, have his left hand cut off, and that to be nailed up in the openest place of such market, and that every person or persons eftsoons offending against this statute shall be adjudged a felon, and shall suffer death as in cases of felony [hanging].'

There was a rapid sequel to this proclamation for, on 16th September 1564, the Lords of the Privy Council charged one Richard Patrike, Comptroller of the Subsedye in the Porte of London, with receiving certain woad from Flanders, contrary to the proclamation, and committed him to the Fleet prison.

Another act of the Privy Council dated 8th November 1565 was intended to suppress piracy. Returns were required of all ships, giving details of their names, the trade they were normally engaged in, the number of crew and shore officials and whether they were seamen or fishermen. Victualling of the ships was to be strictly controlled and the Customs officials were ordered:

'to have good consideration that they give no assent or allowance in those cases, but where they shall perceive planelye the same victuell to be made redye or provided to be employed for the use of shippes to be used for good and true merchauntes, or for the trade of fyshinge or where passage shal be for honest passengers, and in no wyse for any men of warre other than such as shall manyfestly be knowen to belonge to the Queen's Majestie and shall have speciall commission of Her Majestie for the same.'

It appeared that the government of the day was far from satisfied with the collection of the Customs revenue at this period for in January 1565 a document was issued under the Great Seal which laid down quite firmly the system that was to be adopted. Following the preamble the document runs:

'Forasmuche as heretofore oure Customes and Subsidies of Merchandises goying owte and comyng into this oure Realme of Englande and Wales have not bene nor cannot be so duly and justely answered unto us as they might and oughte to have been, for that the waye, manner and order heretofore appointed and used in and abowte the levying and answering thereof, are not so certayn as in that case are meete and convenient, to oure great losse and hinderaunce, as we have perfect understandinge whereupon, we have devised and made certain reasonable and necessarie articles, ordinaunces, rule and orders to be kept . . . by the officers and ministers of all oure said Ports, Havens and Creeks . . . and for the better corroboration and full testimony of this oure will and pleasure, we have caused oure Great Seale of Englande to be sette to this present booke. Witness ourselfe at Westminster, the 29th daye of January, the seventh yeare of oure Reigne.'

In general, previous practice was consolidated and made applicable to all ports. In the first place the Port of London was dealt with, and then the outports. The Rules for preparing the Queen's Books, generally known as the Exchequer Port Books, were confirmed and the rules for exportation, importation and coastwise traffic were laid down. The merchants had to make entry of their cargo and give all particulars. The quantity of ship's stores also had to be stated even though they were not liable to any Customs duty. When a merchant was unable to give exact details of the cargo which he was importing he was able to enter them on a 'Warrant ad Visum'. This procedure still exists today and is known as entry on 'Bill of Sight'. Because of the danger of coastwise goods being diverted into the export trade without payment of duty, bond had to be entered into in respect of coastwise goods. Careful directions were also given with regard to the weighing of wool at the Beam prior to exportation.

A list issued in 1571 throws light on the duty-free concessions allowed in the wine duties. The quantities granted free of duty to certain persons were as follows:

10 bishops	3 to 12 tuns each
7 deacons & provosts	3 tuns each
Ambassadors of France and Spain	12 tuns each (more if required)
The Nobility	4 to 12 tuns each
Privy Councillors, Law and other State Officers	1 to 10 tuns each
Noble Ladies, 33 Knights and 1 Esquire	1 to 10 tuns each

As a matter of course, all wine for the Queen's household could be imported free of duty, on certificate by her household officers.

A levy on shipping for the upkeep of Dover harbour consisted of a tonnage duty on the tonnage of vessels loading or discharging and a duty of a penny-halfpenny on every chaldron of sea-coal or grindstone. In 1585 Sir Francis Walsingham undertook the farm of all the outports apart from those farmed by Sir Thomas Smythe. New instructions and orders were issued to officers and Customers in the ports and creeks and the principal deputies John Dawes and Lisle Cave were constantly engaged in travelling from one port to another.

An order issued to the officers at certain ports to care for soldiers arriving from the Netherlands shows that the practice of assigning non-revenue tasks to the Customs officials was already being followed. Similarly, in the eventful year of 1588, on 22nd August, the Privy Council ordered that a payment be made to Mr. Customer Smythe for 'providing certain barkes and crayers laden with bavens, faggottes and pitch appointed to be sent to the Lord Admirall at his coming into the Narrow Seas, to be employed in some speciall service'. Again on the following day, the Lord Treasurer wrote to Mr. Customer Smythe ordering him 'to joyne with Mr. Wattes, the marchant, for the provision and speedy sending down, with the victualles provided for the shippes at sea, 400 weight of brimston and 40 barrells of pitch to be employed by the Lord Admirall's direction'. A 'Convoy' duty levied in 1590 was to provide protection for English shipping bringing wine from La Rochelle and Bordeaux. The rate imposed amounted to 3s. a tun on all wine.

When Thomas Smythe died in 1589 Henry Billingsley, Alderman of London, became Customer in his place but did not, however, take over his duties as Farmer. This practice was discontinued and Thomas Middleton was appointed as Receiver General. In 1590 Billingsley wrote to the Lord Treasurer begging that he might be relieved from the collection of the Customs, or that he might at least have such allowance as he was entitled to. He also suggested that it would be much more profitable to her Majesty to put the said Customs to Farm as before, than to keep them in her own hands, the profits being very uncertain and casual. The following month Billingsley wrote again to Lord Burghley, beseeching him to appoint some other.

Surveyors had been appointed to cover the outports and instructions were issued to the surveyors who were to be next in rank to the Customers and were to be present with the Collectors and Comptroller, cognizant of all that went on in the office. They had to keep their own books and sign all the controller's cockets, warrants or certificates. They could go on quays or on the ships at their discretion and they had to see that all entries were made in the Custom House, and generally ensure that the officers carried out their duties. Instructions were also issued to customers, controllers, searchers and waiters, and the Customer in each outport was made responsible for providing 'convenyent Custome-houses in fytt places, as neare unto the open wharfes and places of ladyng and discharging of marchandises as may be reasonably obtained'.

In 1594 Lord Treasurer Burghley asked Billingsley, the Customer, and Richard Carmarden, the Surveyor of London Port, to investigate and report on the advisability of producing a new book of rates. They stated that while some values had increased, some had also decreased and that the new rates would bring but small gain to the Treasury. The labour involved in preparing it would be 'a long piece of work and yet in the end be imperfect'. The question of a new book of rates again came up in 1599. In a letter from Thomas Fanshaw, Queen's Remembrancer of the Exchequer, to Sir Thomas Robert Cecil who had succeeded his father as Lord Treasurer, it was said that, 'Queen Mary in the last year of her reign caused all merchandises then known to be rated for the paying of customs and subsidies and to be published in a book under the great seal . . . But of the book or anything that was done in that matter, I suppose Mr. Carmarthen can best inform you.' By the end of Elizabeth I's reign it was argued that a new rate book should be prepared, as a result of which the Customs would be 'augmented yearly at least £20,000 inwards', but steps were not taken to draw one up until the next reign.

An insight into the farm of the Customs and the relations between the Queen's officials and those of the farmer is given in the correspondence of Sir Robert Cecil. In a letter to the Officers of the Custom House in 1602, he informs them that he has made a very small profit that year from his farm and that his deputies cannot prevent frauds because the Book of Orders is not observed. A letter from Bernard Hide to Sir Robert Cecil in 1602 tells him of certain demands by the Collector, Alderman Moore, and the Comptroller, and goes on to say that the discontented waiters 'that wronged your Honour last year cannot make their profits as in time past, and these stir up the merchants to make clamour against us your deputies'. Later in the letter he states that he has taken into Cecil's service two of Her Majesty's waiters, 'who in consequence are discountenanced by the officers and get hard measure from the discontented waiters, as Mr. Bellot can tell you'.

There is a further letter from Cecil to the Customs of London on this subject in 1602. The letter commences:

'I have heard that you that are Her Majesty's officers of Her Custom House have found some cause to take exception against the proceedings of some of my deputies in the execution of the farm which I have taken upon an improved rent of £1,200 a year more than Her Majesty had before for the custom of some kinds of silks and other small merchandise. I thought it my part to move you, and it is your duty to inform if anything be done by them prejudicial to Her Majesty in honour or benefit, or to the injury of the common subject . . . I will then intreat two or three of you to come to me, at which time I will also cause them to attend, to see if upon such a conference the execution may be so well ordered that neither they may be discouraged from doing their duty, nor you have cause to find fault. As long as the report goeth that they deal injuriously, so long my reputation is called in question . . .'

Chapter 3

THE STUART PERIOD

JAMES I AND CHARLES I

This was a most eventful period for the Customs and Excise for it saw the civil war brought about, to some extent, by the quarrel between the king and parliament over Customs duties, and the imposition by parliament of the Excise on the outbreak of the war. The Restoration led to the firm establishment of a Board of Customs in 1671, of Excise in 1683, and the enforcement of quarantine by the Customs. After the London Custom House was burnt down in the Great Fire of 1666 a new Custom House was built in its place, designed by Sir Christopher Wren.

On the accession of James I parliament set about making financial arrangements for the new sovereign and passed an act granting a subsidy of tonnage and poundage to the king. James, for his part, appointed a committee under the Great Seal to enquire into the reasonable values and prices according to which goods should be rated for the purposes of the Act and to arrange for a copy of the Book of Rates to be delivered to the Customs officials in every port. By bringing the valuations up-to-date James was able to ensure a higher revenue from the ad valorem duties.

The issue of this new Book of Rates had a curious sequel. A Levant merchant called Bates who dealt in currants claimed that the higher valuation given to this commodity was tantamount to an increase in taxation and could not therefore be imposed without the consent of parliament. The case was heard in the Court of Exchequer, and after lengthy discussion the decision was given against Bates. The court decided that 'he who had power over the cause must have power over the effect. The sea-ports are the King's gates which he may open and shut to whom he pleases.' It is interesting to reflect that at a later date the Customs used the portcullis as its emblem and it may be seen impressed on many of the early volumes of orders and letter books. Today the port-cullis is still represented on the uniform caps of the Waterguard officers and on the official flag.

A new Book of Rates was again issued by patent in 1611. The particular interest here is that the patent authorized the payment of a drawback – that is, a refund of duty – on the exportation of goods which have been previously imported. This is a system which still exists today and it has played a great part in easing the development of the processing trade in this country.

An early reference to the payment of drawback is contained in two letters patent of James I in 1611 where it was stated that any impost paid on importation would be repaid by the Collector upon proof of export. Wine was, however, excluded from the arrangement.

The practice of using Customs officials to carry out non-revenue work was becoming more extensive during this period. For example, early in James's reign, arrangements were made for officers to accept the oath of repudiation of the Pope which was required from everyone going abroad.

The text of Section 21 of 3 James I, cap. 4 runs:

'XXI. And that for the due Execution of this Branch of this present Law, it shall and may be lawful to and for the Customer and Comptroller of every Port, Haven or Creek, or one of them, and their or either of their Deputy or Deputies, and none other, to receive and accept all and every such Bond and Obligation to and for the Uses aforesaid, and to minister and give the Oath afore-said, according to the true Intent of this Statute (taking for such Bond Six-pence and no more, and for the said Oath no fee at all). (2) Which said Customer and Comptroller shall register and certify all and every such Bond and Oath so taken, into the Court of Exchequer at Westminster once every year, upon pain of five pounds for every Bond not so certified, and twenty shillings for every Oath not so certified. (3) Provided always, That this last mentioned Branch shall not extend to any Person or Persons which are already gone or shall go beyond the Seas to serve any Foreign Prince, State or Potentate, before the tenth Day of June next coming, for his said going or passing before the said tenth Day of June.'

James's concern with obtaining more money by taxation is thus reflected in the Customs records of this reign. His son Charles was involved in an even more bitter struggle with parliament over these matters. His quarrels with parliament resulted first of all in dissolution of that body in 1629, and eventually in the Civil War. In 1626 Charles appointed a 'Committee for Trade' whose task was to revise the Book of Rates and reorganize the Customs. During his eleven years of rule without parliament, the King attempted to obtain the money he required by imposing taxes himself. He ruled by Order in Council and Proclamation and imposed, inter alia, a duty of four shillings a chaldron on coal exported. He also restricted the landing of tobacco to the London Custom House, prohibited the landing of tobacco seed, and the planting of tobacco in England and Ireland. Eventually, however, he was forced to summon parliament once again, and found the members more obdurate than ever. A new Book of Rates appeared in 1642 which also included Rates and Directions for the Governance of Merchants and Customs Officers.

Among the Customs Officer's varied duties was included the control of smuggling. In 1614 the Privy Council found it necessary to draw attention to the export smuggling of wool 'notwithstanding the many laws and statutes now in force, prohibiting the exportation of wooll out of these his Majestyie' dominions, the same is notwithstanding dayly practised, and the wooll of this kingdom (even in very greate quantitye) transported unto forraigne partes . . .'

But a sign that smuggling was still rampant is shown by the report in 1624 that William Davis, Collector of Customs for the Ports of Sussex, raised fourteen men to watch a suspicious bark near Pevensey. Twenty-three horses laden with wool, leather and cloth and guarded by twenty well-armed men came alongside and, after a long fight with Davis's men, succeeded in shipping the goods.

The collection of Light Dues on behalf of Trinity House was by this time regarded as a normal Customs function, and in 1615 we find a reference to this in the letters patent for a licence to Sir Edward Howard to erect and maintain a lighthouse at Dungeness and to receive 1d. per ton on all ships passing there, to be collected by the farmers of the Customs.

An interesting sidelight on Customs affairs is provided by the story of John Prettyman, Customs officer at Dover, who seized some books which had been unlawfully imported. The sailor who had introduced them into the country from Calais claimed that he had brought a box and a bundle for another person, not knowing that they contained books. The reason for the embargo on their importation is not stated, but even today obscene and seditious books may be seized by Customs Officers, as well as in cases where copyright has been infringed.

THE CIVIL WAR

The Civil War involved both sides in great expense and in 1643 the Long Parliament imposed the Excise. This was a new tax in England, although it existed in various forms in other countries; in France, for example, as the *gabelle* and the *octroi*, and in Holland as the *accijs*. It was intensely disliked right from the start, and later became even more resented since it was imposed on imports in addition to the Customs duties, and also on goods produced in England, for example, strong waters [spirits], beer, cider and perry. In 1643 parliament appointed a Board of Commissioners of Customs consisting of four city aldermen and four merchants. In the same year an Excise duty was also imposed by Charles I at Oxford. The Excise was intended to be a temporary tax for the duration of the war at the most.

An early move towards preference may be seen in an Ordinance of 1647 which exempted goods consigned to the Plantations from export duty and also from import duty in the colonies. A new edition of the Book of Rates was issued and this included rules concerning coastwise traffic, the giving of bond that goods would be discharged in this country and certificate of discharge supplied. The landing of goods was not permitted except in the presence of a Customs officer and during lawful hours.

The civil war proved so costly that the Excise duties were retained during the whole of the Interregnum, and this in spite of many complaints and objections. Among others, William Prynne argued strongly against the tax in his tract of 1645 entitled 'A Legal Vindication of the Liberties of England against Illegal Taxes' in which he endeavoured to show that Excise was illegal. It is interesting to note that in 1666 William Prynne occupied the position of Commissioner of Excise.

The system of direct collection by the Commissioners of Customs was not working to the satisfaction of Parliament, and in 1657 an Ordinance made provision for the appointment of a Committee of Parliament 'to treat, contract, and conclude with any person or persons for the Farming all or any part of the Duties and Subsidy of Tonnage and Poundage . . .'

THE RESTORATION

At the Restoration Parliament passed a new Tonnage and Poundage Act, and a new Book of Rates was issued with a set of rules for the officers. Rule XVIII stipulated that the officers who sit above stairs at the Custom House of the Port of London should attend from nine to twelve o'clock in the forenoon and that one officer or one able clerk should attend with the book in the afternoon during such time as the officers are appointed to wait at the waterside. Rule XXII ordered that the Searcher should not detain any vessel on pretence of searching for prohibited goods for more than three tides at Gravesend, after her arrival there, nor more than one tide after she was fully laden, unless there were reasonable grounds for suspicion. At the same time the Excise was granted by Parliament to Charles II, one half for his personal use, and one half for himself and his heirs in perpetuity.

Elias Ashmole, founder of the Ashmolean Museum in Oxford, became a Controller of Excise at this time. Excise duties were then imposed on strong waters, ale, beer, tea, coffee, chocolate [cocoa] and sherbet. Soon afterwards, however, the hearth tax was imposed and this caused great resentment, mainly on account of the attendant right of search which seemed a threat to individual privacy. The act which repealed it described it as a badge of slavery upon the whole people, exposing every man's house to be searched.

The London Custom House was one of the victims of the Great Fire, and following its destruction a notice appeared in the *London Gazette* stating that the affairs of the Custom House were to be transacted in Mr. John Bland's house in Mark Lane where the farmers and officers of His Majesty's Customs would be ready on all occasions at the usual times for the despatch of their affairs. After the Fire of London a tax was imposed on coal, the proceeds of which were to be devoted to rebuilding the City of London. The original act applied only to coal brought to London and the tax, although it was a domestic levy, was described as a Customs duty. This was probably because at that time almost all coal was brought to London by water.

Discussions about the rebuilding of the Custom House were held, and after some dispute as to the site, Sir Christopher Wren was commissioned to design a new building to be erected on the same historic spot on London Pool. Work on the new Custom House seems to have progressed rapidly, for in 1671 Sir Christopher Wren certified that he was present at a conference in the new building when accommodation was allocated to the various officers. He stated, among other things, that the farmers were to have the west end of the Custom House to themselves, the Great Long Room was to be held in common, and the east end was to be for the accommodation of the King's Officers.

At the beginning of Charles's reign a navigation act was passed which went much further than Cromwell's act of 1651. It entailed a good deal of extra work for the Customs staff and caused discontent in the Plantations, since the colonials were now only allowed to export their produce in British ships and no alien was allowed to be a merchant or factor in the colonies. Certain commodities, which were allowed free circulation within the colonies, could only be exported to continental countries if first sent to England, and bond had to be entered into to cover such exports.

The East India Company received its charter in 1661 and the Customs service was affected by two clauses. One clause made provision for the postponement of payment of duty on imports by the Company, one half to be paid within six months and the other half six months later. Another stated that duty which had been paid by the Company on goods which were subsequently lost, should be returned to the Company.

In 1663 precautions were taken against the possibility of plague spreading to England from the continent. By agreement with the Corporation of London and the farmers, it was arranged that a King's ship should patrol the Thames below Tilbury with the object of preventing the entry of ships from infected ports. A lazarette was to be established where vessels from dangerous areas could be moored in quarantine. From this date the enforcement of the health regulations became a normal part of the duties of a Customs officer.

DIRECT COLLECTION OF THE REVENUE

The Customs service was finally taken out of farm in 1671 and Sir George Downing (Godfather of Downing Street), Sir William Thomson, Sir William Lowther, William Garraway, Francis Millington and John Upton were appointed Commissioners of Customs each with a salary of £2,000 per annum. Richard Sherwyn was to act as their secretary at £400 per annum, and Richard Prowse as solicitor at £300 per annum. It was not until 1683 that the same action was taken with regard to the Excise.

Certain Excise records at this period make interesting reading. We find that, on the orders of the King, the Department was making certain monthly payments; for example, £4,000 was paid to the Forces, £300 to the Secret Service, £1,000 to the House (presumably Whitehall Palace), £500 to Prince George and £500 to Mistress Eleanor Gwynne. At this time the Excise officer's salary was £50 per year. Today an Excise officer would earn thirty times that amount, and if Mistress Gwynne's emoluments were to be multiplied at an equivalent rate, her allowance would now be worth £180,000 per annum. There are also a number of intriguing entries made at a later date allocating £500 to 'Mistress Nellie'.

Soon after the inauguration of the Board of Customs, the Treasury ordered that protections be issued to officers of Customs so that they could not be called for service on juries or inquests, or to act as constables or tithing men. Arrangements were also made to ensure that the King's Customs officers were not impressed for the fleet.

THE GLORIOUS REVOLUTION

The dramatic events of 1688 cannot be better conveyed than by reference to the Customs records of the period. On 5th November 1688 the Customs officer at Brixham wrote to his Collector at Dartmouth as follows:

'About three hundred saile of Dutch came just now into Torbay, several of them landing soldiers, and the Prince himselfe & goeing on shore. The rest of the souldiers and horse will, if they can, be landed this night, there being about 5 or 600 a shore already and are still landing.'

It appears that the collector had already been apprised and had made the following report, which was in the hands of Samuel Pepys, Secretary of the Navy, by the next day.

'This morning, being very hazey, foggie and full of raine, cleared up about 9 of the clock, at which time appeared the Dutch Fleet, consisting of about four hundred or 500 sails as neare as we can guess all standing to the Eastward with the wind at W.S.W., a moderate gale. The capital ships are off Torby abour four leagues from the shore, the small shipps and flyboats, between the Start and Dartmouth about a league and a half off.'

The Glorious Revolution may be considered as a turning point for the Customs Service. England immediately became involved in a long war with France, and Marlborough's victories were not lightly gained for, during the next twenty-five years, taxation was levied on an unprecedented scale. In the first place, the importation of certain French goods was prohibited. The prohibitions included brandy, silk and lace, all of which had become very popular in this country during the seventeenth century. Over and above this, certain specific duties were imposed on other commodities, including tea and tobacco. All these factors – together with technical advances in ships' rigging which allowed greater manoeuvrability – encouraged smuggling which, until this period, had been chiefly confined to the outward carrying of wool. In 1696 an Act ordered the navy to co-operate with the Customs in preventing the illicit exportation of wool, and another chapter of the same Act gave the Commissioners of the Treasury and the Customs power to appoint officers of Customs in the Colonies.

Following the accession of William and Mary a new Board of Customs was appointed. This Board included Thomas Pelham, later Lord Pelham, and Sir Robert Clayton, a colourful figure who had been Lord Mayor of London and had represented the City in Westminster for more than thirty years.

During William's reign provision was made for the unloading of goods at Sufferance Wharves as well as at Legal Quays, and this made it easier for merchants to discharge their cargoes at more convenient places. During the same period an Act was passed which laid down the formula for measuring the tonnage of ships.

At about this time Trinity House undertook the construction of the Eddystone Lighthouse, and the merchants agreed to pay one penny per ton to the Corporation, the money being collected by Customs Officers. Steps were taken to increase the administrative efficiency of the Customs Service itself. In 1696 the Office of Registrar of Imports and Exports was set up which for the first time attempted to keep a regular account of trade statistics. The following extract from the first volume of these trade returns will convey some idea of the detail of the account:

EXPORTS FROM LONDON TO THE PLANTATIONS
MICHAELMAS 1696 to MICHAELMAS 1697
No. 23
TO MOUNTSERATT

London	Quantity	A neer estimate of the original value of first cost of the goods in the countrey from whence imported	The amount of that vallue
	Cwt Qtrs Lbs		£ S D
Druggs Vocat Lignum Vitae	5 0 0	att 3s. 6d. per cwt	17 6
Pimento	840	att 6d. per pound	21 0 0
Suger Browne	1888 2 0	att 12s. 6d. per cwt	1180 6 3
Indico	4013	att 2s. 6d. to 3s. 6d. per pound	601 19 0
Juce of limes	150 Galls	att 8d. per gallon	5 0 0
Wooll Cotton	2 Baggs: 4 cwt	att £3 5s. per Cwt	13 0 0
		Totall	1824 0 3

The Registrar was required to keep an accurate account of the cargo entering or leaving the country, and the resulting records form a most valuable source of research for economic historians. Later this office became the Statistical Office and the present day monthly trade accounts and annual statement of trade contain the information supplied by this department.

A new duty introduced in 1697 was the imposition of a farthing per ton on all coal shipped from the port of Newcastle, which at this time included the east coast from the Scottish border to the river Humber. Regulations were then made for the vessels carrying coal to be so marked that the displacement could easily be ascertained and such ships came to be known as 'keels'. At the same time a new grade of officer known as the 'coal meter' – whose task was to measure the coal and keep an account of it – was established. An act of the following year, the 'Wool Act', had an important effect on the Customs service, for the legislation provided for control of the movement of all wool within ten miles of the coast, and a force of Riding Officers was set up to implement the act.

Under Queen Anne there were a number of important developments affecting the department. An act which provided for Poor Law boys to be indentured as apprentices to masters of ships required Collectors of Customs to make the registrations and supply the boys with 'Protections' against impressment if they were under eighteen. Some of these Registers of Apprentices still survive among the Customs archives.

Of much greater significance, however, was the effect of the Act of Union of 1707. Although at first separate Boards of Customs and of Excise were appointed for England and Scotland, English officers were sent to Scotland as experts. They were rather resented and, because of disparities in the rates of duty, smuggling across the border continued to be a great problem. The Customs officer today is very often concerned with granting diplomatic privileges. This task dates from 1708 when the code of 'Courtesy of Nations' received formal approval although its history reached back further than that.

A new Board of Customs was appointed in 1712 which included Edward Gibbon, grandfather of the historian, and also Matthew Prior, the poet. Another literary figure who was in the Customs service at this period was William Congreve, the playwright. In 1700 he had been appointed Patent Customer of the port of Poole, and in 1714 became an Under Searcher in the port of London.

Interesting from the departmental point of view is the act of 1713 which ordered that tobacco warehouses should be under the joint locks of the merchant and the Customs. Another act of the same year was concerned with wreck. Customs officers had been and still are 'Receivers of Wreck', and at this period it was a most hazardous task. Not all the stories of the 'wreckers' are fictitious.

At the beginning of the Stuart period, Customs affairs had been comparatively calm. There had been no real increase in the duties from medieval times. James I had begun by increasing the values on which the duties were based and had thus increased the tax burden, but it was the Civil War which brought in the Excise, and the necessity of paying for the wars of William and Anne caused the very great increase in Customs duties. By the end of the seventeenth century a complete transformation had taken place. Smuggling had become big business. Profits were great and risks comparatively slight. By degrees, however, the revenue forces were built up and a fleet of armed cruisers and cutters patrolled the coasts of the British Isles. The story of the eighteenth century is one of constant battle between the Customs and the smugglers.

Chapter 4

THE EIGHTEENTH CENTURY

Collectors (or Customers), Controllers, Searchers and Surveyors had been appointed in medieval times and other officials such as the 'peseur' and tronager were appointed to weigh goods at the King's Beam. After 1671 the newly appointed Board of Customs had to replace many of the officials of the 'farmers' by their own staff.

By the beginning of the eighteenth century the staffing of the service had been more or less consolidated and a contemporary account describes the establishment as it was in 1715. There were three main categories: Headquarters, London Port and the Outports. The Headquarters' staff included seven Commissioners all appointed by patent. They were Sir Walter Tong, Sir Matthew Dudley, Sir John Stanley, John Pulteney, Thomas Walker, Sir Charles Peers and Sir Thomas Frankland. The Principal Secretary, Charles Carkasse, attended to the Commissioners, reading such representations, petitions and letters as should be laid before them, receiving their instructions and drawing up answers for the Commissioners to sign. He was also the proper person to make known the Commissioners' wishes with regard to any business. To assist him he had John Manley, Secretary, or Clerk, for the Western Ports which included the ports from London along the south coast up to the west coast to Milford and the Plantations. He was appointed by deputation and was directly responsible to the Commissioners with regard to those places. There was also a Northern Clerk, John Savage, who was similarly responsible for the ports from London northwards along the east coast and down the west coast as far as Beaumaris. A Solicitor, Robert Stephens, was appointed by patent and his business was to prosecute all goods forfeited and illegally imported and all persons offending against the Acts of Trade and the Customs Laws. The Commissioners would also consult him in all legal matters before giving directions. There was also an Assistant Solicitor, George Metcalfe, who was appointed by constitution.

The Receiver-General, Henry Ferne, appointed by patent, received all the revenue money collected throughout England and paid it weekly to the Exchequer. Charles Godolphin, Register-General of all trading ships belonging to Great Britain, also a patent officer, received the copies of the ships' registers which collectors were obliged to furnish him with when they registered ships in accordance with the law. The function of the Inspector-General of imports and exports, Henry Martin, appointed by constitution, was to receive the account of all goods imported and exported at each port, and, by valuing each commodity at its prime cost, draw up an estimate of the balance of trade with every country and enter the details in a ledger. The Surveyor of the Outports, John Byde, patent officer, received from every Customs and comptroller of the Outports the quarterly books of imports and exports and the duties paid thereon. He examined the returns to ensure that the duties were correctly computed. The Inspector of the Outport Collectors' Vouchers, George Langton, appointed by patent, was responsible for receiving the collectors' accounts, and the vouchers in connection with their disbursements were examined and transmitted to the Comptroller General, William Burnet, who was also appointed by patent, and was responsible for keeping a check on collectors' accounts. He ensured that they were correctly stated and properly worked out, and that the remittances agreed with the credit side of the account. He had an assistant clerk, Robert Paul, who was appointed by constitution.

The Inspector of Prosecutions, Robert Wind, patent officer, had to keep an account of all prosecutions by Customs officers and ensure that the king's moiety of all fines and forfeitures was duly paid into the Exchequer. The Register of Seizures, Thomas Woodford, had to be informed of every seizure made by Customs officers, and checked on them to ensure that collusive seizures or compositions were not made.

The establishment of the port of London included two Collectors Outwards, the Earl of Manchester and Sir James Montague, both appointed by patent. They had deputies and clerks in the Long Room whose business was to accept entries, work out the duties and receive them on all goods entered outwards. The two Collectors Inwards, Sir John Shaw and Charles Shaw, appointed by patent, likewise had deputies and clerks in the Long Room who carried out the same work with regard to goods entered inwards. The Comptroller of the Port of London, Charles Downing, appointed by patent, was required to check upon the collection of Customs duties and approve all merchants' securities in connection with duties which were bondable. Such securities could not be accepted without his approval. The Comptroller of the Issues and Payments of the Receiver-General, Arnold Sansem, patent officer, had to ensure daily that the Receiver-General charged himself with the money and bonds he received from the collectors and receivers in the Port of London weekly, and that he charged himself with the money received on the bonds in his weekly certificate to the Treasury.

The Office of Surveyor, a patent officer, was held in trust for two of the Earl of Scarborough's sons and the incumbent was required to keep an account of the duties received and served as a check upon the Collector. The Surveyor-General, patent officer, had deputies and clerks in the Long Room. The Customer of the Petty Customs Inwards, patent officer, had to sign all warrants and keep an account along with the Collector for certain branches of the revenue and for petty customs on goods imported. The Customer of the Petty Customs Outwards, patent officer, carried out similar duties in respect of goods exported. The Comptroller of the Petty Customs, patent officer, was responsible for checking and controlling the Collectors of the Petty Customs. The Customer of the Great Customs on wool and leather exported, patent officer signed all warrants and kept an account along with the Collectors for the duties on wool and leather exported. The Comptroller of the Great Customs on wool and leather exported, patent officer, checked and controlled the Collectors of the duties.

The Usher of the Custom House, patent officer, was also Housekeeper, and was responsible under the terms of his patent for providing the doorkeepers and messengers and for attending the Commissioners. He also made small incidental payments and provided candles, fire and other necessaries, as well as all stationery except that for the Register General of trading ships who, by his patent, provided his own. The Usher also had a seat in the Long Room where he administered oaths, for each of which he demanded twopence but, through the courtesy of the merchants, normally received sixpence.

The Searchers Office was made up of the Chief Searcher, patent officer, six patent Under-Searchers, and five Searchers by deputation. They worked together and were responsible for the shipping of goods at Custom House Quay and for endorsing them on the cocket, which was then sent by a tidesman to Gravesend. There were also two patent Searchers at Gravesend who, however, acted by deputies who had to receive the cockets from the Searchers Office in London, check the cargoes of the outward bound ships against the cockets and then deliver them to the Masters of the ships.

There were nine Land Surveyors who supervised the Land Waiters and King's Waiters and were stationed on the quays between the Tower and London Bridge. They also adjudicated in case of allowance for damage. Land Surveyors were always promoted from Land or King's Waiters, who were responsible for controlling the landing of goods and checking against entries.

There were nineteen King's Waiters and thirty-one Land Waiters. The duties of both classes of officer were identical, but King's Waiters were appointed by a patent from the king, whereas the Land Waiters were appointed by a deputation from the Commissioners, in pursuance of a Warrant from the Lord High Treasurer.

Eight Tide Surveyors supervised the boarding of tidesmen on

ships and visited them from time to time. They attended to quarantine requirements and took it in turn to go to Gravesend, two
at a time, for placing tidesmen on board ships. One or more of
them also went down the river on every tide and cleared vessels
which had discharged their cargoes. Later in the century a higher
official, the Inspector of the River, was appointed. The two hundred tidewaiters or tidesmen as they were often called were
boarded on ships according to the type and value of the cargo,
from two to eight at a time. They had to ensure that no goods
were 'run', that ships were properly discharged and that goods on
which Drawback was claimed were not re-landed.

They were divided into two classes, 'preferable' and 'extraordinary', the first being in constant employment. They were regularly
sent to Gravesend to board ships from foreign and were lodged
at two taverns there. East Indiamen were boarded at Deal and the
tidesmen would journey thence from Gravesend on horseback.

In times of stress the tidesmen on the London Quays were
supplemented by temporary officials known as 'glutmen' and
senior tidesmen stationed at Custom House Quay were known as
'piazza men'.

There were seventeen Land Carriage Men who were appointed
to certain stations, where they could watch the inns to which the
waggons and packhorses came from the various ports of the kingdom, and see that no dutiable or prohibited goods were brought
except with proper certificates and permits or other proof of duty
payment and also to ensure that duty was paid on any goods
liable to the London duty. Lastly, seventeen Coast Waiters had to
supervise the landing and shipping of goods carried in coasting
vessels and ensure that goods consigned coastwise did not go
foreign and thus avoid the export duty.

In the outport headports there was normally a patent Collector
(Customer) Controller and Searcher. The patent officials frequently nominated officials to act in their stead, particularly in the
smaller ports, or creeks when some of the offices were often combined. Each port would have one or more Landwaiters and Tidewaiters and Coastwaiters whose functions were similar to those

of the London officials. As in London Tidewaiters were supervised by Tide Surveyors but in Liverpool there was also eventually an Inspector of the River.

The Wool Act of 1698 had brought about the establishment of a force of 'Riding Officers', supervised by 'Riding Surveyors' and the coal duties had ushered in the 'Coal Meters'.

PATRONAGE AND FEES

Today people think of patronage as an evil thing of the past and a system of appointment without regard to merit. It must be borne in mind, however, that apart from having been the accepted system for centuries, the field from which the revenue services could draw their officials was relatively small. The lowest established grades in the service, the Waiters, had to be able to read and write and keep accounts, as their work involved the checking of cargoes against documents and the tallying of the cargoes. Even more was expected of the higher grades who were called upon to carry out the intricate regulations of the time, to make the most involved calculations and to initiate legal action against offenders. It has often been argued that the appointments of men like Geoffrey Chaucer and William Congreve were mere sinecures, but the terms of Chaucer's first appointment as Comptroller of Customs in the Port of London stipulated that he should write the records in his own hand. Later he was given permission to have a deputy, but this did not necessarily mean that he no longer worked at the Office. Congreve had two Customs appointments, the first in 1700 as Patent Customer of the port of Poole, and it is probable that in this case he merely bore the financial responsibility and deputed a Collector to act for him – an extension of the farming system. Later in 1714 he was appointed an Under Searcher in the Port of London. In a contemporary account of the establishment and work of the London Officers, it was stated that there were six Patent Under Searchers, one of whom was Congreve, whose business it was to attend to the shipping of goods at Custom House Quay and endorse the contents on the cocket. There were also five Searchers by deputation who jointly did the same work as the Under Searchers. Thus it would appear that Congreve's position was not simply a sinecure. The need to recruit literate persons from a predominantly illiterate population may well account for the number of literary people in the revenue services, to mention only John Oldmixon, Adam Smith, Thomas Payne and Robert Burns.

The system of payment by fees has also come in for much criticism and yet, until the beginning of the nineteenth century, it was considered quite normal and not at all an evil practice. It was first and foremost a means of making the customer pay for the services, and it was thought right and proper that the merchant and ship-owner making the profit should in fact foot the bill. Today the cost of these services is spread over the whole community. In a manner of speaking, it was also a method of payment by results, for if trade fell off then so did the fees. The amounts paid by the Crown were nominal and it was expected that officials should raise their salaries to subsistence level in this manner.

There is no doubt that when trade increased certain officials such as the Duke of Manchester, hereditary Collector of Customs for the port of London Outwards, and the Earl of Liverpool, Collector Inwards, benefited from the correspondingly larger number of transactions and were indeed drawing very large sums for little or no actual service. But they carried at least the financial responsibility which the government in those days preferred to delegate to others. The Collector was personally responsible for all money until it was received by the Receiver General, and he was required to give adequate security on first taking up office.

THE FREETRADERS

Although there was a good deal of smuggling in earlier centuries, particularly the outward smuggling of wool, the smuggling of large quantities of goods inwards was hardly profitable before the eighteenth century because of the comparatively low duties and the difficulty in 'running' contraband in square-rigged ships. But the increased number of prohibitions, and the introduction of the fore and aft rig which improved manoeuvrability, lessened the risks involved so that this period has sometimes been referred to as the 'free trade era', and the smugglers described as 'freetraders'. There is no doubt that many people, particularly on the south coast, who, even if not engaged in smuggling themselves, had no qualms about buying contraband tea and brandy. Even the more fastidious did not regard smuggling as particularly reprehensible – much less as a crime.

It must be remembered in this connection that the Customs duties until 1671, and the Excise duties until 1683, had been collected by the farmers and it was well known that their profits had been far from small. Thomas Smythe was not the only one to have made a fortune in this way, and it is hardly likely that Cecil would have undertaken the farm of the Customs if it had not been profitable. During the farming period the population no doubt felt, with reason, that they were being exploited and that taxes were being extorted from them to swell the coffers of the financiers. As Adam Smith said: 'In countries where the public revenues are in farm, the farmers are generally the most opulent people and their wealth alone would excite public indignation.'

This attitude towards Customs and Excise duties no doubt persisted long after the end of farming, and was most probably reinforced by the enormous increase in taxation to finance the War of the Spanish Succession. Furthermore there were those who opposed a war in which they felt this country had become embroiled because of the Dutch connection, and those who as Jacobites resented any tribute whatsoever paid to one they did not consider their rightful monarch. Adam Smith, himself a Commissioner of Customs and whose father and grandfather were Customs officers, gave a lot of thought to this problem. When discussing smuggling he suggested that a smuggler was a person who, though no doubt highly blameable for violating the laws of his country, if frequently incapable of violating those of natural justice, would have been, in every respect, an excellent citizen had not the laws of his country made that a crime which nature never meant to be so. He also stated that not many people are scrupulous about smuggling when, without perjury, they can find an easy and safe opportunity of doing so and that later the smuggler, indulged by the public, is often encouraged to continue a trade which he is taught to consider in some measure innocent, and when the severity of the revenue laws is ready to fall upon him, he is frequently disposed to defend with violence what he has been accustomed to regard as his just property. As is well known Smith was of the opinion that the high duties on almost all goods imported caused merchant importers to smuggle as much and make entry of as little as they could. On the other hand, although respectable citizens may have indulged in smuggling or at least helped to finance it, there was a tendency for smuggling to attract the criminal element to its ranks, both on land and at sea.

It will be seen from the evidence provided by the Customs Letter Books that the Preventive Service had a very difficult task indeed for the officers were expected to cope with adversaries much superior to themselves both in numbers and fire power. The Waterguard service afloat could rarely take on a smuggling cutter unaided in the early part of the century and even much later, when the cruisers were faster and better armed, the smuggling vessels were usually one step ahead. In order to lessen the odds, regulations were introduced limiting the size of vessels and of the packets they carried. It was made an offence for a ship to be fitted with a bowsprit more than two-thirds its length. Naval vessels rendered useful service from time to time but they were often unreliable and were sometimes suspected of being in league with the smugglers, or at least willing to do a deal. Even the revenue officials themselves were not free from suspicion but it seems that, although the Commissioners were aware of this, they relied upon the effect of the rewards to stimulate the revenue zeal of their staff.

With the best will in the world, however, it required officers of great courage and determination to stand up to the uneven odds. The cruisers were regarded as the first line of defence, and ashore or near the coast the tidewaiters under their tide surveyor were expected to intercept smugglers who had escaped the vigilance of the cruisers. Landings were often made at lonely places where no tidesmen were stationed and then reliance was placed on the riding officer who was engaged in regular patrols, often at a considerable distance inland. When a landing of contraband had taken place, it was customary for the 'country people' – as the smugglers were called – to assemble in large numbers and load the contraband on their horses. They were usually armed with clubs, but frequently in the case of the organized gangs such as the Hawkhurst Gang, they carried blunderbusses, fusees, pistols and swords. The unfortunate riding officer, although armed, was usually alone and had no chance against the well-equipped gangs. It has been suggested that the officers were often cowardly, but since they themselves reported their own inadequacy on so many occasions one can only assume that they realized that any attempt to oppose such force was utterly futile. Their superiors, and the Commissioners as well, most probably concurred in this view. In time, and usually after constant petitioning by the Collector, regiments of dragoons were stationed in strategic places, but they usually arrived on the scene much too late to be of any real assistance. In some areas, where the Collectors were particularly zealous and energetic – for example, William Arnold at Cowes or Philip Taylor at Weymouth – their efforts seemed to be attended with a fair amount of success, but it was well-known that smugglers soon changed their scenes of operation if certain areas became too difficult. Even when smugglers were caught it was often very difficult to secure convictions as the juries, if not actually composed of smugglers, were either in sympathy with them or under some compulsion to acquit them.

In addition to these obstacles, the Customs service was expected to carry out numerous duties other than purely revenue ones. Shipwrecks were frequent in many areas and officers were expected to secure cargo, to help in rescuing the shipwrecked crew, and – most arduous of all – to prevent the local populace from looting. Wreck had to be salved and the salvors paid, and there were countless disputes with the lords of the manor over foreshore rights.

The Navigation Laws had to be applied and this took up a great deal of time since it necessitated the taking of oaths, as well as arranging for Certificates of Registry to be issued and ships measured. By the end of the century the registering of British ships had become a complicated and exacting job. The receipt of light dues was by now a regular function of the Customs service, and a number of other minor duties were performed in connection with shipping and seamen; for example, the registering of apprentices. One of the most important of the non-revenue duties was the running of the quarantine service. The cruisers were expected to assist in this, but it was primarily the task of the tidesmen. A vessel was required to bring to at a boarding station where the master was questioned about the health of the crew and passengers. Vessels from known infected areas or suspected areas were ordered to perform quarantine, and it was up to the Customs service to ensure that it was not broken. Soldiers were sometimes called upon for assistance since seamen frequently made violent attempts to go ashore, and heavy penalties were imposed on persons evading or breaking quarantine.

The cutters and cruisers of the service, in the early days called smacks, luggers or sloops, were sometimes called upon to help the navy. Many of the ships were armed and later in the century, when the Customs had built up a large Waterguard fleet, many of the vessels were issued with 'Letters of Marque' so that they could defend British merchant ships from French privateers. This also enabled them to capture enemy merchant shipping, and commanders of Customs vessels were frequently given naval rank. This, coupled with the fact that naval vessels were often assigned to Customs duties, brought the two services into close contact and the effect of this connection is still felt today when naval officers, in certain circumstances, may act as Customs officers, and Customs Waterguard officers still wear naval-type uniform. The revenue craft were expected to remain constantly at sea and the crews constantly acquired an unrivalled knowledge of the coast much of which was charted by them.

The early life-saving methods were also developed by the

Customs service, a tradition which continued until the Coastguard service was finally withdrawn. Press gangs were very active in the eighteenth century and it was part of the Collector's duty at this time to help them by supplying names, handing over smugglers, and paying their travelling expenses and subsistence money.

The Excise service to a certain extent shared the tribulations of the Customs service, since during the greater part of the eighteenth century there were many Excise import duties to be collected and in many ports the revenue was protected by both Customs and Excise cruisers. Although there was a fair amount of rivalry between the two services, they did quite frequently co-operate with each other, particularly in the Cowes area during Arnold's time as Collector. Although the Excise still retained a service afloat, it was, however, essentially a 'riding' force, and its districts were divided into 'rides'. Strangely enough, the Excise service always seemed to arouse much more hostility than the Customs, and Dr. Johnson's definition of Excise as a 'hateful tax levied upon commodities, and adjudged not by the common judges of property, but by wretches hired by those to whom the excise is paid' was not an opinion peculiar to the great lexicographer.

A number of eminent people were employed in both revenue services during the century. Adam Smith, author of *The Wealth of Nations*, was a Commissioner of Customs at Edinburgh from 1778 to 1791, Robert Burns, Excise Officer at Dumfries from 1789 to 1796, and Thomas Paine, author of the *Rights of Man* and *The Age of Reason*, was twice dismissed from the Excise and twice condemned to death, once in England for sedition and once in France, when as a member of the National Assembly, he disagreed with Robespierre.

The beginning of the Hanoverian period was an uneasy time for the members of the Customs and Excise both at the top and the bottom of the scale. Many were known to have been Jacobite sympathizers, or were suspected of being such, and at the time of the first Jacobite rebellion officers were liable to be denounced and stood the risk of forfeiting their employment. Mathew Prior, the poet, who was a Customs Commissioner at this time, was dismissed on impeachment by Sir Robert Walpole. An Excise Record of 1715 sheds some light on the means the Old Pretender adopted in order to pay his way through England without resorting to pillage; he merely collected the Excise receipts at Carlisle.

On the 24th September 1715, the Commissioners of Customs wrote to the Collector at Liverpool instructing him to inform all the Customs Officers in his port to use all endeavour to apprehend and secure Sir William Wyndham. Sir William, a Jacobite, was a former Chancellor of the Exchequer. At this period an order was issued to the service enjoining members 'to use their utmost care and diligence to detect all secret practices whatever which may at any time be carrying on to the disturbance of the Government'. In November 1715 the Collector at Liverpool expressed concern about the money, books and bonds in his custody as the Old Pretender was said to be at Lancaster and was expected at Preston. He told the Board 'and for cash I have but about £160 by me which I have just received, and hope the rebells will not come this way to meddle with it'. He also assured the Board that 'for my part I shall not be wanting to venture my life and all I have for His Majesty King George'.

A year later the rebellion still occupied the attention of the Customs service. Its members were instructed by the Board 'to make diligent search as to all passengers and to be as watchful as possible for discovering Mr. Foster who has this morning made his escape out of Newgate, to prevent his getting out of the Kingdom'. Then followed a description of Foster, who was the Member of Parliament for Northumberland, and a leader of the Jacobite rising. The same year a tidesman at Lancaster, Edward Hunt, was dismissed when it was reported that he had drunk the Pretender's health, and in October 1716, the Board wrote to the Collector at Liverpool stating that, 'we are informed that William Purchase, Waiter and Searcher at Meals, his wife is a roman catholick and that he suffers his children to be educated in the same religion, you are to examine and report to us the truth thereof with your opinion'. A month later the Board instructed the Collector to dismiss William Purchase.

Chapter 5

SMUGGLING IN THE
EIGHTEENTH CENTURY

The pattern of smuggling which had evolved in the latter part of the seventeenth century relied to a large extent on the inability of the Customs vessels to cope with the larger, better-manned and more heavily armed smuggling craft. It was usual for the smugglers to approach a lonely part of the coast where they had a rendezvous with their confederates ashore and to transfer the contraband to small boats. If they were challenged by Customs officers they would either attempt to make a run for it, talk their way out of the situation by making some excuse for their presence in the area or, if these expedients failed, resort to violence.

The Customs officials were generally resented, and some of them, no doubt, were only too ready to turn a blind eye to smuggling activities rather than risk their lives, but there were, nevertheless, some very conscientious officers who did not spare themselves in their attempts to combat this menace. Mr. Mears, Commander of the yacht *Calshott* which was attached to Southampton, appears to have been such an officer. At 2 a.m. one Sunday morning in June 1715 he came across a vessel at Hell's Head which, on sighting him, immediately 'tacked about and stood for sea'. Mears gave chase and brought it to anchor. On board he found 'sixty-three anchors and three half anchors containing about 600 gallons of French brandy'. Leaving two men on the vessel, he went on shore at Hell's Head where he discovered a wherry and eight men armed with clubs. Close to the waterside he noticed a set of waggon-tracks. Several houses and barns in the area were searched but nothing was found. On being questioned, the master of the vessel, Charles Jacobs, a notorious smuggler, claimed that he was bound for Ostend. This did not convince Mears, however, who took the smuggling vessel in charge and brought her to Southampton.

For much of the time the smugglers seem to have been a step ahead of the revenue forces, and in the early part of the century were able to outsail and out-manoeuvre the Waterguard vessels. Philip Taylor, the Collector at Weymouth, drew attention to this in a letter to the Board on the 18th March 1716. He stated that the Poole and Dartmouth smacks had been of very little service to the revenue of his port which would not suffer by their being 'laid aside'. He did, however, press for the appointment of a riding officer and maintained that this would be of service in detecting the 'the great runing of goods as most of the goods runed in these parts are conveyed by way of Sherborne to Bristol and other great towns'. He went on to say that 'it would be very condusive to ye service of the Revenue to fix a riding officer at Sherborne who is a resolute honest fellow and knows the roads and buyways from the sea to that place . . .'

Less than a year later the Weymouth Collector was pressing for additional riding officers, one for Cerne Abbas, one for Dorchester and one for Piddle Town. After suggesting the areas to be covered he gave his opinion as to the type of man to be recruited. He considered that 'as the smuglers ride with companys of armed men twenty, thirty and forty in a gang and very dangerous to the officers in the night time, wee are humbly of opinion that ye persons imployed in this service be men that are hardy, unmarryed and are well acquainted with the country soe they maynt have the clogg of a family and may be capable from their acquaintance to cultivate a friendship with the country people to have their assistance on occasion without which the service will not be soe well performed'.

The appointment of additional riding officers did not seem to have had the desired effect for in the following year we find Philip Taylor once again pressing the Board, this time for military assistance. He told them that the 'smugling traders in these parts are grown to such a head that they bidd deffiance to all Law and Government. They come very often in gangs of 60 to 100 men to the shoar in disguise armed with swords, pistolls, blunderbusses, carbines & quarter staffs & not only carry off with the goods they land in deffiance of the officers but beat, knock down & abuse whoever they meet in their way soe that travelling by night neer the coast & the peace of the country are become very precarious and if an effectual law be not speedily passed, nothing but a military force can support the officers in the due discharge of their dutyes.'

Sometimes the religious and political feeling of the period seems to have been tied up with smuggling activities, if we are to judge by yet another communication of the 11th April 1719, from the conscientious Philip Taylor. It appears that the Board had instructed him to arrange for the search of Lulworth Castle belonging to Mr. Weld, a Roman Catholic, as well as many other suspected houses in the area. After making some seizures of brandy, pepper, wine and vinegar the revenue officers proceeded into the Isle of Purbeck to continue their search. Mr. Taylor then explained that 'as Blackmore is the most disafected part of this country abounding with great numbers of dangerous rogues, two whereof wee hear were thursday last committed for declaring themselves for the Pretender, & consequently a place very fitt to be searched we have accordingly narrowly searched severall houses & there seized yesterday in the house of Jacob Fox, two anchors of Brandy!'

No doubt a brisk trade in contraband goods was carried on with London. The Collector told the Commissioners that, as a result of their letter, he had consulted his informer who said that he was not too well acquainted with London, but that after going from Knightsbridge to Charing Cross, 'he did not keep streight to the road but turned to the left hand and left the goods at the sign of the Bell a grocers shop & one Mr. Rawlings keeps the same – that this shop is a magazine for receiving of runned goods of Chas. Weeks . . .'

Although Mr. Taylor was obviously a dedicated revenue man, he did sometimes give his mind to other things, and we find him putting in a word for one of his officers. Mr. Oldfield, the Riding Officer at Dorchester, had received a letter that 'his elder brother (who is a gentleman of Fortune & from whome he has a great expectation) lyes dangerously ill in the smallpox near London & desires to see him'. The Collector allowed him six days' leave and supported his request for a further ten days. Mr. Taylor ended his letter, 'As his fortune on this occasion seemes to be at stake and he not haveing been absent from his duty since an officer, I am humbly of opinion it may be highly reasonable to grant him the further leave of tenn days under such abatement of salary as your Honrs. shall think reasonable.'

At this period the revenue officers on the East Coast were also stretched to the utmost in contending with the illicit traders. We find the Collector of Newcastle reporting on the 21st August 1724 that Captain Robinson of the *Spye* sloop had brought into the port a French dogger of about 50 tons burthen called *La Mouche* of Calais, with 56 half ankers of brandy on board. Captain Robinson met the dogger 'hovering on ye Lincolnshire coast with a French snow in company'. They fired several shots at the *Spye* but 'at last all ye crew save two boys quitted ye Dogger and made their escape in ye Snow'.

The lack of adequate equipment and staff to protect certain parts of the coast was also a problem. It was found that the two boatmen at Blythnook were not making use of their boat, and when the Collector enquired the reason he was told that it was rotten and not fit for service. Finding this to be true, he wrote to the Board and asked for a new one, at the same time telling the Commissioners that he had reason to believe that more goods were run in Blythnook than all the rest of the Port. He also informed them that one of the boatmen there 'by a lingering distemper & old age together is become a perfect skeleton & not fit for service either by land or water'. But it appears that his request for more capable officers at Blythnook was not acceded to for, on 19th June of the following year, he was impressing upon the Board that 'Blythnook is become a place of great trade both for coasting and oversea vessels & that a very great smuggling trade is carried on almost without ye least disturbance there being only two officers.'

Conscientious revenue officers sometimes had difficulty in establishing seizures, and this was the case with Captain Robinson of the *Spy*. When he sent into Hull a Dutch dogger which had on board 180 casks of brandy, 13 English guineas and some English silver, the Board informed the Collector that Captain Robinson should be called upon to justify the seizure, and that the goods be delivered to the master, unless Robinson would undertake prosecution at his own risk. In reply to the Board Captain Robinson declared, 'I'll not stand tryal at my own charge, and I've sent to Mr. Grant, ye Dutch merchant's Solicitor, to know how he would propose to bring ye matter to an Amicable agreem^t. His ans^r shall be handed to your Honble Board, on whom I shall throw myself entirely, to be made clear of all Charge, litigious Cavill, & law-suit, for I have done no more than my duty in bringing ye vessell in your suspicion.'

Evidence of a good deal of activity by the Waterguard and Navy vessels is provided in a letter acknowledging the orders that the *Deal Castle* sloop was to cruise between Newcastle and Leith, and the *Spy* sloop between the 'Firth of Edinburgh' and Newcastle. Captain Mead of the *Deal Castle* was reported to have brought into Shields four French vessels which were smuggling on the coast. From these ships were taken 790 half ankers of brandy and gold and silver coin worth about £180.

Customers, Controllers and Searchers were appointed by patent or Treasury Warrant, but although the patent officers in their turn had the right to appoint deputies, the Treasury frequently wished to influence their choice. Many of the Collectors had other interests, and it is interesting to note that in 1726 the Board was informed by the Collector that the Deputy Collector at Blythnook had been acquainted with their decision that 'he should not for the future receive any salary or reward from ye proprietors of the severall collieries &c and he has assured us that he has not received anything from them since the time he was acquainted therewith which was on ye 25th March last nor will for the future receive from them any gratuity or reward whatsoever.'

On the north-west coast of England revenue protection was made very difficult by the proximity of the Isle of Man, which at that time was overrun by smugglers. The Collector at Whitehaven was particularly concerned about this. On the 18th October 1723 he told the Board that as ships from Virginia and abroad had arrived, and more were expected, he would have to recall the officers he had sent to Millham (Millom) to help combat the smugglers who were running brandy, tobacco and other goods from the Isle of Man.

The Collector had even more serious business to report in May 1730, for the crew of the cruiser he sent to assist the officers at Carlisle in seizing two wherries were attacked at Annan by the smugglers and 'several other wicked persons' as they were waiting for the tide to bring up their boat. The smugglers 'beat them most unmercifully and after giving them several wounds, left them for dead and carryed away their arms.' In a later letter the Collector reported that examinations on oath had been taken from the assaulted men before a Commissioner in the King's Bench and had been sent to the Scottish Commissioners at Edinburgh. He went on to say that he had been informed that one of the wherries which was seized and rescued by the smugglers was now in the Isle of Man and might be easily secured there by leave from the Lord Derby (at that time Lord of Man).

Although the Collectors generally seem to have been tough with the smugglers, and also with their staff, instances occur of a humane attitude towards the peccadilloes of their subordinates, and sometimes, too, they put in a good word for the smugglers whom they have had convicted. When the Board asked the Collector of Whitehaven to report on John Swinburn, late waiter and searcher of the port, who had been dismissed and had petitioned the Commissioners for reinstatement, the Collector said that he had carefully examined the petition and had found that the statement, that Swinburn's wife had formerly sometimes sold ale but on account of lack of credit had been obliged to discontinue the trade, to be true. He continued 'since that time they have not only been forc'd to dispose of their household goods but even wearing apparell, to preserve 'em from starving. Mr. Swinburn was born to an estate and marry'd a Baronet's daughter, but by misfortune fell into decay and has not now anything we know of to support him. We humbly are of opinion he is a person truly within the rules of qualification laid down in your Honrs letter of the 27th of July, 1721 and that he is a proper object of your Honrs Charity.'

In 1731 the Board asked the Collector at Whitehaven to report on the services given by Captain Roper, commander of the wherry employed in the area, and also to ask Roper to give his his opinion as to the possible usefulness of such craft on other parts of the coast, and in particular to guard the River Thames. The Collector explained that a year previously Captain Roper had brought the wherry from Dublin, where she was built, and since then had captured two smuggling boats from the Isle of Man, each carrying 24 casks containing in all 409 gallons of brandy. He had also picked up from the sea some casks containing about 40 gallons of brandy. These had been thrown overboard by another boat so that the smugglers could make their escape. The Collector went on to point out that when they had used open boats, which were not good sailing ships, to guard the coast they had been at a serious disadvantage since the smugglers at that time used large wherries of ten or twelve tons which easily outsailed the Customs boats. 'But', he continued, 'since this wherry was employed we observe that this clandestine trade is now all managed in open boats with good oars which draw little water, thrust into any place, over any bank, and can easily, if it do not blow, out-row the cruiser which is built for sailing and rather too heavy to be managed by oars with any success . . .' In order to deal with this new situation it was suggested that a small boat should be constructed for 'rowing swiftly with four or six oars and with some alterations to be made on the wherry's deck so that the boat could be stowed there'. In conclusion, it was stated that 'if Mr. Roper do but duly exert himself and do his duty in the service, there cannot be anything that we can think of more effectually to detect or deter these runners . . .' The Commissioners appear to have been impressed by these recommendations, for on 21st August of the same year they asked for a further opinion from Captain Roper as to the advisability of employing a wherry type of boat to guard the River Thames below Gravesend, rather than a larger vessel, and he was also asked how far on each side of the channel such boats should be stationed.

An insight into the strength of the Waterguard in this vulnerable area of the north-west coastline can be gained from the details of a crave for arms by Whitehaven in April 1732:

The names of the officers humbly proposed to have arms.

	Case of Pistols	Horseman's Sword
Thomas Pearson, Riding Officer at Allonby	1	1
William Yair, Riding Officer at Flimby	1	1
Timothy Fisher, Riding Officer at Workington	1	1
For the use of the Tidesmen and Boatmen at Workington who are often occasionally sent to watch the coast at night on each side of the River	2	2
Thomas Dickenson, Waiter & Searcher at Parton	1	1
Thomas Peirce, Riding Officer at Cutherton	1	1
Edward Herring, Riding Officer at Ravenglas	1	1
Walter Graham, Riding Officer at Annaside	1	1
Robert Hewetson, Riding Officer at Millam	1	1
	10	10

In a letter to the Board in October 1736, the officials at White-haven went into greater detail about the revenue danger from the Isle of Man. Having been asked to report on the present state of the smuggling trade, they told their Honours that they were aware that the town and country 'are still mostly supplied with brandy, rum, tea, tobacco, soap and other high duty goods illegally imported'. They were 'apprehensive they are furnished with these commodities from Ireland but chiefly from that "warehouse of Frauds",' the Isle of Man. Since the island lay close opposite and in open view of the coast, the boats there could easily row or sail over and unload their cargo in the night at almost any place on the open shore. They could pick the state of the tide, bury the contraband and return to sea in two hours without alerting the preventive staff, unless they were seen before dark; but they usually avoided the daylight. The goods were then left in the hiding-place until the owner found a purchaser.

Other boats, called 'bumboats', were also used by the merchants of the island. These would lie about a mile off the coast in day-time, loaded with brandy and rum, awaiting the return of the light colliers or other vessels from Ireland and elsewhere, bound for the Cumberland or Scottish coast. The bumboats sold their goods to these ships and then returned to the island for fresh supplies. The practice was for the vessels which had received the contraband either to pass it off as stores or, if there was too much for this, to sink it in the sea and mark it. Sometimes they also hid it on the ship or buried it in the ballast.

Further south, the Customs officials at Liverpool were also troubled by the Isle of Man smugglers. In 1726 we find that Captain Richmond of the *Royal George* yacht had complained about the bad reception afforded to himself and his crew by the people of the island. This was reported to the Board, and they were also informed that the island was full of foreign goods ready to be run into Great Britain and Ireland. Later in the same year Captain Richmond pursued a boat near Scotland and captured her. There were 84 casks of brandy on board. Papers were produced covering a coastwise journey in the Isle of Man, and it was claimed that the vessel had been blown off course. The following year the Commissioners were told that Richmond had been threatened with imprisonment if he searched any vessel in Manx ports. The Board had ordered that all ships which cleared out at Liverpool with goods requiring a certificate should be notified to the Customs officer in the Isle of Man. It appeared that this could only be done safely by the Customs sloop. In 1732 Captain Richmond was still active around the Isle of Man, and reported that he had found there thirty vessels loading brandy and other goods which he thought were intended for north Britain and Ireland.

In August 1743 the Board of Customs gave consideration to the question of the powers of officers stationed on the Isle of Man. When the Collector of Liverpool was consulted, he gave it as his opinion that they were of scarcely any service to the Revenue. He said that the main reason for an officer being placed there was to give an account of the trade of the island in general, and also to report when any foreign goods were shipped for any part of Great Britain. The Collector claimed that these advices never came to hand in time to prevent any fraud, as they were of necessity sent by the smuggling vessel itself. Five years later this problem was still occupying the minds of the Commissioners, and as a result of their command the Collector of Liverpool offered some observations as to the means of dealing with this clandestine trade. He stated that goods such as brandy, wine, rum, tea, soap and other foreign goods were imported into the island by foreign ships from Holland, France, Sweden and other countries. The tobacco there was mainly exported from Great Britain and entered out as foreign. It was then relanded in the island. The rum was usually imported directly from the Plantations. The remedy suggested by the Collector was the purchasing of the Revenue there from the Duke of Atholl, who had inherited the island from the Earls of Derby in 1736. He estimated that the revenue received by the Duke of Atholl amounted to £1,400 or £1,500 per annum. If the British government were to give the Duke £2,000 or even £3,000 the Revenue would save as least £40,000 per annum. In case this should not materialize, he made some other suggestions such as the limiting of the size of vessels in respect of which drawback should be allowed, the forfeiture of vessels in the case of the relanding of goods which had been entered outwards, and finally a reduction in the tobacco duty. It was seventeen years before the first of these suggestions was acted upon, and in the meantime the Manx smugglers were to continue to trouble the revenue forces of the north-west. A letter to the Board in November 1750 stated that the goods were run at night-time, and that the officers on the coast could do nothing as they were single-handed and placed five or six miles from each other.

That the smugglers had become even bolder was obvious from the report of George Dow, Commander of the revenue cruiser *Sincerity* who, in July 1750, had seized a Dutch dogger loaded with India goods, only to be attacked by armed people in the Isle of Man. His boat and firearms were seized, and his cruiser turned adrift. Four of his men were taken prisoner and were still being held there in October. The Collector appealed to the Board to do something to set the poor fellows at liberty, for otherwise they would perish as the prison was not a place 'for a christian to be confined in'. The Collector received a letter from Mr. Sidebotham, officer in the island, in February 1751, announcing the release of the mariners belonging to the *Sincerity*, and also stating that the pernicious trade there was increasing daily.

In Whitehaven, too, the officers had the mortification of seeing fleets of smuggling vessels from the island making for the Scottish coast. The Custom House sloop was unable to get near them among the sandbanks and shoals, for the 'people in that Wicked Island' were still holding on to the boat they had seized from Captain Dow. Even in 1764 the memory of Captain Dow's mishap had not faded, and John Burrow, Collector, pointed out to the Commissioners that since that episode no person dared offer to molest the ships landing their cargoes in the island. The merchants there continued in safety to pack goods for running, or to send out bumboats to meet the coasters.

The sovereignty of the Isle of Man was re-vested in the crown in 1765. Compensation was paid to the Duke of Atholl and the crown was able to take immediate measures to prevent the landing of foreign cargoes there. This seems to have achieved the desired effect, for the island no longer figured prominently in smuggling reports. The ultimate effect, however, seems to have been merely the diverting of smuggling from one area to another. When the Collector at Beaumaris was asked his opinion about smuggling since the annexation of the Isle of Man to the crown, he declared that vessels were now fitted out from Ireland, and that large vessels had been built for this trade in Liverpool. He cited the case of one large cutter which landed her cargo at Ormshead. Twenty well-armed men were sent on shore to make good the landing, but the vessel had suffered some damage and was obliged to leave. When the Customs officers searched the area they found in a house near the sea six blunderbusses, five muskets, seven horse pistols, thirteen cutlasses and fifty pounds of gunpowder. Others found three carriage guns and other equipment buried in the shale on the beach.

Eight years later the Collector reported to the Commissioners that a large Irish smuggling cutter had been landing tea and spirits at places on the Welsh coast and Anglesey. The smugglers had threatened any officer who should seize any of the goods landed that they would 'demolish such officer and burn his house'. They had also expressed the wish to meet with the Customs cutter, the *Pearl*. On account of this, the captain of the *Pearl*, Gambold, asked for four carriage guns to be sent for the use of the cutter. In the same letter the Collector suggested that, as a sloop of war and two Admiralty cutters were stationed at Douglas in the Isle of Man, one of these might well be spared for Beaumaris so that it could cruise along the Welsh coast and assist the *Pearl* to deal with the powerful smuggler.

In 1783 the Collector at Beaumaris reported a great increase in smuggling, stating that many vessels belonging to various parts of Ireland had been built with the purpose of smuggling. They were very well-manned and carried between ten and twenty guns, as well as a great number of small arms. After the contraband had been landed, the crews of the smuggling vessels escorted the 'country people' and defied the king's officers. Later the same year the Collector reported that a vessel laden with brandy and geneva was lying off Pwllheli. He had informed Captain Foukes of the *Lynx* cutter but did not think she could seize the vessel, which carried fourteen guns, since she was only equipped with small arms.

During this period, officers at the Bristol Channel ports were concerned about smuggling from Barry and Lundy Islands, off the coast. It seems that this smuggling had been interrupted by the war with the French, for on 15th October 1748 the Collector at Barnstaple felt it his duty to inform the Board that the smuggling trade had begun once again. One or two vessels had run brandy, claret and similar goods in Lundy Road, and he was very apprehensive that 'this pernicious trade of smuggling' would again be carried on with great impunity, unless a smack were ordered to prevent it.

In September 1751 the Board was told that Mr. Benson, proprietor of the island of Lundy, wished to send sundry provisions and also four or six hogsheads of tobacco to the island, and offered to give a Coast Bond if the Collector should send over an officer to certify the landing. The Board was asked for directions, and it was also pointed out that the produce of the island was brought to Barnstaple from time to time; particularly wool, sheep and bullocks. Four years later the Commissioners wrote to the Collector stating that they had received information that a new trade was being carried on in the Island of Lundy. Many ships bound outwards from Barnstaple Bay unloaded there and the cargoes were afterwards returned in other vessels. It was also reported that a gun platform had been erected there and shots fired at ships to force them to bring to and explain who and what they were. The Commissioners feared that unless an immediate stop was put to this business, the island would become a 'magazine for smugglers'. Commenting on this information, the Collector replied that it was difficult to prevent this clandestine trade. Since the island was not within the limits of any port and was upwards of four leagues from any shore, he felt that the legality of seizures made could be disputed. He again pointed out that many applications were received for despatches to convey goods to the island for the use of the inhabitants, but he was at a loss to know how to act as there was no officer there to certify the landing or to discharge the bond. The proprietor of the island had complained that he was deprived even of the common privileges of a subject.

The officers on the other side of the Bristol Channel were also very much concerned about Lundy, and the Collector at Cardiff even went so far as to say that he believed, 'There never lived yet a man on the Island of Lundy who was not concerned in smuggling.' He pointed out that, owing to the extensiveness of the coast, the officers could not prevent landings, nor had they any boats or force to cope with the smugglers at sea. He, too, considered that the only effective way of stopping the smuggling would be to provide a good cutter, well-manned, and mounted with a few guns to sweep the Channel from Lundy to Bristol. He stated that there was in the Channel at that time a smuggling vessel with at least forty men on board. There were a number of danger spots, but he thought that the principal place was the Island of Lundy which he considered should be purchased by the Government.

About this time, a report was made to the Commissioners of Customs by the Collector at Swansea of a seizure by Captain Dickenson of the *Lady Mackworth* on the Island of Lundy. It appears that Captain Dickenson was on his way to Swansea when he saw a small cutter off the Island of Lundy and immediately gave chase. He was unable to come up with the cutter but, as he had reason to believe she had landed part of her cargo, he gave orders to search the island. In cavities in the rocks and in small huts, his crew found 128 ankers of brandy and 4 bags of Bohea tea. Two years later the officers at Cardiff felt that they had successfully coped with the smuggling in the Island of Barry, as they had driven away from there the notorious smuggler Knight and his armed brig. But it was at the expense of Lundy, since they suspected that he had established himself there 'on the same bad business'.

On the south coast, smugglers seemed to rely mainly on their well-armed ships and crews, and the officers at the ports frequently reported their helplessness in the face of great odds. The Collector at Penzance, for instance, 'acquaints their Honours that the smugglers are carrying on a greater trade than ever', and, 'that the officers dare not do their duty for fear of being knocked on the head because of the vast numbers of smugglers that assemble together'. Years later Penzance still complained that though there was a great deal of smuggling in Mounts Bay, little had been seized for want of a cutter.

The smugglers on the south coast seem to have been exceptionally violent. The murder of one of the officers stationed at Porthleven is recorded after he and another officer had seized some prohibited goods. A month later it was reported that two of the murderers were in Guernsey and the other two in France. In October 1776 another officer, Thomas Davies, gave an account of his treatment at the hands of the smugglers. He was on his way home from duty at Breage when he met seven or eight smugglers who were carrying goods, and 'wished them a good night'. Three of them immediately ran across a cornfield, headed him off and, hurling stones, knocked him off his horse. They then jumped over the hedge and beat him with great whips and stones. They left him for dead and threw a rock weighing fifty-nine pounds on his back. Davies thought he must have lain there senseless for more than an hour. It was later discovered that he had six cuts on his head, two pieces off one of his ears, and the bone of his nose was broken.

In 1755 the Board were informed of the death of John Hurley, Riding Officer at Branscombe, who was killed by falling over the White Cliff near Seaton as he was on the look out for a smuggling boat. It was reported that at the time of the accident a great number of women, the wives of smugglers, were on the edge of the cliff making fires as a signal to the expected boat and it was suspected that they were responsible for his death. But at the inquest the women were carefully examined by the Coroner, and stated on oath that the deceased 'accidentally fell over in running from one fire to another to put them out'. The jury brought in a verdict of accidental death, but as there had been many threats by smugglers against both Hurley and Mr. Boots, Riding Officer at Beer, it seems more than likely that Hurley was in fact pushed over. Soon after this incident the Collector appealed to the Board for a supply of arms for the officers, pointing out that the smugglers bid them defiance when they are in gangs. Oddly enough, one of the men for whom the arms were requisitioned was William Hurley, Riding Officer at Branscombe, possibly a relative of the dead officer, but nothing deterred by his fate.

Officers frequently reported their failure to prevent smuggling. An instance of this occurred when, during the hours of darkness, George Langden, preferable tidesman, met a party of smugglers with thirty horses loaded with tea entering the West Gate of Exeter. He attempted to seize one of the horses but was surrounded by the smugglers who used 'dreadful threats, oaths and imprecations and obliged him to desist'. He followed them and noticed that they went through the city and out into the country. Afterwards officers were sent to search but without success. It was thought that the goods had been landed in Torbay by the Beer smugglers.

The same gang is credited with accomplishing another successful run in 1766. Some of the officers were on watch during the night of 19th of April, and between midnight and one o'clock fell in with a body of smugglers of more than forty men and fifty horses apparently loaded with tea. The officers, considering the odds too great, tried to escape but one of their number, William Hunt, a boatman at Exmouth, having but an indifferent horse fell into their hands and was 'most barbarously wounded and beat insomuch that his life is in great danger'. It was estimated that they were carrying about 5,000 lbs. tea. In July of the same year the Collector transmitted the surgeon's bill for treating Hunt and described how the surgeon had replaced his dislocated shoulder. He was 'carried to an apple engine and being fastened round the body to a stake in the ground it was by the meer force of that screw brought in again'.

The lengths to which smugglers were prepared to go, and their sheer effrontery, are evident from the account given by the Weymouth officers of the adventure of Captain Lisle of the *Beehive* cutter. He saw a small vessel stand in for Portland, which altered course on sighting the Revenue cutter. The *Beehive* gave chase and came up with her after five hours. She refused to bring to and Johnson, chief mate of the *Beehive* signalled to the *Diamond* tender belonging to the *Lenox* man-of-war to come to his assistance. Hough Forbes, Lieutenant of the man-of-war, and John Johnson boarded the smuggler. When the tender's boat got loose, the *Beehive*'s boat was used to go after it so that the whole party was weakened. John Hastings, master of the smuggling vessel, took advantage of this and 'finding means to get the lieutenant, Johnson and the other persons in the great cabbin, shut 'em in and nail'd them up'. The smuggler then put before the wind, carrying the revenue and naval people with him. Later in the month a further letter to the Commissioners gave information about the smuggling vessel and its crew and stated that the officials who had been carried off had been landed at Boulogne.

One of the few King's Warehouse accounts which has survived gives some idea of the size of seizures made in this area:

31 July 1743	by Thomas Packer	4 lbs. Tea
1 Aug.	by S. Templeman (Surveyor)	8 gallons Brandy
12 Aug.	by Barker Russell (Tidesman)	4 lbs. Tea
19 Aug.	by Barker Russell	$4\frac{3}{4}$ gallons Brandy
25 Aug.	by William Biles	56 lbs. Tea 10 gallons Brandy 25 gallons Rum
26 Aug.	by Warren Lisle (Searcher)	452 gallons Brandy 53 gallons Rum
30 Aug.	by William Biles	95 gallons Brandy 4 gallons Rum 100 lbs. Tobacco
3 Sept.	by William Biles	109 gallons Brandy 10 lbs. Tea 60 lbs. Tobacco

A year or so later the Weymouth Collector reported that he had put 3,994 lbs. of tea up for sale but had sold no more than 1,020 lbs. at 6s. 0d., 6s. 1d. and 6s. 2d. per lb.

The most gruesome of all the outrages committed by the smugglers at this time resulted in the murders of a Customs officer and of an informer. A number of smugglers who had had tea seized from them by a revenue cutter broke open the Custom House at Poole and carried away a large quantity of tea. On the 6 February 1747 Mr. Till, the Collector of Chichester, told the Board of Customs that John Diamond (alias Dimer), one of the persons concerned in the affair had been apprehended and committed to gaol. The Commissioners instructed Mr. Till to find the informer Daniel Chater and have him sent to Chichester to Mr. Battine, Surveyor General of Sussex, who would arrange for Diamond's committal. The Collector of Southampton arranged for an officer, William Galley, to accompany Chater to Chichester. By the 20th of February the two men had still not arrived at Chichester and it was feared that some mishap had befallen them. Eventually the Commissioners instructed the Southampton Collector to offer a reward for information about Chater and Galley.

In due course informants came forward and arrests were made. It appeared that on the way to Mr. Battine's residence they had called at a public house for refreshment. The landlady was suspicious and warned some smugglers of their presence. The latter managed to get hold of the letter which the two men were carrying to Mr. Battine and realized what it would mean if Chater were allowed to give evidence against Dimer. They seized the unfortunate men and lashed them with whips. Other smugglers who had been concerned in the Poole raid arrived and, after some discussion, it was decided that the two should be done away with, whereupon they were tied to a horse and taken into the country. All the while the two men were lashed pitilessly until at length Galley died. Chater managed to survive a little longer, but eventually he was taken to a dry well and hung there and, to make sure he was really dead, the smugglers threw earth and stones on him. In due course six men were charged with these murders and were condemned to death, the bodies of all but two of them being hung in chains. The trial received great publicity and the judge, Mr. Justice Foster, took the opportunity of making a long speech against the evils of smuggling. One result of this affair was the issuing of a proclamation listing the names of many known smugglers and threatening them with outlawry unless they surrendered themselves by a given date. A reward of £500 was also offered for the apprehension of anyone who should subsequently be convicted. However, the tragic and gruesome fate of those smugglers involved in the Poole murders does not seem to have acted as a deterrent. In October 1763 two of the Poole officers, together with Mr. Wood, an Excise Officer, went to the North Shore at Bournemouth to look for run goods. At Watering Chine they saw a boat loading tea from a cutter, and as they watched from the top of the cliff, noticed the boat leave the cutter. By the time they had got down to the shore the tea was all landed, and upwards of forty men were loading it on to their horses. The officers attempted to secure the tea, but the smugglers took Mr. Wood by the collar and 'with several oaths and imprecations threatened to beat his brains out'. The smugglers then forcibly rescued the tea and carried it all off with them. The officers later estimated the quantity at about one ton.

Thomas Coombes, Riding Officer at Kimmeridge in the Isle of Purbeck, also suffered severely at the hands of the smugglers. He and a servant were attacked, near Holme, by a gang of sixty smugglers with eighty horses laden with tea. The servant escaped through a hedge, but the smugglers violently beat Coombes with huge sticks. They knocked him down and rode their horses over him, causing great injury to his leg and thigh. The smugglers were believed to be the gang living near Downton and in the New Forest.

Very often the smugglers went out of their way to threaten over-zealous officers. Mr. Florence, Riding Officer at Wareham, received this letter in August 1789:

'Mr. Florence, I do desire you would not trouble yourself so mutch with the smuglers as you have don for if you do you may depend upon it that I will blow your brains out by night or day, I do not care whitch it is but by all that is good I will do it . . .'

Another letter, couched in even more insulting terms, was sent from Fordingbridge to Captain Bursack of the *Speedwell* revenue cutter. 'Sir, Damn thee and God damn thy two purblind eyes thou buger thou death looking son of a bitch, O that I had bin there (with my company) for thy sake when thou tookest them men of mine on board the "Speedwell" cutter onn Monday ye 14 Decr I would drove thee and thy gang to Hell where thou belongest, thou Devil Incarnet, Go down, thou Hell Hound unto they kennell below & bathe thyself in that sulphurous lake that has bin so long prepared for such as thee for it is time the world was rid of such a monster, thou art no man but a devil, thou fiend, O Lucifer, I hope thou will soon fall into Hell like a star from the sky, there to lye unpitied & unrelented of any for ever and ever which go grant of His infinite mercy Amen.'

Smugglers did not confine their violent activities to recovering seized goods, but frequently attempted to rescue their confederates who had suffered the misfortune of being caught. In November 1770 the Collector at Cowes received a Capias from the Solicitor against John Hall. On the night of the 10 November two officers, William Mouncher and Thomas Duke found Hall at the 'Plume of Feathers' and arrested him. While they were conveying him to the Watch House they fell in with John Parkman, a notorious smuggler, and some of the crew of the smuggling lugger. They fell upon the officers and rescued the said Hall who, upon getting clear, fired two pistols at the officers. Eventually, with the assistance of the Excise Tide Surveyors and boatmen, six of the lugger's men were captured and the Constable took them to Portsmouth where they were delivered to Lieutenant Newnham on board the *Hunter* cutter.

In 1778 William Arnold, father of Dr. Thomas Arnold, later Headmaster of Rugby School, became the Collector of Customs at Cowes. He proved to be a very able administrator and was extremely active in organizing the struggle against the smugglers from the Channel Islands. In April 1781 he gave the Commissioners his opinion about the situation, pointing out that the smugglers had become more daring than ever, that they assembled in large numbers, carried arms and wore disguises, and that there were many cases of officers being 'wounded, beaten, opposed and obstructed'. He attributed this to some extent to the mildness of the Law which merely subjected persons convicted of obstructing officers or of rescuing goods after seizure to the punishment of the House of Correction or to his Majesty's service by sea or land for a limited time. The following year, when asking for a supply of tuck sticks, Arnold emplained that it was the practice of smugglers in the area to 'conceal their goods under the shingles on the beach or bury it in the sands on the shore or cellars underground. The officers are in want of stout strong tucks to enable them to find out such concealments. We therefore humbly pray your Honours will be pleased to direct a dozen tucks of about four feet in length to be sent to us.'

In October 1783 Arnold and the Comptroller furnished information about smuggling vessels operating between the Needles and Peveril Point. The *Cornish Ranger* belonging to Cawsand was described as a lugger of about 300 tons, mounting 26 guns, which frequently landed goods between the Needles and Christchurch Head. This vessel had recently landed 300 casks of foreign spirits and 10 or 12 tons of tea, and at the same time had convoyed three other luggers. The *Wasp* of Folkestone, of 270 tons and with 22 guns, also worked between the Needles and Christchurch. The report went on to say that, 'The *John and Susannah* of Folkestone is also about the same size and has the same armament as the other two and frequents the same area. They carry about 60 to 80 men and each trip smuggle from 2,000 to 3,000 casks and 8 or 10 tons of tea. If they go to Guernsey they return once a fortnight, if to Dunquerque, once in three weeks. A new cutter is being built for Sturgess of Hamble, a noted smuggler. She is of 220 tons burthen and mounts 20 guns.' It was explained that these vessels usually landed their goods in the daytime, sometimes in sight of the revenue cutters 'whom they will not suffer to come near or board them'. They added that it was the war that first gave a sanction to the arming of these vessels, as their masters had taken our commissions as privateers although, in actual fact, they followed no trade other than smuggling, and 'though the war is now at an end they still continue their illicit practices'.

Arnold had felt the need for an extra cutter based on Cowes and, with the help of some friends, had financed the fitting out of a cutter, the *Swan*, under the contract system by which the Crown paid 4s. 6d. per month for upkeep and repairs. Under this system the contractor was supposed to make his money out of his share of the proceeds of seizures. A local man, George Sarmon, was given the command of the cutter. His brother was already commander of the Excise cutter which operated under the Excise Collector at Newport. The *Swan* was lost the same year at Hurst, and was replaced by another *Swan* the next year. In May 1784 Captain Ellis of the *Orestes* sloop of war seized the cutter *John and Susannah* which was condemned and advertised for sale. Arnold described her as 'fast sailing and as compleat a vessel as ever went to sea'. He said that he was apprehensive that, as cutters of this kind were built only for His Majesty's Service or the smuggling trade, the smugglers would get her again on their own terms, unless the Government took her at the appraised value of £1,700.

Not long after this, Captain Ellis of the *Orestes* was himself in trouble with the smugglers after he had seized a large smuggling boat west of St. Alban's Head. Before he could get it to port, the *Orestes* was attacked by a large cutter mounting 22 guns which came in from the offing and endeavoured to run it down. The cutter opened fire, killing one of the navy men and wounding two others. In their report, Arnold and the Comptroller described this as 'another instance added to the many which occur almost daily of the outrageous and piratical proceedings of the smugglers on this coast'. In July 1790 the Collector complained that, as the *Swan* was employed under the Admiral at Plymouth and the *Rose* cutter of Southampton was under repair, the coast was left without any revenue cruisers, and the smugglers had therefore great opportunities for carrying on their illicit trade. Again, in August, the Board were urged to direct the return of the *Swan* to her station, and this time the request seems to have been successful, for on the 15th of December 1790 Captain Sarmon reported an outrage committed by the master and crew of a large smuggling lugger who had compelled the crew of the *Swan*'s boat to go on board the smuggling vessel, and had kept them prisoner while they used the *Swan*'s boat to land their cargo. Many of the smugglers had blackened their faces with gunpowder, and from their conversation it appeared that they came from Guernsey, where they would return as soon as all the cargo was landed. In the morning they let the *Swan*'s boat and men go free after taking their stores and materials, but put two small casks of spirits in the boat.

It must have been rather embarrassing for the officials of Cowes to have to report to the Commissioners in July 1791 that, among papers found on a smuggling vessel, was a letter written by Mr. Weston to John Early, a noted smuggler, which gave an account of the military force stationed at Poole. Mr. Weston was the Comptroller at Poole and it appears that this letter resulted in his dismissal, since the Board was asking for recommendations for his successor in September.

In July 1793 the Commissioners were asked to provide larger guns for the *Swan* cutter. It was maintained that although she was sufficiently well-armed to cruise against the smugglers, now that she was fitted out as a privateer she might have to contend with vessels belonging to the enemy as well as with those smugglers who, availing themselves of the opportunity afforded to them by the French war of taking out Letters of Marque, would probably attempt to carry on their trade with an armed force. Their fears were well-founded, for in 1795 the *Swan* was captured by the French and the wives of the crew were asking for help for their families. In January 1796 Captain Sarmon was released by the French and reported again for duty. A new *Swan* cutter had been built and Captain Sarmon was again given the command. But the career of this *Swan* was very brief, ending in tragedy a few months later when it fell into French hands and Captain Sarmon was killed.

On the other side of the Solent the numerous inlets and harbours in the vicinity of Portsmouth provided smugglers with ample opportunities for evading the vigilance of the revenue officers, who also had to contend with smuggling by the crews of the numerous naval vessels. In December 1772 the boat of the *Princess Caroline* cutter, cruising in Stokes Bay, observed a large open boat going ashore near the brew-house. On drawing alongside, Peter Peat, the mate in charge, saw that she was full of casks. He seized the boat and her cargo and was about to take her away when a gang of men on foot and on horseback 'came down and took hold of the boat and hauled her on shore'. The men were unknown to Peat and many of them were in disguise 'having on blue carters frocks and handkerchiefs wrapped round their heads which covered part of their faces'. The revenue officers put up a long resistance against violent opposition, and eventually managed to secure and take to the Custom House 121 casks of brandy, 25 casks of rum and 11 casks of Geneva. But the smugglers 'rescued and carried off the boat and the remainder'. Peter Peat stated at the end of his report that the gang were armed with clubs, and he believed that it would have been impossible for his seven men to have done more than they did.

An example of co-operation between the Customs and Excise and the Navy is provided by an incident which occurred in Sandown Bay in May 1782. Captain Stiles of the Customs *Roebuck* cutter was on a cruise in company with Captain Sarmon, commander of the Excise cutter when they observed a large cutter hovering in the bay. They considered that the force of the smugglers was too great for them, and so the Excise cutter went off to seek assistance from the naval frigate, the *Monsieu*. As the naval vessel approached, the smugglers took to their boat and landed in Sandown Bay. The revenue officers took possession of the smuggling cutter, called in a Letter of Marque the *Kite* and belonging to Folkestone under the command of William Bate. Most of the contraband had been landed and only sixty gallons of spirit were found on board.

There have been instances of smugglers' wives attacking officers but in June 1782 we find that when a riding officer, William

Newnham, was being attacked his wife tried to defend him and, as a result, had her arm broken in two places. The Collector thought the surgeon's bill of £6 14s. od. for treating the wounds of the husband and wife was very reasonable.

Mr. Peat, by now mate of the *Roebuck* cutter, reported a frustrating encounter with smugglers off St. Helens. Seeing a large cutter making for Chichester harbour, he made sail towards her, but on coming up with her, noticed a large boat, apparently just loaded, making for the shore. Three well-armed men in the *Roebuck*'s boat were dispatched to board her, but they were opposed by 20 smugglers, all carrying muskets and cutlasses, who obliged the boat to sheer off. As the smuggling cutter was some 300 tons burthen, carrying 18 or 20 well-manned guns, the *Roebuck* was 'under the necessity of remaining at a distance, a tame spectator of this fraudulent transaction'.

Naval vessels were frequently assigned to revenue work, and in December 1784 one of these vessels, the *Hebe*, had been so successful that the Collector felt obliged to inform the Board that, 'the very great exertions by Captain Thornbrough, Commander of His Majesty's Frigate the *Hebe* whose activity and zeal for the Revenue deserve the highest commendations, has proved of great advantage in diminishing the practice of smuggling'. He went on to say that, in spite of large captures, the spirit of the smugglers did not seem to decrease, and that to the east of the port it was carried on with impunity since the Admiralty cruisers stationed there could not sail fast enough to come up with the smuggling cutters, and in any case were not sufficiently strong to take them on. Since the *Hebe* was so fast sailing that she could come up with any vessel she chose, he suggested that it would be of benefit to the revenue if her cruise were extended as far as Beachy Head.

A report from the officer at Stubbington on the 13th of April 1796 told a strange story. The officer explained that in pursuance of a writ he arrested Sarah Harris and conveyed her to the County Gaol. On the way she became very distressed and confessed that the goods which had been seized in her house on the 21st of September 1789 were the property of Mr. Tribbeck of Stubbington.

She stated that after the goods had been seized, Mr. Tribbeck came to the house and said that she must leave with him, or else be sent to prison, and that she must stay away a fortnight. She was taken to the Isle of Wight and detained there two years. Then a Mr. Wade came and said that the officers knew where she was and that she must go along with him. She was taken to Alderney and kept there under watch and it was only after a considerable time that she was able to make her escape. It is to be presumed that the smugglers were worried about what she might say to implicate them.

The early Letter Books for Dover and the Kent ports have not survived but fortunately some details of the smuggling in the early eighteenth century have been found among the papers of John Collier, who was Surveyor-General of the Riding Officers for the County of Kent from 1733 to 1756. Among these, for instance, a brief has survived in connection with the violent rescue of two prisoners who were being held in the custody of the constable of the hundred of Rolvenden on suspicion of smuggling. It was stated that the inhabitants of Rolvenden were famous for hiding wool in the woods of the area, and that some wool was found in the possession of one of the prisoners. A certain William and others 'in disguised dresses' broke into the alehouse where the prisoners were being held and rescued them. The record of a coroner's inquest held in 1715 on the body of W. Beeching, a smuggler who was killed in an affray with Customs officers at Telham near Battle, tells a similar tale since the jury found that Beeching came by his death by misfortune, and that the officer who shot him did so in his own defence. In 1720 two men, Borer and Tomkins, were suspected of being implicated in the murder of Mr. Reeves, Customs officer at Langley Bridge near Eastbourne. They were said to be members of the famous Mayfield gang 'that defied the laws relating to the running of goods', to which the principal witness against them also belonged.

On 22nd March 1720 Nathaniel Pigram, Commander of the Revenue sloop, reported an affray at the 'George' Inn at Lydd and enclosed a deposition by Philip Levermore, the Supervisor of Customs there. It appeared that two men, Jacob Walter and Thomas Bigg, had landed from a French sloop at Dungeness lighthouse and went to the 'sign of the Three Mariners' at Lydd. They each hired a horse and pistols and commanded Levermore forth 'with abundance of ill language'. The latter immediately loaded his 'ffuzee' and, going into the yard, found that the men had left for Camber Point. Together with three other officers Levermore went after them and caught up with them about a mile from Lydd. He asked Walter what his business was with him, whereupon Walter drew his pistol and 'snapp'd at him several times'. Bigg did the same. At length Walter fired at Levermore and Bigg hit him with a stave. Levermore then fired at Walter's horse, but missed, and Bigg clapped his pistol to the officer's breast and snapped it but it failed to go off. Levermore succeeded in bringing Bigg's horse down, and eventually both men were captured and taken to the 'George' Inn at Lydd, where a guard of six officers and two others were set over them. On the Sunday evening, '9 well-mounted and well-armed men' rode up to the 'George', forced their way upstairs, firing all the while at the officers, and carried the prisoners away.

An insight into the conditions prevailing in the gaols of the period is provided by a report of Mr. Collier about a visit to prisoners in Horsham gaol. They were an Englishman and four Frenchmen who had been convicted of smuggling and fined, but were unable to pay the fines. Collier remarks 'They really all five lye in a very miserable starving condition, not having shirts to their backs nor hardly any other cloathes, nor have they had noe remittances from France or elsewhere ever since they have been in gaole this I am assur'd of by the gaoler and the townespeople of Horsham, whose Charity has hitherto kept them alive. They have been in Gaole a year the latter end of this month and there being no manner of probability of their being ever able to pay a penny of their fine, I must say in my humble opinion their case deserves compassion . . .'

Among Collier's papers is a letter written in 1734 from the

Secretary of the Excise Commissioners to the Customs Commissioners giving an account of a report from Mr. Dodd, their officer at Romney. Dodd stated that, since the extra Custom officers had been sent to Dymchurch, the chief place for the running of goods was now Lydd. The smugglers – forty and fifty to a gang – could be seen in the daytime passing back and forth, carrying tea, brandy and dry goods. One night more than two hundred mounted smugglers were seen on the beach waiting for the loading of six boats, and at least a hundred, loaded with goods, were observed to go off together. They marched in a body from the beach about four miles into the country, and then separated into small parties. A few weeks earlier, twenty-one loaded horses had set out from Lydd between twelve and one o'clock in the afternoon. The smugglers, who were armed with blunderbusses and other weapons, 'waited above half an hour at the Warren House in sight of the whole town and declared they would be opposed by no Body'. In Collier's own report to the Commissioners for the year 1734 he says: 'I humbly observe to your Honours that the Smugglers in Romney Marsh are associated into very large formidable Gangs and that without the assistance of the Dragoons believe the Riding Officers will not be able to guard the Coast to prevent the clandestine running of Goods.' It is pleasing to see that Collier's proposals were implemented to some extent, since he noted at the end of his annual report: 'Since my survey and the report made thereon, there are nineteen Dragoons come into Romney Marsh on the application of the Commissioners of the Excise and are quartered at Hythe, Romney and Lydd. The Cornet who is the Commanding Officer has intimated to the Customs Officers that he has orders to assist them in the execution of their Duty.'

It has been seen that the smugglers were often in such force and so well-armed that the Customs officers alone could not cope with them. Even the soldiers did not find it easy to take action in concert with the revenue officers, since the local populace was so hostile to them, and this extended to the juries before whom offences were brought. A striking example of this occurred in

1735 when two soldiers were indicted for the murder of a smuggler. Collier tells us that Thomas Elgood and Robert Biscoe were two private sentinels belonging to Brigadier General Cope's Regiment of Foot and were stationed at Hastings under Serjeant Angell to assist the Customs officers in the execution of their duty. On Friday, 24th October 1735, it was suspected that a large quantity of goods would be run, and three Customs officers assisted by Serjeant Angell and his men went to a place called Hollington, three miles from Hastings, where they divided into two groups and hid in the hedges and trees bordering the high road. At about twelve o'clock – 'the moon shining very bright' – they saw a person approaching whom they assumed to be a 'forerunner' sent ahead of the smuggling gang to see if the coast was clear of officers. This assumption appeared to be correct, for in less than a quarter of an hour they heard a great number of horses coming along the 'road from the Seaside'. The party nearest the shore, made up of Hide and Bourne, Customs officers, and the two soldiers Elgood and Biscoe, let the gang go past them. There appeared to be about thirty horses laden with goods and a great many men. When the smugglers arrived at the place where Mr. Carswell and the remainder of the soldiers were concealed, Carswell went out and asked the front person what goods he had. The man answered with a great oath 'None for him', and so Carswell attempted to seize the bridle of the leading man's horse, but he turned round and called to the gang to retreat. Carswell and his men gave pursuit and at the same time called out to Hide and Bourne to stop them. This they attempted to do but the smugglers 'struck at the Officers with the great ends of their whipps and the clubs they had in their hands'. As the revenue men were unable to stop the gang, or seize any of their horses or goods, Hide called out to the soldiers to fire. This they did, but the smugglers got away, and as the officers and soldiers were pursuing them they saw something lying in the road at some distance from where the action had taken place. It was a body, and the officers carried it to a neighbouring alehouse. The Coroner 'sat upon him' and the jury, 'without any proofe that the deceased was in that Gang', found that the soldiers (without naming any in particular) were guilty of manslaughter. The case was committed to the assizes. The dead man, Peen, was a carpenter who lived at Hawkhurst in Kent but it was not known how he came to be at Hollington, nor on what business.

An affidavit by Thomas Pettit of Battle affirmed that on the day of the affray he was at the 'Black Horse' at Battle, 'an alehouse much frequented by Smugglers', and there he saw a great many persons he knew to be smugglers. He suspected that there would be a run and therefore went to Hollington to watch them. He saw them pass and then heard shots and watched the smugglers return in great disorder and confusion. He heard two of them propose to go to Whatlington and conceal their goods in 'Turner's Hole', a barn belonging to John Turner who kept an alehouse at Whatlington. He sent this information to the Hastings officers, who went to Whatlington and seized a quantity of tea. Pettit gave other information and agreed to give evidence in the Hollington matter – though fearing for his life as the Hawkhurst gang were 'bloodthirsty fellows' – on the condition that he was provided with some new clothes to go in. Later, because of threats from the Hawkhurst gang, Pettit left Battle and betook himself first to Cranbrook and then to Biddenden. The result of the Hollington case is not recorded.

The following year Thomas Pettit again gave some information to Collier. It appears that he was on his way to Hastings from Rye when he came upon a gang of smugglers unloading tea at Fairlight. Some of them knew him and at first threatened to drown him but later decided to spare his life if he would swear not to betray them. He promised not to do so but later told Collier 'I shall Breack my promas in what I promased them for it is a fost promas'. They placed him on a horse, bound him to one of their number, and took him to Hawkhurst where he was released and told that if any of the gang saw him in the county of Sussex they had made an oath to kill him.

There are many references in Collier's papers to the Hawkhurst and the Groombridge gangs who were said to strike terror into the 'whole country'. John Bowra of Groombridge was charged in 1737 with carrying off tea which had been landed at the Red House between Pevensey and Eastbourne and transporting it to the Ashdown Forest. The witnesses, who were members of the gang, said that they met in the Ashdown Forest armed with pistols. Groombridge was described in the case as 'a place several years noted for entertaining and harbouring the most notorious desperate persons concerned in carrying on the Smuggling Trade in defiance of the Laws, and got to such a height of insolence that there was a necessity of sending down a detachment of soldiers to curb them, for they strick terrour into the inhabitants of that part of the country'.

Collier occasionally received complaints from the Board about the large quantities of tea landed at Dungeness, and he was directed to examine the journals of the riding officers and the waterguard officers and report 'whether it appears by these journals that each officer was on duty'. Collier's inspection showed that the officers were all on duty on both the days and nights mentioned in the Commissioners' letter and he also mentioned that the revenue cutter was cruising in Rye Bay on one of the nights in question. The Commissioners were still not satisfied and Collier was told to 'excite' the officers to the more careful performance of their duty. The Board had been informed that not less than two hundred half ankers of brandy had been 'lately run' in two days in the vicinity of Dover, and that not one of the officers at that port, being related to the smugglers, 'will meddle with them'.

In 1740 General Hawley addressed a memorial to the Lords of the Treasury criticizing the way in which the dragoons were being used. He accused the Customs Officers of actively helping to promote smuggling in various ways, and suggested that they ought to be used as 'advanc'd Spies' to give the Army Officers information about parties of smugglers working in the area. Collier was told to enquire into the matter and make a report. He consulted General Hawley and a number of the dragoon officers, and his conclusion was that there were no 'particular facts or particular charges against any of the Customs Officers'. Collier was of the opinion that more troops should be stationed on the coast as those stationed at a greater distance 'have not answered the intentions'. He ends the report by stating that he had given 'strict charge to all your Honours Officers to behave with respect and civility to the Officers of the Dragoons and to go out on duty with them on all occasions and when required and to exert themselves in the due execution of their duty . . .'

The magistrates of Kent do not appear to have been very co-operative in dealing with the problem. In his report of 1741 Collier stated a large gang of smugglers had been camped down near Lydd for two or three nights, expecting some run goods, and that in the mornings they went off into the country to Sandhurst, Newenden and the Isle of Oxney. The Customs were aware of this and for some time all the riding officers stationed at Lydd, Romney, Dymchurch and Scotney House, as well as the dragoons quartered there, met together and watched at 'proper places' to detect them, but without success. Collier went on to say that the riding officers complained that the magistrates of Lydd were 'regardless of putting the Act of the 9 of his present Majesty into execution against persons found lurking on the coast'. He there-fore applied to several of the magistrates and represented to them the ill consequences to the nation by the Act not being put into execution. In the same report he mentioned the refusal of the Justices of the Peace of the port of Dover to convict a man in whose house some smuggled tea was found. Again in connection with a seizure of tea and brandy in the Isle of Sheppey he reported that the Justices would not fine the two men involved. Reference was also made to a similar result in the case of a seizure at Birch-ington.

In 1740 Daniel Barker, the Customs officer at Tunbridge, re-ported that 'we are very much infested with Smuglers that go in such large Bodies armed with Blunderbusses and other ofencive Weapons, severall of which have called at my House, swaring they would kill me or any other Officer they should meet with. About a fortnight past we had an Excise Officer shot at Placksteed, with-in five miles of Tunbridge, by 16 or 17 men armed as aforesaid, and last Wensday the Excise Officer of Seven Oakes was taken Prisoner by uperwards of 20 Smuglers, who beat him and Caried him to the Bull head at Sprats Bottom near Farnborow, ware they unloaded their goods, kept him all night till they loaded again, and went clear of, and last night Mr. Griffin, Supervisor of Excise, was going his servay with the Excise Officer of Tunbridge, was Beat and Cutt in so Violent a manor that his life is Dispard of by a Large Parcell of Smuglers within a mile of Tunbridge. They likewise Beat and Missuses severall Private People in the road, making them kneel down in the mud and beg their Pardons. Sir I Humbly Beg your utmost Endevours we may be suply'd with some Soldiers.'

A letter written the next year described the forcible detention of Customs Officers at Folkestone by the smugglers of 'Peak's Gang'. Mr. Cadman and his fellow officers approached a smuggler's boat and were told to keep off. On their advancing further the smugglers, who were carrying small arms, fired a volley at them. They afterwards obliged the officers to go on board Peak's cutter, where they were confined all night while the smugglers used the Revenue boat to land their goods. In the meantime they gave the officials 'very abusive language' and threatened to cut off their ears and 'carry them to France for French soldiers'. At three o'clock in the morning Cadman was allowed to go on deck. As he observed the boat of the Customs cutter rowing towards them, Peak's boat discharged a volley at it. Later the Customs cutter came up and Peak fired a swivel gun at the cutter and 'bid them bear off or they would destroy them'.

The sheer effrontery of the smugglers at this period is illustrated in a report of October 1743 by Mr. Clare, the Supervisor at Hythe. He explained that he went to Lydd, surveyed the Officers and examined their books. He was told that there was a large gang of smugglers in the parish and therefore thought it safer to stay at Romney. He arrived at Romney at about six o'clock and went to the 'Rose and Crown', but to his surprise found that the stables were filled with smugglers' horses. He went to his room, sent for the Romney officers and examined and signed their books.

Apparently the officers were aware that a run was taking place and were powerless to do anything about it. In Clare's words: 'We lamented our condition, that such quantitys of goods must be suffered to be run before our faces, and we not able to prevent or take any of it.' At eight o'clock in the morning the smugglers arrived with sixty horses all loaded with dry goods, which he took to be tea. They were armed with brass muskatoons, brass 'ffuzees' and pistols, and immediately took possession of the two inns, the 'Dolphin' and the 'Rose and Crown', where they breakfasted and baited their horses for about two hours. They then left the town in a long procession.

Later in the year Mr. Clare interceded with Collier on behalf of Darby, the officer at Lydd, 'who has been obliged to leave Lydd with his wife and family as the smugglers have threated to murder him. He has gone to Hythe and dare not go to Rye to meet Collier as arranged for fear of being murdered.' Clare pointed out that the naval and revenue frigates and sloops could not be of much help as the danger came from the smugglers on land, and only military assistance would do any good. Apparently orders were given for three regiments of marines to assist as required, but this did not satisfy Clare who thought foot soldiers insufficient to deal with the smugglers. To show what the Customs had to contend with he gave a list of known appearances during the month of January 1743. On nine occasions gangs of smugglers, who had from thirty to one hundred horses at a time, had been seen and they appeared to have been well armed.

At this time, Collier was required by the Commissioners to furnish an account of obstruction and assaults upon Customs Officers within his survey from 1st April 1743 to 1st April 1744. The Collector at Rochester reported one assault. Five cases were reported at Hythe, only one at Deal, none at Faversham, none at Canterbury, four at Sevenoaks. Eight cases of obstruction were reported from Dover, and one case of assault in which a dragoon was killed. The Collector and Comptroller at Sandwich told Collier that there were large gangs of smugglers in the neighbourhood, but the Officers had not been assaulted because they had been afraid to attack the smugglers. It may be assumed that this was also the case at New Romney and Dymchurch, since armed smugglers were observed on thirty-one different occasions during this period (in one case to the number of fifty-five) either in Romney itself, or passing through the town with their goods. In the case of Dymchurch there were thirty-five entries. One of these was dated July 7th and stated: 'At 7 in the morning on duty with Mr. Lake near the Street. We fell in with the outlawed gang loaded with Oylskin Baggs which we believe was full of Tea. They had fire Arms and Swoards drawn in Hand and bid defiance to us. The gang consisted of upwards of 40 in number.' A week later there was another entry: 'July 14th, 4 morning on the wall, the mound called Dymchurch Wall, with Mr. Lake. Saw the outlawed gang loaded with Oylskin Baggs which we believe was full of Tea: number 70 horses with fire Arms.' As no obstruction or assault was reported, it is to be presumed that the officers made no real attempt to molest the smugglers or to seize the contraband, but simply restricted themselves to a watching brief.

Mr. Patrick, Collier's clerk, visited Lydd and told his senior that large gangs of armed smugglers frequented the town as much as ever. He said that the Transports (an association of smugglers) and one Betts of Rye had leave from the French government to go in and out of the French ports and harbours, and that since the beginning of the war with France there had been great quantities of run goods landed in Romney Marsh and places adjoining. The smugglers had been 'so impudent as to publicly drink the Pretender's and his Son's health, with Success to their Arms and confusion to his Majesty King George, and swore they will murder Darby wherever they meet him'. It is interesting to note that in this case the smugglers were actively allied to the Jacobite cause, and a number of similar incidents show that they frequently refused allegiance to the Hanoverians.

The officers at Hythe reported that the Hastings outlaws had run their goods between Brockman's Barn and Hythe and the goods were immediately carried off by the Hawkhurst gang, who were armed and of a great number. It was reported that the

Hastings outlaws had taken an Oath of Allegiance to the King of France, and that they frequently brought people from France and carried people from England thither.

In 1744 a Hastings Customs officer, Thomas Carswell, was shot dead and two dragoons were wounded when defending some tea which they had seized from smugglers at Hurst Green. One of the smugglers, John Macdonald, was captured and there were great fears that an attempt would be made by the Hawkhurst gang to rescue him. On this account he was escorted to prison by a lieu-tenant, forty foot soldiers and eleven dragoons as well as by some Customs officers. Even so, Collier was apprehensive and said: 'Great rumours of upward of 200 smuglers assembled to rescue. I hope to hear of his being safely delivered into Goal and to send more particular account of this affair to the Board by next post as this part of the Country is in a ferment on the occasion.' After-wards Collier was able to inform the Board that Macdonald was safely lodged in gaol.

A more detailed account of the way the smugglers operated and the distances they covered is supplied in an affidavit made by one of them on the 29th November 1744. In his statement Richard Bunce of Thames Ditton said that, together with a person who went by the nickname of 'Tugg' and one James Blackman who lived at Hooe in Sussex, he went to the house of James Blackman and there loaded on a drove-horse four half anchors of brandy and about a quarter of a hundredweight of tea, and he placed a further two half anchors of brandy on the horse he was riding. The other two loaded their horses and the three went to Ninfield, each of them carrying a brace of pistols. At Ninfield they were joined by others, including 'Long Charles' armed with a blunderbus and 'Saucy' armed with a carbine, and there were also a great number of drove-horses. The whole party went to Wych Cross. From there Bunce and 'Tugg' and Thomas Wayte of Hooe went on to Thames Ditton where they unloaded their goods. In July, Bunce went again to Wych Cross, this time with his brother John and two others, and they again loaded brandy and tea. In November he went to Pevensey Bay with his brother and some others, and there they aided and assisted in the landing, running and carrying away of about 8,000 pounds of tea. Having loaded their horses they went to Ninfield, and then to Bucksted Bridge where they were joined by John Dagger, commonly known as 'The Hoo Farmer', and the party proceeded together to Wych Cross where they separated. On a further expedition with Richard Edwards of East Grinstead and John Bevin of Watford, he went to Felbridge Water in Sussex where they loaded their horses with tea and returned to Thames Ditton, where Bunce remained while the other two went on to Watford.

In referring to Macdonald's prosecution Collier told the Solicitor to the Board of Customs that 'the Smuglers are got to an amazing height on the Kentish and Sussex coasts . . . the Civil Magistrates fully decline putting the Laws in Execution against them'. He explained that in September he had had a great deal of discourse with the Chancellor of the Exchequer on the situation, and referred to a recent incident when the house of a Customs officer, Mr. Bayley of Bexhill, was plundered and pillaged by smugglers. The officers of the regiment were informed, and they pursued the smugglers and shot dead one of the gang. Collier also mentioned this incident when writing to Mr. Fremantle, a member of the Board, and told him that on the following night the smugglers ran a very large quantity of tea and carried it through the country 'firing, making huzzas and threatening and striking terror to the places they went through and it was computed that, at a small town called Hailsham not eight miles from the sea, there were seen about 300 loaded horses together'. About the shot smuggler Collier went on to say: 'I gave my utmost assistance to Mr. Coppard the Collector in the affair and conducted it as well as I could, but in the present situation and the menaces and insults I have received, I shall decline acting as Solicitor in any proceedings against the Smuglers.' He added that the vessel used to run the goods was said to be the large cutter lately built at Folkestone, the largest of its kind and equipped with 10 or 12 carriage guns and about 20 swivel guns. This cutter, and the other smuggling vessels there and at Rye, bought their goods at Boulogne and were permitted to enter the harbour, though the crews were confined under a guard of soldiers until loading was completed.

On the 12th March 1746 Mr. Ketcherell, Customs Officer at Canterbury, wrote to Collier acquainting him that on the 7th instant a gang of about 150 smugglers landed their cargo between Reculver and Birchington. Sixty-three men and eighty or ninety horses went by Whitstable and Faversham and the rest over Grove Ferry. He also mentioned that the Rev. Mr. Patten of Whitstable had let the Commissioners know when gangs went through Whitstable for Faversham. He added that it was reported that the Doctor formerly received 'tyth' from smugglers.

Although the gangs of smugglers frequently joined together to outwit the revenue forces, there is at least one instance recorded of dissension among them, mentioned in a report sent by Mr. Ketcherell, Customs Officer at Canterbury, to Mr. Collier. There seems to have been a common agreement among the smugglers that, when running goods, each party should stay by the shore until everything had been loaded. In practice, however, those that completed their loads first 'shifted for themselves'. On this occasion, the Customs officers, with some fifteen volunteers, appeared before the last of the smugglers had loaded, and their goods were seized. There were some Sussex and Hawkhurst men among them, who went home and returned with an armed band of ninety-two men carrying fuzees, pistols and broadswords. They apparently intended to make up for their earlier loss by capturing the contraband from the smugglers who had left the coast before the rest. The two gangs met at Wingham where a pitched battle took place, leaving seven men wounded, two of them seriously. In the end the Sussex and Hawkhurst gangs were 'masters of the Field' and carried off forty horses belonging to the Folkestone men and others.

Meanwhile, groups of local inhabitants, determined not to let the smugglers have it all their own way, were forming voluntary associations, such as the 'Goudhurst Militia', with the object of bringing to an end their terrorism of the countrywide. One such association is referred to in a letter from Collier to Mr. Simon, the

Customs Solicitor, in 1747. He tells him that the 'Cranbrook Associators' had apprehended William Gray of Hawkhurst, one of the 'Gang of Smuglers who have so many years Triumphed over the Officers of the Revenue and struck Terrour into the Country for so many years'. It appears, however, that Gray was released by the Justice of the Peace for lack of evidence of any offence. Another member of the Hawkhurst gang was a certain Trip, *alias* Stanford, who had been indicted for the murder of the Hastings officer, Carswell, but not apprehended. The chief witness had vanished and Collier thought that the smugglers had either bought him off or murdered him. Another member of the gang called Austin was in custody awaiting trial and Collier was arranging for the two witnesses against him to appear in London, and was of the opinion that 'they should have something of a Guard'.

In December 1747 Mr. Simon gave Collier an account of the proceedings against two members of the Hawkhurst gang who had taken John Bolton and two other officers prisoner at Shoreham, and had carried them to Hawkhurst, where they had been whipped and abused 'in the most unmercifull manner'. Finally they were taken to the coast, confined in chains, and forced to assist the smugglers in working goods at Lyddlights. The two prisoners in this case, Tickner and Poison, were found guilty and sentenced to transportation. Simon then referred to the trial of Samuel Austin, who had killed a sergeant while resisting arrest. His principal witness was a young man called Thomas Cook, who swore that he saw the prisoner at another place when the offence was committed. It was suspected that Cook was related to the prisoner, but he denied it. Eventually, under the Attorney General's cross-examination, he admitted that he was the son of the wife of the prisoner by a former husband. He was committed for perjury and the prisoner was convicted. Later Simon told Collier that Austin was to be executed and his body hung in chains. The government does appear to have been taking firmer measures to deal with the smuggling menace, in view of the violent attacks against Customs officers.

The pattern of smuggling was much the same in the Dover area as it was further to the west. Proximity to the French coast facilitated smuggling in time of peace, and there is reason to think that in time of war the smugglers were even more welcome in France on account of the information they could supply. In 1783 the Collector reported an increase in smuggling during the previous three years and put it down to the fact that the smugglers were employing vessels of much greater burthen than formerly, and had therefore augmented their complements of men to double the number carried by the Revenue cutters. He further pointed out that during the war they were equipped with carriage guns and were to some degree protected from the Revenue vessels by virtue of their Admiralty Commissions. On the cessation of hostilities, the smuggling cutters should, of course, have discontinued carrying heavy armoury but in fact scarcely any of them had disarmed, and the recent encounter between the Deal shallop and a smuggling vessel off Dungeness in which Captain Haddock was killed, and a similar engagement between His Majesty's cutter, the *Nimble*, and a smuggling cutter were proof that these vessels were still very formidable. The Collector went on to say that the smugglers still continued their practice of 'making blazes on the coast' at night-time so that they could discover any officers on duty by land or sea.

In February 1785 Captain Hills of His Majesty's Sloop the *Wasp* in company with His Majesty's Sloops *Flirt* and *Echo* and the Revenue cutters *Tartar*, *Hound* and *Nimble*, captured the *Long Splice* cutter after a chase of seven hours, 'during which time the *Long Splice* was seen to throw overboard a great number of bags and half ankers supposed to contain tea and spirits'. Captain Hills requested that the cutter might be prosecuted for being found armed and rigged contrary to Act of Parliament within the limits.

Another instance of instant retaliation by smugglers occurred when John Gill, Riding Officer at Folkestone, reported that two dragoons who had assisted him to seize some tobacco were attacked in their quarters. When Gill was informed of the assault he rescued the men and took them to his own house but the smugglers soon followed them there, whereupon they broke in, and 'behaved with unparalelled insolence' until the mayor of the town came along with some assistance and 'dispersed the rioters'.

Dover was already an important port for travellers to and from the Continent, but the majority of passengers in those days were people of 'quality' who no doubt were able to procure some concession from Customs duties. But a letter sent to the Board in 1787 indicates that the officers did not always allow a passenger's rank to deter them from carrying out their examination, for the Collector assured their Honours that the Lady Sussex's baggage was examined with every degree of respect and attention, that nothing liable to stoppage or seizure was found, and that afterwards the baggage was repacked in as careful a manner as possible. Furthermore he knew of 'no instance of the officers neglecting to examine any baggage in consequence of the offer of a large fee'.

By this time the custom of allowing diplomatic immunity had become established and there were some who would have liked to take undue advantage of it. For instance, the King's Messenger, Thomas East, arrived in Dover from Ostend on the 26th May 1793, carrying among his baggage a box which he refused to allow to be examined, claiming that it contained dispatches from the Duke of York. The officer insisted upon examining the portmanteau and in it was found one India silk handkerchief and two pieces of nankeens. In reporting this incident to the Board, the Collector stated that East had frequently brought such boxes which were alleged to contain dispatches, and submitted that they should be examined by the proper officers before delivery.

Today there are special regulations governing the treatment of theatrical effects in baggage by Customs Officers, but in the latter part of the eighteenth century such importations were still dealt with on a 'particular instance' basis. One such case arose in 1791 when Madame Auberval and Mademoiselle Gervais de Troche petitioned the Board for the return of their clothes and thirty-two pairs of silk covered shoes which had been seized on arrival as passengers from France. They explained that they had been engaged by Mr. O'Reilly, the proprietor of the King's Theatre in

London, under the authority of the Lord Chamberlain, as 'first dancers for His Majesty's entertainment' at the King's Theatre in London. They had never doubted that they would be permitted to bring their wearing apparel and in particular their shoes, being 'implements of their profession'. The shoes were of a particular fabric and could not be had in this country at any price. As they were hurried from Paris by Mr. O'Reilly they had had no time to obtain a supply to bring with them and had arranged for the rest to be sent after them in the charge of Mr. Lauray, from whom they were seized. They needed a large supply, as the shoes were as thin as paper, and a pair seldom lasted more than one night. The articles were claimed as *bona fide* wearing apparel, and the Board were asked to order them to be delivered on payment of the carriage and customary fees.

In 1788 the Collector pressed the Board for 'one or more additional cruisers' for the district, pointing out that the tide surveyors and their crews were so busy visiting and rummaging the packet boats and other passenger vessels that 'they can scarce find time to go to sea and Sandgate Castle is now much resorted to by the smugglers'. The following year the Collector received an account of an affray with smugglers at Sandgate from James Childs, Sitter of the boat there. When two of his boatmen were attacked by a gang of smugglers on horseback, one of them, Cook, fired at and seriously wounded a member of the gang; 'since then Cook's life has been threatened'.

On the 7th March 1789 the *Tartar* cutter returned to port from a cruise and landed Stephen Gowland, a mariner who had been beaten by smugglers. The surgeon examined him and reported that his skull was fractured and that he could not live. He died the next day, and the Coroner and Jury who 'sat on the Body' returned a verdict of death as a result of wounds received by blows on the head from persons unknown. On learning of the incident the Board ordered that an advertisement be inserted in the county newspapers offering a reward for apprehending the offenders.

In June 1789 the Collector was informed of a complaint from the Marquis de la Luzerne of a violation of territory by a Custom

House cutter pursuing a smuggling vessel off the coast of Boulogne on the 6th April. A strict examination of the journals of the *Tartar* cutter showed that she had not sailed from Dover until the evening of the 6th April, and that for several days after sailing had confined her cruise close to the English shore off Dungeness, not once crossing the English Channel.

A tobacco factory had been allowed, perhaps unwisely, to function close to the seashore near Sandgate, and in September 1789 it was the scene of a skirmish between officers and smugglers. Leggatt and Bateman, Riding Officers, had received information that tobacco had been clandestinely run on shore and concealed in the factory, and so they obtained a warrant from a Justice of the Peace and, taking a constable with them, went in the daytime to search the suspected premises. They were opposed by a company of armed men, and 'being overpowered by numbers', were obliged to desist from making any further attempt. The officers represented that Richard Castle and William Major, the proprietors of the factory, 'were very active in encouraging and abetting sundry persons in resisting the officers'.

A letter to the Collector dated 2nd October 1789 from Captain Thomas Rouse of HMS *Myrmidon* throws some light on the method of disposing of seized smuggling vessels. He stated that the *Tartar* cutter, which he had seized and left in the Collector's charge on the 29th August 1786, was condemned in February 1789 and he understood that it had since been taken into the service of the Customs. Rouse went on to say that he had no doubt that the Board had settled with the Collector for the seizure, and he would like to know at what amount the vessel and materials it contained had been valued and when he could expect to have his money as the seizing officer.

The hardships occasionally suffered by members of the staff are conveyed by a complaint in October 1791 from Eleaxer Moule, Sitter of the boat at Dungeness, that as their accommodation had been taken away from them, he and the crew of the boat were obliged to live in tents in an exposed position. It would be impossible for them to remain much longer without better accommodation and 'an essential station for preventing illicit trade' would be left entirely unguarded. In December they were still in the same plight and Moule said that it was impossible to remain at Dungeness Point any longer as the people were ill with colds, having no fire-place to dry themselves, and their clothes were 'nearly rotten' with being wet so long.

Instances are found in the records of churchwardens making appeals for convicted smugglers. These appeals were not all inspired by humanitarian motives. For example, the churchwardens and overseers of the parish of Lydd petitioned the Board on behalf of John Jackson, one of their parishioners who was under prosecution for having hidden uncustomed goods in his house. They said they believed him to be a very 'peaceable' and industrious man but in very low circumstances, and he had a wife and ten small children. He was unable to pay his fine, and if he should be thrown into prison or obliged to leave his family, the 'burthen would fall upon the parish'. Jackson had offered the Board £20 and this offer had been refused. The churchwardens and overseers therefore offered the Board £20 more to be paid by the parish 'to save a large family from ruin and the parish from a heavy expense'.

During the French wars it had become common for Customs cutters to apply for Letters of Marque to enable them to capture enemy shipping and also to defend our own merchant ships against the French privateers. The *Tartar* cutter was one of those which had been ordered by the Board to assist in defeating the efforts of the French privateers. She was duly surveyed by the Tide Surveyor and application made to the admiralty for a Letter of Marque. In September 1799 Captain Worthington of the *Tartar* reported that his vessel was now refitted and ready for sea, but he asked for more men. He said that the coast between the South Foreland and Dungeness was continually infested with French privateers and that the destruction to trade was considerable. On the 2nd November the *Tartar* sailed for the Heldar under the command of the mate and was not heard of again. Captain Richards of the revenue cutter *Vigilant* had earlier asked the Collector to solicit the Commissioners 'to indulge him with a

Letter of Marque as is usually allowed to revenue cruizers'. In anticipation of this he also asked for an increase in the number of the crew, and requested some equipment for boarding vessels and securing prisoners, as well as a French Ensign, 'as it may happen to be requisite to deceive the enemy'. In August 1799 the Collector received a letter from Walmer Castle, signed W. Pitt. He was desired by the writer to deliver the *Fox* lugger, under detention, to William Crooks, the master, together with her ammunition and tackle. The vessel was wanted for the service of the government and regular authority would be sent afterwards in due form.

In connection with Captain Richards' appointment to the *Vigilant* an account of his expenses in coming from Falmouth is furnished.

27th January 1798. Expenses of Captain F. Richards in consequence of his appointment to the *Vigilant* Cutter.

	£	s	d
My expense of the coach from Falmouth to London	5	17	0
Attended at the Custom House London, 17th August remained in London one day		10	6
My expense of the coach from London to Dover	1	11	6
My expense on the Journey		6	0
Remained in Dover 10 days at 7/6d. per day	3	15	0
Arrived in London the 28th August and remained without orders on expenses 27 days at 10/6d.	14	3	6
Still remained on shore on expenses previous to having necessaries on board to the 22nd October it being 29 days at 10/6d. per day	15	4	6
10 days wages and victualling from 23rd October to 1st November	1	17	4½
	£45	7	4½

A bold attempt to trade with the enemy – by running tin plate on board a French vessel which had brought prisoners from Dunkirk – was reported by the Collector on the 15th September 1799. Some British manufactured cottons, woollens and hardware were also found on board the ship. The tin plate had come from the works of an 'eminent ironmonger', Mr. T. Ismay.

A Lydd smuggler was shot dead by a naval party from HMS *Anacreon* when he and others were attempting to 'rescue' the *Ann* lugger of Folkestone which was laden with tubs of gin. At an inquest the verdict given was 'wilful murder', unless the officer of the boat had authority to seize. In that case, the verdict was 'justifiable homicide'. The commander of the *Anacreon* stated that his boat's crew claimed that the smugglers fired at them, and he hoped that the Board would take every step towards apprehending the people concerned, who were all inhabitants of Lydd. He added that two of his crew were assaulted by the people of Lydd, threatening to murder them, and he had heard that the coroner (a very respectable clergyman) had inflamed the minds of the mob by speaking against his authority.

TOBACCO FRAUDS

The illicit trade in tobacco caused a great deal of trouble and anxiety to the revenue officials. The basic position was that, under the Navigation Laws, tobacco, like other commodities from the Plantations, had to be brought to England before it could be shipped elsewhere. On the re-export of the tobacco, duty was re-paid or 'drawn back', and this drawback system led to a great deal of chicanery on the part of the merchants who saw an opportunity of making an easy, though illegitimate, profit by shipping tobacco waste or other waste camouflaged as tobacco. It was then claimed as duty-paid tobacco which was being re-exported, and the Searcher very often was unable to discern the deceit. Another method of obtaining duty-free tobacco was to clear it out to a place which qualified for drawback and then to land it on the coast or transfer it to coastal vessels for landing. If the worst came to the worst, and they were intercepted by revenue or naval vessels, they could always claim that they had been blown off-course – a reasonable enough excuse in the days of sailing ships and one sometimes difficult to disprove. The main tobacco ports were Bristol, Liverpool and Whitehaven, but other ports such as Dumfries had regular though infrequent importations.

The Collector at Liverpool described an attempted fraud in a letter to the Customs Commissioners in 1724, telling them that he had discovered 'a most notorious fraud in this port in the exportation of roll tobacco to the Isle of Man'. He considered that the Revenue had lost £10,000 per annum by the shipping of tobacco stalks rolled up in a large twist and thinly covered over with tobacco, so that most of the rolls were filled up with sand, dirt and 'all manner of rubbish'.

It was customary for drawback on exported tobacco to be paid if the cargo was lost. The Collectors sometimes appeared rather liberal in dealing with incidents of this kind, as in the case of the *Freedom* which on the 7th April 1744 sailed with a cargo of tobacco for Rotterdam. On the same night she ran into a storm and was dashed to pieces on the North Rock near Donaghadee in Ireland. Some of the crew were lost, and most of the cargo driven on to the Irish coast where the country people came in large numbers and took possession of it. The Collector asked the Board whether he could issue debentures for the tobacco as if it were really exported to Holland.

Precautions were frequently taken to prevent the illegal landing of tobacco, and information about shipments was sent from Collector to Collector. The Collector at Alloa, for instance, notified the Board in August 1734 that the *George* of Kinghorn had loaded 41,047 lbs. of tobacco, claiming it was bound for Holland. But he believed the intention was to run the tobacco on the coast near Montrose. The Board directed the Montrose Collector to put all his officers on guard to prevent the intended fraud.

Another method of evading tobacco duty was simply to avoid entering it. In September 1734 the Collector at Alloa reported that he had received information that tobacco was brought and lodged without clearance, so he decided to check on all the cellars in his Collection. In one of the cellars he found 126 hogsheads which, taken at 700 lbs. each, amounted to 88,200 lbs. of tobacco. But they only had credit for 72,405 lbs., which left a balance of 15,795 lbs. unaccounted for. In another cellar he likewise found 16 hogsheads which had not been credited with him.

WRECKS AND WRECKING

An example of the difficulties experienced by Customs officers in their capacity as receivers of wreck is given in a report by the Board of an incident at Barnstaple. The Tide Surveyor was looking after the wreck of the ship *Beulah* when a 'buero' (a chest or bureau) was driven ashore. As he was about to examine the contents, the wife of Richard Budd approached him 'in a most outrageous manner' and, with a ladle in her hand, made several attempts to strike him so that the boatmen and some others were obliged to hold her down while the officer 'persevered in his duty'. In the drawers of the chest he found three tea spoons, some old gold lace and a silver candlestick, all of which were claimed by Richard Budd, the tenant of the lord of the manor, who maintained that whatever was cast on the shore was his property.

On 30th April 1752 at about ten o'clock at night in foggy weather the *Indian Prince* of Bristol was stranded on the coast to the west of Aberthaw. Coming from Guinea and St. Kitts, she had brought a cargo of 117 hogsheads of sugar, 6 husses and 35 bags of cotton, 20 tons of ebony, about one ton of elephants' teeth and a few puncheons of rum. The wreck was reported to the officers at Aberthaw and Barry at noon the following day. But when they arrived at the scene they found that hundreds of 'country people' who had got there before them had destroyed and wasted all the rum except for one small keg. The cotton, which was floating along the shore, was also carried off by the country people, while the sugar was quickly dissolved in the saltwater. All that the officers managed to save were some elephants' teeth, Indian goods and ebony.

Eventually three people were caught with cargo from the *Indian Prince* in their possession and were committed to the County Gaol pending trial. They were indicted for felony at the Assizes and acquitted under a law passed in Queen Anne's reign since they had delivered up the goods as soon as demanded. The Collector complained that unless the offence of taking away or having possession of stranded goods was made a 'Felony without Clergy' (see glossary) there would be more such outrages.

Friction frequently arose between the Customs officers and the lord of the manor, or his agents, over the ownership of salvaged goods, since the legal rights of the matter were in some doubt, but when the *Princess Mary* of Glasgow was cast away on the sands between Briton Ferry and Aberavon in January 1752 there was a surprising instance of co-operation. The Collector at Swansea reported that the master and two passengers were lost overboard and perished; since he did not mention the crew it must be presumed that they survived. It appears that the agents of the Lord of the Manor gave ample assistance to the officers, and they were able to salve 98 raw hides, 493 dozen raw calves skins and 10 hogsheads of tallow. Since the skins and hides were perishable, they were sold by the agents once security had been given for the duties. Their bill for salvage, settled by three justices of the peace, amounted to £79 0s. 5½d., and the Collector asked the Board's permission to sell sufficient skins duty-free to cover this charge.

On the day after Christmas in 1753 the Collector at Swansea had occasion to reprimand one of his officers, Mr. Matthews, for not informing him about the wreck of the French vessel *Levain Coeur* at Sear, in Mr. Matthews's district. The French ship, which belonged to Havre-de-Grace, was making for her home port with a cargo of oranges, lemons, figs and timber, and so was well off-course. The Collector said that although he had heard a rumour about the wreck he did not at first credit it, since he had had no report of it, but when he heard that large quantities of fruit were being brought to Swansea for sale he realized that it was true. He admonished Mr. Matthews for having no regard for his duty to the Crown and for making no attempt to save any goods for the owners. He ended his letter by pointing out that if timely warning had been received they could probably have 'intimidated a parcel of ruffians from so horrid and shameful a plunder as by all accounts they have been guilty of'.

When a ship, carrying cargo on which export duty had been paid, was wrecked on her outward voyage, it was customary to repay the duty if reliable evidence was furnished. The Collector reported such an incident to the Board for directions after Thomas Dibden, Master of the *Gloucester Lass* of Gloucester, had claimed that his ship, loaded with eighty chaldrons of coal at Swansea for Boston, New England, had foundered between Swansea and the Mumbles, and the cargo been entirely lost. The Master asked either for repayment of the duty or for permission to carry the same quantity in some other ship or ships for New England duty-free.

In June 1770 the Collector gave an account of a successful salving operation carried out after the Dutch ship *Planter's Welfare* of 700 tons burthen was wrecked at Newton. She was laden with sugar, coffee, cocoa and cotton from Surinam for Amsterdam. The officers were able to report that thirty-one out of a crew of forty-five had been saved, but added that they had had to keep a constant watch on the wreck, 'to prevent the cargo from being embezzled by the Country'. Although they were doing their best to save the ship and cargo, they were finding it no easy task as 'the Country people are quite outrageous and threaten our lives'. Eight horses loaded with coffee had been seized, and the officers requested orders for their speedy condemnation before the Justices of the Peace.

The officers were given some assistance in protecting wreck when the Italian ship *Caterina*, bound from Leghorn to Ostend with a cargo of cotton and marble, was stranded on the Sker rocks. Soon after she was cast on the rocks, the 'country people' came down and carried off most of the cargo. Fortunately, however, the 'country gentlemen' came to the assistance of the officers and the 'mob was quelled'.

In December 1723 the *Helena* was wrecked on the coast near

Swansea within the manor of Mr. Windham who had seized part of the cargo. The officers immediately attached the King's locks to it, and Mr. Windham threatened to strike them off. The Board referred the matter to the Solicitor who reported that it was doubtful if the Officers had the right of custody of goods really wrecked.

In the eighteenth century the north-west coast of Wales, including Anglesey, was one of the most dreaded in the country; the rocky headlands, shifting sandbanks, dangerous currents and lack of lights all contributed to a disastrous toll of shipping. Most of the ships wrecked in this area were trading between the port of Liverpool and the Plantations. It does not appear from the reports of the Officers that the local inhabitants indulged in anything like the wrecking which was customary in South Wales and Cornwall. There was, however, one incident of this kind when the *Neptune* was stranded at Criccieth and the officers were driven away by the violence of 'the mob which was raised by Robert Mordecay of Llanarmon, Ismail Hughes and Robert Thomas of Llanstynding and George Esmes of Cricketh'. The Board ordered the Collector to transmit an affidavit against these offenders which was to be sworn before a Commissioner in the King's Bench.

The officers were successful in saving all the crew except one man when the *Swallow*, on its way from Jamaica to Liverpool, was driven on to a sandbank and sank. The man who was left behind was sick and lying in the tween-decks, and the officers had no time to get him out. The vessel was carrying 46 hogsheads and 8 tierces of sugar, 284 bags of ginger, 10 tons of logwood, 1 barrel of guin grain, 50 bags of cotton, 10 puncheons of rum and 50 teeth. The officers went out in boats to salve as much of the cargo as possible.

There was a more tragic ending to the wreck of the *Love's Increase* of Workington on the Dutchman's Bank off the entrance to the Menai Straits. As the wind was blowing towards the Carnarvonshire shore, the Collector ordered the officers to go there but none of the crew was saved. The vessel was in ballast from Dublin, but a few articles from the ship were salved on the Carnarvonshire coast.

A report from the officers of Carnarvon who went to attend the snow *Hibernia* of Dublin which had been wrecked between Abermenai and St. Trinals, reminds us that officers were empowered to use arms to protect wreck. They were insulted and abused by the country people when they attempted to prevent them from plundering and since they had no firearms they were at a great disadvantage. The vessel was carrying a cargo of linseed flour, beeswax and rum, and Mr. Quellyn, the Tide-surveyor, reported that despite local opposition he had nevertheless succeeded in bringing it to shore.

During a particularly stormy period in November 1772 three vessels were wrecked on the rocks in Holyhead Bay. On the 21st the *Friends* of Liverpool had her bottom torn out, without loss of life, and on the same night the *Charlotte* of Chester, laden with coal and passengers, was blown from her anchorage onto the rocks. The subsequent fate of this vessel is not reported. On the 27th the snow *Carolina Planter* of Greenock suffered the same misfortune, but unfortunately neither the ship nor cargo could be saved. She was bound from Greenock to Morlaix with 219 hogsheads of tobacco.

Another double tragedy was reported by the officers at Holyhead on 10th January 1785. At 2 a.m. on the previous morning, the *Nelly*, of about 300 tons burthen and carrying a cargo of rum, sugar, cotton and pimento from Jamaica for Liverpool, ran ashore and was jammed between two rocks under Rhoscolin Church in Holy Island. They hoped to save some of the cargo but do not mention the fate of the crew. At about the same time the brigantine *Custin*, bound for Liverpool with a cargo of wine and fruit from Lisbon, was totally lost on the rocks to the north of the same church. In this case the Master and two sailors were drowned.

Over eighty people were lost in a catastrophe on 3rd December 1785. There had been a fair at Carnarvon and the ferry-boat which was bringing back the merrymakers to Anglesey ran into a hurricane when she was half-way across the Menai Straits, and was driven on to a sandbank. The passengers were stranded on the bank for about three hours before they were carried away by the flood tide. Among them was Hugh Roberts, Coast Waiter, Coal Meter and Riding Officer at Aberffraw who perished with the rest.

The Cornish wreckers have won for themselves a deservedly notorious reputation, but it does not appear from the reports of the Collectors that they were any worse or any better in this respect than the 'country people' of North Wales and South Wales. In February 1740 the Board demanded to know what action had been taken by the Officers at Penzance to prevent the 'embezzlement' of goods from the wreck of the *Lady Lucy* and ordered the Collector to make a strict search for the offenders. The Collector informed the Board that the ship was stranded at three o'clock in the morning about three miles from Porthleven, where the officers resided, but they did not hear of the wreck until almost noon, by which time all the goods had been carried off. A diligent search was made in the area, and as a result they found four casks of wine in the possession of the Rev. Thomas Whatford of Curey, three casks of wine with Thomas James of the same place, one cask of wine with John Betty of the same place, one cask of wine in the house of John Brailley of Gunwallo and one cask of wine in the house of Thomas James of Mullion.

An indication of the attitude of the local magistracy towards the wreckers is contained in the report of the wreck of the *Jonge Alcida* in 1748. She was carrying a cargo of 167 tons of wine from Bordeaux to Amsterdam, and was stranded near Porthleven on the 3rd December. As soon as he received the report of the wreck, the Collector himself, with the Surveyor, went to the scene and together with the local Officers tried to secure the cargo. The 'violence and barbarity' of the country people was such, however, that their lives were in some danger and they were unable to save one cask. But the Commissioners were not entirely satisfied with these results and ordered the officers to redouble their efforts to secure the wine. The Collector explained that the officers had indeed from time to time taken a number of hogsheads, whereupon the mob had once again seized them by force. He explained

that a week earlier the officers of Porthleven had found two hogsheads of wine which were immediately removed from them, and
'the Officers were forced to fly to save their lives'. The Collector
ends his report by insisting that 'it will be in vain for the officers
to attempt to do their duty in these caves without the assistance
of an arm'd force'.

Part of the duties of Customs officers acting as receivers of
wreck were concerned with health. Wheat contaminated by sea
water was considered dangerous, and so we find the Collector by
order of the Commissioners instructing his officers to take all the
wheat salved from the *Friendship* brig out to sea and sink it in deep
water where it would be 'irrecoverably destroyed'. They should
then let him have a certificate to show that this had been done.

Thomas Davies, sitter in the boat at Porthleven, was severely
harassed by the 'gentlemen and common people' when he
attempted to lock up goods which had been thrown ashore. It was
claimed that the Customs officers had no right to do this, and the
Collector sought a ruling from the Commissioners. The Commissioners stated that, 'if such goods are flotsam the Officers of the
Customs have no right to interfere and "of consequence, no prosecution can be commenced for resistance for flotsam goods are
now within their jurisdiction", but if the goods are stranded the
officers of the Customs should secure them for the owners and if
there be any reason to suppose them run, they may be seized . . .'

A number of ships came to grief in the vicinity of the Isle of
Wight. In April 1753 the Collector reported the stranding at the
Needles of HMS *Assurance*, which had sailed from Jamaica and
Lisbon under the command of Captain Scrope. He explained that
part of the money on board was saved and taken to Yarmouth,
and that the officers had been instructed to give what assistance
they could to secure any customable goods and place them under
the King's locks.

The Collector at Cowes furnished an account of the tobacco
which had been salved from the wreck of the *King George*, carrying
a cargo of this commodity from Whitehaven to Rotterdam when
she was stranded on Southmore Point on the Isle of Wight. In all,

280 hogsheads of tobacco had been brought to the King's Warehouse in 101 waggons and three sloops, and a number of waggons had also been used to cart loose tobacco and ships' materials.

Sugar was by now a regular import, and the ship *Howe* had been stranded in the Cowes area with a cargo of that product. It was decided that the only way to save the cargo would be to tranship it from the wreck to other ships and send it straight to London. The Collector intended to send a tidesman on each vessel for the security of the revenue, but as the shippers intended to let the vessels go without convoy, the tidesmen objected to the risk of being captured and taken to France.

An outward bound East Indiaman, the *Henry Addington*, commanded by Captain Wakefield, was stranded on 3rd December 1798 on the Bembridge Ledge on the eastern tip of the Isle of Wight. The Deputy Comptroller went to the scene, and finding there was no probability of getting the vessel off, gave directions to the boatmen at St. Helens and other officers on the coast to render what assistance they could in saving goods, preventing embezzlements and securing for the owners as much of the property as possible.

The Collector at Poole reported on 21st November 1795 that the troop transport *William Pitt*, on a voyage from Southampton to the West Indies carrying troops and naval supplies, had been driven ashore at Chapman's Pool in the Isle of Purbeck. No lives were lost, and they were able to bring some of the stores to the Custom House at Poole. But although it was hoped that a good part of the cargo would be saved, it was feared that the vessel itself would be lost.

In January 1786 the officers were able to salve from the wreck of the East Indiaman *Halswell* 54 barrels of foreign red wine, three trunks of stationery, three half bend tanned hides, five partly full hogsheads of porter and a quantity of nails, hoops and sundry other articles of ironware. As they were in a perishing condition the Directors of the East India Company ordered them to be sold.

An early example of wrecking on the south coast is described in a letter from the Board in January 1702 to the Collector at

Weymouth commenting on his report of the wreck of the *Katherine* of Brest. It appears that the ship was carrying a cargo of chestnuts when it was driven on shore at Portland, and broken up. On this occasion, the 'country people did not only imbezle and carry away ye chestnutts but beat and abusd ye officers in ye execution of their duties'. The Board asked for particular proof on oath against 'some of the most notorious offenders' so that they could then endeavour to make them an example 'for deterring others from the like barbarous practices'. The Master of the *Katherine* was in some distress, and wishing to sell what materials he could save from the ship in order to defray the charges and passage home of himself and his crew, the Board felt that it would be hard in this case to insist upon the duty being paid.

Chapter 6

SCOTLAND IN THE
EIGHTEENTH CENTURY

It had been the practice in Scotland to put the revenues out to farm, and the system continued in force here after it had come to an end in England. When the question of the Union of England and Scotland was being considered, it was found, in 1705, that while the English Customs brought in a revenue of £1,341,559 per annum, the Scottish Customs was being 'farmed' for £30,000. At the same time the Scottish Excise was farmed for £35,000 and it was estimated that the yield could be as much as £50,000 if the same method of collection as in England were employed. Arrangements were therefore made to take the Scottish revenues out of farm and the Commission for the Union decided that there should be the same Customs, Excise, and all other taxes and the same prohibitions, restrictions and other regulations of trade throughout the United Kingdom of Great Britain.

As a result a Scottish Board of Customs was established by royal letter patent, to collect, from 1st May 1707, both the Scottish Customs and the Excise duty on salt. Another Commission was appointed to collect the Excise duties apart from the salt tax. The duties collected by the Scottish Customs were to be remitted to the Receiver General of Customs in England, the salt duties to the English Salt Commissioners and the Excise duties to the English Commissioners of Excise.

In 1723, when an act was passed providing for the English and Scottish Customs to be put under the management of a single Commission for the whole of Great Britain, the existing patents were cancelled and a single Board set up. Seven of the Commissioners were ordered to reside in London to control the English Customs, and five in Edinburgh to look after the Scottish Customs and salt duties. In 1742, however, separate Boards for England and Scotland were restored, and the position remained like that until 1823.

In 1823 there were five revenue Boards covering the whole of the United Kingdom; the English and Scottish Boards of Customs, the English and Scottish Boards of Excise, and the Irish Revenue Board which dealt with both Customs and Excise. An act of that year formed two commissions out of these five bodies, a United Kingdom Board of Customs and a United Kingdom Board of Excise.

After the Act of Union in 1707 the new Commissioners set about bringing the Scottish system of collection into line with the English system, and skilled staff from England were sent to introduce the new procedure. One of the inherited difficulties in Scotland was the practice of confining overseas trade to the Royal Burghs so that legal quays were appointed only within their boundaries. The result was that foreign trade could still only take place within the limits of the burghs even though the rivers connecting them with the sea were often no longer navigable. For this reason, goods had to be transhipped into barges at the nearest convenient place and carried to and from the burgh, at considerable extra trouble and expense. The Royal Burgh of Dumfries provides a good example of this kind of situation for in the years immediately following the Act of Union, Dumfries was the head port of an area stretching from the boundaries of Carlisle to the Mull of Galloway. Already by this time the channel of the river Nith was too shallow and rocky for the vessels of the day, which had to use quays on either side of the mouth of the river at Carsethorn and Glencaple. The inhabitants of the area participated in the smuggling from the Isle of Man, and because of the lower rate of duty on spirits in Scotland were able to thrive on the smuggling of spirits into England.

A few years after the union, the Collector reported in a letter to the Commissioners of Customs that, since the business of the port was chiefly to prevent the running of goods from the Isle of Man, Ireland and other places, he had recently taken the opportunity of riding round the coast. His enquiries had shown the need for a tide waiter and a good boat to be provided for the Water of Orr and for Carsethorne, as well as a tide waiter and a small yawl for Kelton, and a tide waiter for Rivell.

On 11th July 1711 the Collector of Dumfries took a statement from Robert Stewart, Riding Waiter at Carsethorne. Some servants of the Laird of Arbigland had rescued a cargo of rum after Stewart had seized it from a Manx boat. The story he tells, in the quaint language of the time, makes interesting reading.

'*11 July 1711*. Att Carsethorne. – Ane Copie of the examinatione of Robert Stewart, Ryding Waiter, touching a Manks Boat which rune a parcelle of Brandye upon the tenth July current and deforced the officer in executione of his office. – Robert Stewart being examined saieth that he, haveing discovered a small boott hovering along the Cooste, the grounds for his jealousing him for a rogue. He the said Robert Stewart did watch hir all that day from eleven of the clock in the forenoon till eleven of the clock at night, still moving from place to place, att last the sd. little boat cam to the werry creek where he was watching being about half a mile distant from the dwelling house of the Laird of Arbigland, he the said Robert Stewart beholding this lay undiscovered to observe what would be done, and so soone as the watter fell from about the boat, the crew who were all strangers excepting on Jacob Turner, a quaker, who formerly used to practice the running trade fell immediately to disload the boat which so soone as the said Robert Stewart he went to and boarded her which he seazed with hir cargo consisting of twelve runlets containing about ten gallons each. So soon as the said Robert Stewart had made the seazour, the boat men all went away and left him alone in the boat where he stayed till about four a clock in the morning when the boatmen returned with three horses and two servants belonging to the said Laird of Arbigland, the boatmen no sooner cum on board but the two of them laid violentt hands on him and held the said Robert Stewart untill the other third disloaded the cargo when itt was cleared he could not discover but does suspectt that seing Arbigland's Servants and horses were present, it probably may be lodged wither in or near his dwelling house.'

During the same month another officer, James Young, had an even more disturbing experience. He had gone to the foot of the Water of Nith to a place called Glenhowen and there he discovered that a certain John Morrow, a smuggler, had recently come from the Isle of Man. He asked the Constable of the Parish to give him assistance and went to Morrow's house, where he found one large pack and two trusses of leaf tobacco. While he was attempting to remove them to the Queen's Warehouse, he was attacked by a 'multitude of women' who carried away the pack which was in the custody of the Constable. Young, leaving the two trusses with the Constable, went after the women who laid violent hands on him and kept him prisoner in John Morrow's house until they had managed to remove all the tobacco.

At this period, the Collectors of Customs were also usually responsible for collecting the salt duties and, in answer to an enquiry from the Commissioners relating to the salt pans within the port – which were numerous at this time on the Solway Firth – the Collector gave a very detailed description of the various installations. He also described how salt was made in one particular area, explaining that sand was gathered in dry weather after the sun had 'congealed the saltish particles with the sand after the overflowing of the sea, which sand after being mixed with sea water makes a very saltish liquor and this liquor makes a very good and strong salt though not so very fair as other salt'.

In July 1718 Thomas Louden, Tidesman at the foot of the Water of Orr, sent a message to the Custom House at Dumfries stating that a boat from the Isle of Man had landed at Cowend with a cargo of brandy and tobacco. The boat belonged to James Willson, a tenant at Macks, and Louden who had already managed to seize ten trusses of tobacco, knew where the rest of the goods were located. The same day William Sutherland, Landwaiter, together with three Tidesmen hurried to Cowend, about eighteen miles from Dumfries. They joined Thomas Louden and William Gracie, another Tidesman, only to find that Willson's son, with some servants, had forcibly entered Louden's house, dragging his wife outside and carrying away the tobacco. When Louden heard this he assembled some of his friends and together they managed to recapture the tobacco and return it to his own house. But James Willson, his son and a number of companions, later returned with about 120 women and carried off the whole cargo while Louden and Gracie stood by, not daring to attack. When reinforcements arrived from Dumfries they searched the country, without success, and so returned to Dumfries with the two trusses of tobacco they had been able to secure. But when they arrived at a place called Whiteside, they were attacked by about twenty or thirty men in disguise and by about forty or fifty women, who 'with long poles, clubs and staves, beat and abused the officers and their horses' and kept them prisoners till the tobacco was carried off.

During a plague scare in November 1720 the Dumfries Collector reported that he had heard of three large vessels which were hovering off the Isle of Man since the inhabitants would not allow them to land. He was very much afraid that they might try to land on the Solway coast, although the Justices had appointed watches there, as the smugglers had convinced the country people that the plague rumour was just a trick of the Customs to prevent the landing of goods. The greatest danger was in Kirkcudbright Bay, where sometimes as many as twenty or thirty ships were windbound, and the Collector insisted that unless soldiers were sent there it would be impossible to implement the quarantine laws.

A letter written a few years later from Glasgow, presumably by a business man since the writer described himself as a 'fair trader', throws light on the extent and organization of the smuggling trade. The letter runs:

12 April 1744. Glasgow. – 'We fair traders are much surprised at the neglect of severall of the officers to let such an illicit trade be carried on by severall of this Kingdom and so much encouraged by those of England. We shall only mention some which to our knowledge is a very great detrement to the Government and also to us Fair traders. –

There are three in company at Annan, The first is John Johnston, Postmaster, the 2nd is one William Hardie, the other is Tristram Lowther. This John Johnstone is indulged by being Postmaster, Hardie is Brother-in law to Mr. Bryce Blair who has a post in the Government and is so much indulged by Blair that none dare meddle. Lowther is a Cumberland man and well acquaited with the officers at Carlisle. There is one John Carlyle, one of the greatest smugglers from the Isle of Man, he has a near relation whose name is John Little. The traders in this place often drink his health and tell us how kind he is to them.'

PERTH

The situation of the ancient port of Perth was similar to that of Dumfries, since the river Tay had so frequently changed course that the channels were obstructed with dangerous sandbanks and navigation was extremely difficult. In spite of this, a fair amount of foreign trade was carried on in the eighteenth century, although larger vessels had to discharge a few miles below the town.

In the early part of the century, immediately after the Union, there was a good deal of hostile feeling towards the revenue officials in this area, who had to rely on military support for their safety. In March 1722, for instance, the Collector of Perth wrote to the Commissioners telling them of the forthcoming election 'of a Barron for this shire to represent them in Parliament'. As a result, Captain Wright, commander of the garrison troops, had been told to march out of the town and not to return until two days after the election. The Collector begged the Board to intercede with the Commander-in-Chief to allow the Captain and half the garrison to remain to protect the King's Warehouse. His entreaties cannot have been unsuccessful, for a week later, when the King's Warehouse was broken into by unknown persons who carried off a variety of goods, he and some soldiers gave pursuit and rescued some of the goods. The magistrates were asked for assistance but, said the Collector, 'they laugh at us, ney, when our officers in the night are in their duty in looking after the tide, they are almost murdered by knocking of them down with clubs'. A year later, the garrison once again marched off to Inverness, leaving the port unprotected, but although the Collector asked the Provost and magistrates for a guard, they could only supply a constable.

Later in the year in reply to an enquiry from the Board as to whether any of his officers were suspected of disaffection, he assured their Honours that he suspected none of the officers, all of whom frequented 'the Established Church where King George was prayed for and no other'.

One evening in September 1735 the Comptroller and some officers were walking along the street when they met some people 'running' two hogsheads. They took no notice when called upon to stop, so the Comptroller sent for the guard and attempted to bring them to a halt by placing himself between the casks. In spite of his endeavours, one of the hogsheads was carried off. When the soldiers arrived he placed one as a sentinel to guard the other hogshead, and then demanded access to the 'Thistle' in order to search the cellars. William Duncan, the landlord, let him in but while he was making his search he was told that the sentinel had been killed. He immediately ran to the gate and found that the four grenadiers had been shut in the inn-yard by the maid. He opened the gate and hurried to the sentry, who 'appeared to be dead'. The rest of the guard ran up, and the drum 'beat to arms', whereupon all the soldiers hurried from the garrison to the scene. This frightened the 'runners', causing them to abandon the hogshead near the town cross and make their escape. The 'dead' soldier recovered, but was terribly bruised.

Another savage attack on the Customs Officers at Perth was made by a group of sailors in April 1755, after five ankers and six half-ankers of foreign spirits had been seized from a ship at Newburgh. Fortunately a party of soldiers once again came to their assistance. In the skirmish the Sergeant's regimental sword was broken, and the Collector was worried about having it repaired at the public expense, since the soldiers had already been rewarded for their help.

An odd remedy for headaches is described in a report of 1760. The Comptroller, who had been afflicted with headaches for many months, was advised to drink 'Goats Whey' as the 'most probable way of re-establishing his health' and the Collector on his behalf, asked the Board whether he might have five or six weeks' absence to take advantage of the remedy, while his son took over his office. The request was acceded to.

During the winter it was often extremely difficult to transport dutiable and seized goods. In February 1767, the Collector, who had already been held up for some time waiting for the snow to clear before arranging for tobacco and snuff to be brought from Blairgowrie, decided to send for the goods before conditions became any worse. He therefore directed the Surveyor, a boatman, and a corporal and four men of General Rufane's Regiment to set out from Blairgowrie.

A letter was written to the Commissioners in August 1768 by the Collector, Lawrence Craigie, which is worth quoting in full for the light it throws on the Collector's character.

'Yesterday I received your letter of the 10th instant imposing a fine of £5 upon me and £2/10/- on the Comptroller for our having admitted to entry four hogsheads of wine of which we ought to have made a seizure. May I entreat your Honours to review your sentence and withdraw those marks of your displeasure, the bitterness of which I feel the more sensibly as I have on so many occasions been honoured with your Favour and approbation. But with whatever shall be the fate of this application with regard to myself, I must do the Comptroller the justice to acquaint Your Honours that he was sick and confined to the house when the proposal was made to me of receiving the French duties and that the whole demerit of this transaction belongs to,

Your most humble servant, LC.'

The Collector had been in the habit of keeping his balance of cash in the Perth Bank but in January 1788 the Board ordered him to keep it in the King's Chest. The Collector explained that this was an old wooden box, and therefore asked their Honours to order an iron chest for the purpose. He pointed out that the duties were almost wholly paid in banknotes and if these should be lost by robbery or fire, while in the King's Chest, the loss necessarily fell on the Collector. He ended by asserting that he would cheerfully submit to the expense of insurance rather than run any risk.

In May 1752 the Commissioners issued a report concerning the famous Appin murder in which they instructed the Collectors to 'examine very strictly every person offering to take passage on board any ship going out this Kingdom'. Later in the same month they provided a detailed description of Allen Breck Stewart, suspected of the crime, as follows:

'He is about five feet ten inches, long visage very much mark'd with the small pox, black bushy hair, a little in-kneed, round shouldered, about thirty years of age, came to this country in February last from Ogilvies Regiment in France. His dress when last seen which was upon the 18th instant was a blue bonnet, a Blue coat (Lowland Dress) with red lining, waist-coat and breeches and a brownish colour'd great coat over all and no visible arms.' The Appin murder was vividly described by Robert Louis Stevenson in *Kidnapped*.

DUNDEE

At the request of the Commissioners of Customs, the Collector of Dundee, in December 1725, described how he had seized eight casks of wine in a barn about five miles west of the town. As no cart was available to convey the goods to Dundee, he left the soldiers who had accompanied him to guard the wine and returned to the town to procure a boat. At about nine o'clock in the evening a mob of about forty people armed with forks and staves attacked the barn from all sides, but were speedily repulsed by the soldiers' gunfire. The sergeant in charge of the party was badly wounded in the head in the course of the struggle.

The following year in September, the Tide Surveyor and four

boatmen seized six ankers of brandy in the loft of John Smith's house at South Ferry, near Dundee. As they were carrying them to the nearby Custom House hovel for temporary safe keeping, they were attacked by a 'mobb who carried off ye said six ankers brandy and beat the boatmen'.

The Collector and Surveyor of Dundee met with a rebuff when in May 1729 they went to search a house belonging to my Lord Kinnaird for uncustomed goods. They took a party of soldiers but were refused access by George Kinnaird, who alleged that they had no privilege of searching Peers' Houses. They then applied to Mr. Drummond, Justice of the Peace and Member of Parliament, for a warrant to search the house. The Justice refused saying that he had no authority for granting 'warrant for searching Peers' houses'.

MONTROSE

In the years following the Union, the Customs Officers of Montrose had to be particularly circumspect as the people in the area were strongly Jacobite in sympathy. They also had difficulty in protecting both themselves and the King's Warehouse. The effect of the first Jacobite rebellion is shown in a letter sent to the Commissioners by the Collector on the 20th September 1715, which ran:

'On Saturday in ye afternoon after ye proclamation was over, Severall Gentlemen and others came to ye Custom House and brook it open and took away all the bonds and then brook ye warehouse and took away all the goods that was seized one Friday, and Saturday last Samuel Lothian, Surveyor, William Dennison, Landwaiter, John Huddart and Allan Gordon, Tydesmen deserted ye service and went for Edinburgh, There is now off the Harbour mouth a ship loaded with tobacco from Virginia bound to this Port but does not design to enter her cargo till she sees how things will go, which we are very glad of for if any money or bonds should be paid or given here it would be infallibly taken away immediately.'

The Collector informed the Board in July 1723 that two French barques loaded with brandy were hovering off the coast. He had reliable information that the masters of the vessels had been offering the brandy to a number of merchants, with the promise of an armed force of thirty or forty men to escort the goods six or seven miles into the country. As there were no troops or magistrates in the area, the Collector claimed that it was impossible to hinder the smuggling. He suggested that one of His Majesty's sloops should be able to catch them.

The King's Warehouse was repeatedly broken into and robbed On one occasion two sentries were badly beaten up by a mob armed with clubs, and on another sixty ankers of brandy were taken without alarming the guard. The thieves apparently broke through the cellar door of the neighbouring house, and then through the wall of the warehouse. The owner of the house next door, Mr. Dunbar, according to the Collector, 'pretends that he knows nothing of it which is very odd'.

Chapter 7

THE NINETEENTH CENTURY

At the opening of the nineteenth century the members of the Customs and Excise service could scarcely have foreseen the great changes which would take place during the next few years. Smuggling continued unabated and possibly had even increased, since so many revenue cruisers were kept busy on naval duties. The Act of Union with Ireland in 1800 had some effect on Customs work as the many prohibitions and restrictions on Irish trade – formerly part of the department's jurisdiction – were abolished. Another act of the same year suggests that Customs officers may have been guilty of some dereliction of duty in connection with public health, for it included a clause that, 'if any Officer of His Majesty's Customs . . . shall desert from his duty . . . or shall knowingly and willingly permit any person, ship, vessel, goods or merchandise, to depart or be conveyed out of the said lazarette, ship or other place unless by permission under an order of His Majesty . . . he shall be guilty of felony and suffer death as in cases of felony without benefit of clergy'. In 1801 an act was passed authorizing Customs and Excise cutters to take out Letters of Marque against enemy shipping. As Letters of Marque had already been issued to revenue cutters for a good many years, some doubts may have been raised about the legality of the practice.

A further consolidation of the Customs Laws was made necessary in 1803 as so many changes had taken place since the 1797 consolidation that the business of interpreting the laws had become exceedingly complex. Another important piece of legislation passed at this time was the Warehousing Act which allowed merchants the privilege of placing their goods in bonded warehouses and delaying the payment of duty on them until they had arranged a sale. This obviated the onerous procedure whereby merchants had to pay immediately on import, before they had sold their goods, and were thus liable to incur heavy debts. This procedure had already been applied to certain goods, such as tobacco from 1714 and British Plantation Rum from 1742, but only now was it given general extension.

The Excise duty on salt caused a good deal of ill feeling at this time since it had been greatly increased during the war, and was especially detrimental to the fishing industry. Although fishermen were entitled to drawback, they were required to pay the duty if they returned to a port other than that from which they had sailed. As a result, many catches were ruined because fishermen neglected to take sufficient salt, and consequently there was an enormous increase in the smuggling of salt. However, the duty was not repealed until 1825.

At this period one or two changes were made affecting the staff of the revenue services. Among these was the abolition of the payment of fees. Previously merchants had had to pay for the various services concomitant upon importing goods, as well as further customary fees to ensure that the officers would carry out the complicated procedures and calculations on their behalf. These payments had become an intolerable burden as trade had increased, and their abolition was long overdue. Numerous official holidays enjoyed by the staff were a cause of great delay, and steps were taken to reduce them. The official hours of attendance were also revised, and became nine a.m. to four p.m. in the winter and eight a.m. to four p.m. in the summer. The tables of fees and lists of official holidays were ordered to be publicly exhibited.

Steps were taken in 1810 to build a new London Custom House as Ripley's building had become extremely dilapidated and was no longer large enough to meet the needs of the day. It was decided to erect the new building to the west of the existing Custom House, but before work could commence the complicated process of acquiring the land and quays had to be completed. These matters were only finally settled in 1813. John Rennie, the famous architect and civil engineer, had surveyed the site and in his report of 1812 he recommended that the building should be on piles driven two feet into the stratum of hard gravel. David Laing, the Departmental Surveyor of Buildings, was the architect of the new building and the construction contract was allocated to John Miles and Henry Peto. In October 1813 the foundation stone was laid by Lord Liverpool, the Prime Minister, who had previously been Collector of Customs Inwards for the port of London. At about six a.m. on 12th February 1814 it was found that the old Custom House was on fire. At the time the only occupants were the housekeeper, Miss Eleanor King Kelly, her sister, her brother General Kelly, some other relatives and domestic servants and some Customs Watchmen. A little after seven a.m. some barrels of gunpowder blew up; at about half past nine there was a tremendous explosion, and by twelve o'clock the whole building was in ruins. Two domestic servants lost their lives in the blaze, and General Kelly and a young man named Carlisle who rescued him were badly burned. General Kelly died a few days later but Carlisle recovered and was afterwards made a Customs weigher. Many who were in the area came to help and the Custom House Volunteers and East India Company's Volunteers rendered valuable service in preventing looting and plunder. The Aberdeenshire militia and a company of artillerymen came from the Tower of London and gave assistance. It was said that the explosion was so great that official papers and records were carried away as far as Dalston, Shacklewell, Homerton, Hackney and Highbury and all the adjoining villages. Miss Kelly later received £1,200 for the loss of her furniture and effects and a messenger £100 for very special services in the rescue of important documents and valuables.

One disastrous result of the fire was the almost complete loss of the department's headquarter archives and the library of printed books which had been gradually assembled from 1671 onwards. Fortunately, some volumes of extracts from the Board's Minutes which had been compiled by Sir William Musgrave were rescued, and these have helped in the reconstruction of the history of the department.

The history of the new building was not itself without incident. In January 1825 the floor of the Long Room fell in and the Custom House had to be closed. After an inquiry the Crown took action against the builders, Miles and Peto. Much hinged on whether or not the piles of the building had been driven into the hard stratum of gravel, as required by Rennie's survey. When they were drawn out, they were found to be too short to reach the gravel, and consequently the Commissioners put the builder's bond of £33,000 in suit. The case lasted for more than ten years, by which time both builders had died, and the Board finally agreed to pay £10,000 to their families. Sir Robert Smirke was called in to rebuild the central part of the building, which survived in this state until the last war, when the east end was so badly damaged in an air raid that that part of the Custom House had to be dismantled.

An act of 1814 which gave authors copyright of their works for twenty-eight years or for life, whichever should be the longer, also provided that the task of controlling the importation of pirated editions of English works should remain with the Customs service. Another act of the same year required the master of a ship to hand over all ship's letters to the Post Office, and Customs officers were not to allow the discharge of cargo to commence until the master had furnished an oath that he had handed over such letters. Officers were also required to search for any ship's letters that might not have been handed over.

On 28th April 1815 the captured Napoleon was sent to Elba, and arrangements were made for representatives of the victorious allies to visit England. The department was ordered to afford every possible facility to these 'august personages', who included the Emperor of Russia, the King of Prussia, Prince Metternich and General Blücher, and to forgo examination of their own and their suites' baggage.

In 1786, Richard Frewin (later a Customs Commissioner), had

proposed a scheme for the repealing of obsolete Customs acts, but this had been considerably delayed by the war. For some years, however, Nicholas Jickling, Collector of the port of Wells-next-the-Sea, had been working on the scheme and in 1814 it received Treasury sanction. In 1815 Frewin and Jickling produced a tome of 1,375 pages which became known in the service as 'Jickling's Digest'.

The methods used to determine the strength of spirits had proved somewhat unsatisfactory. A hydrometer devised by John Clarke of London, which had been in use from the early part of the eighteenth century, was statutorily recognized in 1787, but in 1816 an act was passed giving legal sanction to the use of a hydrometer invented by Bartholomew Sikes, then Collector of Excise at Hertford. In submitting his instrument for trial, Sikes states with due modesty, 'and hereupon I speek with the greater confidence, as, if there be any part of knowledge in which I am more versed and fully grounded than in any other, it is on the subject of hydrometers.' Sikes's instrument certainly proved itself, for it is in use even today.

In the same year a private act was passed establishing the 'Customs Fund'. It was described as an act for establishing and regulating a fund for the widows, children and relatives of officers or persons belonging to the department of Customs in England. The idea was originated by a clerk in the Custom House, Charles Ogilvy, and he also suggested that, in order to provide a source of income, the right of publication of the *Bill of Entry* should be purchased from the patentee. The *Bill of Entry* – a daily news-sheet published for the benefit of merchants since the days of Charles II – gave details of vessels arriving in and departing from the Port of London and information about the cargoes carried. In 1760 George II had granted the patent to publish it to a certain Henry Lewis, and it was renewed in 1791 to John Lewis. It was not until 1822 that the Fund was able to purchase the patent from Lewis's widow for £28,000. In 1880 the patent was again due for renewal, but the Crown took over publication without compensation to the Fund. The *Bill of Entry* continued to be published until 1939, when it was discontinued for strategic reasons, and so the merchant community lost a valuable source of information. During the nineteenth century the *Bill of Entry* was gradually expanded to include the principal ports of the country. Copies have survived in various places, but the most complete sets are in the possession of the Commissioners of Customs and Excise and provide a valuable source of material for research into the trade of the last century.

A new Customs Consolidation Act was passed, as well as an act which dealt with the tonnage measurement of steam vessels. This made allowance for the space occupied by the engine room.

Although legislation had already been passed, in 1806 and 1807, to prohibit the taking of fees by Customs officers, merchants continued to offer sums of money to expedite their business. One of the first acts of George IV's reign imposed a penalty of £500 on anyone offering a fee to an officer. At this time, a number of items of dutiable goods, including tea, coffee and tobacco, as well as the staff responsible for them, were transferred to the Excise's control.

The following year an attempt was made to deal with 'wrecking' and the looting of wrecks – still a constant cause of anxiety to the Customs service in certain areas. Customs officers were given authority to allow salved goods to proceed to their port of shipment, and were permitted to enter private lands in order to preserve wrecked goods.

An important change was made in the management of revenue business in 1823 when the three Boards of Customs (England, Scotland and Ireland) were consolidated into one Board. The same policy was undertaken for the three Excise Boards. The new Customs Board consisted of thirteen commissioners, with two assistant commissioners in both Dublin and Edinburgh, though these local boards were abolished in 1829. The following year the salaries of the entire Board were reduced.

A new consolidation of the Customs laws, completed by James Deacon Hume, Comptroller for London Port, Samuel Thackeray and Sir Thomas Tomlins brought untold benefit to the service, 443 Acts being repealed and replaced by 11, dealing with management, regulation, smuggling, navigation, ship's registry, duties, warehousing, bounties, colonial Customs, the Isle of Man and passenger traffic. In the same year, the Board approved the establishment of certain offices in the Plantation territories of Ceylon, Mauritius, Sierra Leone, Gambia, New South Wales and Van Diemen's Land, all of which were to be administered by the United Kingdom Board of Customs.

In 1825 the Customs finally became responsible for the duties on cocoa, coffee, foreign spirits, tobacco and wine, so bringing to an end the curious practice by which two revenue services collected import duties, often on the same commodities, and maintained two separate port organizations, including revenue cruisers. There had often been rivalry between the two services, and from time to time both Boards would instruct their staffs to cooperate, though, of course, the government or the Treasury may at times have considered an element of competition desirable. More probably, however, the system evolved gradually, and the division arose because Excise duties were regarded as temporary, even though they had been granted to the monarch in perpetuity at the restoration of Charles II. The revenue cruisers belonging to the Excise were handed over to the Customs service at this time.

The Customs Acts which came into force in 1826 were still largely restrictive, and did not really foreshadow the great relaxations in the offing. The regulations governing the report of ships and the entry of cargoes were restated, and certificates were still required for goods shipped in the Plantations or in British ships in foreign ports. Goods liable to both Customs and Excise duties still had to go through the procedure of being dealt with by both departments, and a number of prohibitions – such as those on the importation of cattle, sheep, swine, malt and tobacco stalks, and on the exportation of machinery – remained in force to protect home industries and agriculture. A number of measures were taken to counteract smuggling. If prohibited goods were brought within four leagues of the coast between the North Foreland and Beachy Head, and within eight leagues of any other part of the coasts of the United Kingdom, both ship and cargo were made liable to forfeiture. Similar penalties applied to square-rigged ships found with illegal-sized packages of tobacco or spirits on board within one hundred leagues of the coast, and to cases where goods were thrown overboard during chase, or where a vessel which had previously been carrying cargo on board was discovered to be unaccountably light within the limits of a port. Three or more smugglers with firearms were liable to punishment for felony, and those assaulting revenue officers to transportation for three years. The provisions of the older Navigation Acts were re-affirmed. Trade with the Plantations, as well as inter-Plantation trade, was still restricted to British ships, although foreign ships were allowed to carry produce from the country to which they belonged direct to the Plantations, and to take goods from the Plantations to any foreign port. Certain ports in the Plantations were designated 'free ports' and foreign trade into the Plantations was limited to them. Certain goods from Europe, such as wine, timber, corn, brandy, tobacco, oil, dried fruit, salt, flax and hemp, could only be brought to the United Kingdom in British ships or, directly, in ships belonging to the country in which they had been produced. There were many new rates of duty, and provision was also made – in cases where it was considered that a country was discriminating against British goods or shipping – for additional duties to be imposed by Order in Council.

On the ending of the East India Company's monopoly on the importation of tea in 1834, the duty on tea was transferred to the Customs. It was now possible to import tea into certain ports other than London which had been approved for the importation and warehousing of goods from China and the East Indies. The Excise department still remained responsible, however, for licensing the retailing of tea.

In January 1825 a directive was issued by the Board of Customs about the uniform worn by the commanders and mates of the cruisers. A further order was made in December of that year with regard to the uniform of chief officers, riding officers and others. Before this time, there had been no acknowledged uniform, although many of the officers of the cruisers, who frequently had naval rank, wore naval uniform; and it had been customary for the Board to issue distinguishing buttons. Early in the reign of William IV the allowances for duty-free stores for use on board ships were prescribed. Previously such allowances were confined to naval ships, and to Plantation rum on board merchant ships. Under the new act, all vessels of less than seventy tons going on voyages expected to last more than forty days were allowed to ship duty-free stores. The Board issued a list of articles which could be shipped for the use of passengers and crew. This included tea, coffee, cocoa, spirits, raw sugar, molasses and British manufactured tobacco for all persons, and wine, cigars, refined sugar and beer for officers and passengers.

In response to petitions from merchants and shipowners asking for a relaxation of the quarantine laws, the Privy Council decided to appoint medical superintendents at the regular quarantine ports. This empowered the Customs officers to admit to Pratique, that is, to release certain vessels from quarantine on receipt of a certificate from the medical superintendent. The superintendent of quarantine, on releasing a vessel, was required to deliver a certificate to the master who had to show it to the Customs officer when making entry. At the same time he had to pay the quarantine fee of £5 14s. 6d. These certificates were the forerunners of the present-day Certificate of Pratique issued to a master by the Customs boarding officers, which he must produce when 'reporting' his ship. An epidemic of cholera in 1832, which lasted for most of the year, caused a deal of alarm and gave the department much concern about the enforcement of the quarantine laws. The following year the epidemic reappeared in London, but the port was 'declared free' on 11th September. At this time a steam vessel was introduced for the first time into the revenue fleet. She was the *Vulcan* of 325 tons and had been specially commissioned at White's yard at Cowes. Her crew consisted of a commander, two mates, two engineers, four firemen, seventeen mariners and four boys.

An unusual entry in the Minute Book of the Board of Customs in 1835 refers to a substantial grant of money, £500 to buy a library of 'Useful and Religious Books' for the Coastguard, and in the following year two more grants were made for the same purpose. In 1840 £50 was allocated to the new churches at Rotherhithe on condition that accommodation was provided for the inferior officers of the Customs, and in 1841, £40 was allocated to Fairlight Church on condition that thirty-five seats were provided for the inferior officers of the Coastguard. During the next few years there were also similar grants to Lulworth and Bexhill, and also a grant to the Isle of Arran for the religious instruction of the Coastguard and their families.

In the new reign a further act which affected the Customs Service dealing with copyright made provision for the officers of the Department to have lists of copyright works in order to prevent the importation of pirated works and in 1842 there were further regulations directing that pirated copies should be seized and destroyed.

In 1839 Collectors of Customs were asked to report about their methods of enforcing the Emigration Acts after an inspecting physician in Canada had complained that the medical supervision on emigrant ships was defective. The lists of passengers certified by the British Customs officers were seldom correct, and it was therefore difficult to ascertain the number of deaths during the voyage.

The Customs Amendment Act of 1843 which permitted the export of tools and machinery marks the beginning of one of the great changes in the trade policy of this country in the nineteenth century. This was a far cry from the act passed in George I's reign which prevented skilled artificers finding employment abroad so that this country might retain its industrial advantages.

A Select Committee to inquire into the tobacco trade set up in 1844 found that although smuggling by specially built cutters had ceased, the actual amount of tobacco smuggled was greater than ever before. To some extent this is reflected in the quantity of tobacco seized by the revenue officers, for obviously this could only have represented a small proportion of the whole amount illicitly imported. It was, in fact, estimated that only about one-third of the tobacco finding its way into this country was legally imported.

A change was introduced in the system of appointing ports and legal quays in 1846. From the earliest times Customs ports had been sections of the coast extending up rivers and seawards within certain defined limits. The Court of Exchequer had been accustomed from time to time to appoint a Commission to survey these area and to make recommendations about the limits and places of landing and discharge. The Treasury was now empowered to appoint ports and legal quays, and to alter them under Treasury Warrant.

Another duty allocated at this time to the Customs service sometimes caused difficulty and occasioned embarrassment. This was the seizure and destruction of obscene prints, paintings, books and literature. Attitudes have changed considerably since the act was passed and it is quite likely that some of the matter which would have been seized then would be passed today.

In 1849 the Excise, the Office of Assessed Taxes and the Stamp Duties Office were amalgamated, and although the change did not affect the day-to-day running of the service, it greatly altered the management of the Excise. During the previous sixty years, many of the multifarious Excise duties had been gradually relinquished. When the Office of Assessed Taxes was first set up in 1785, for instance, it took over the duties on coaches, and later the duty on male servants. Many duties had been transferred to the Customs, including those on imported spirits, tobacco, rum, coffee, chocolate, pepper, tea and wine. Many Excise duties had also been repealed, such as those on beer, cider, perry, tea, coffee, chocolate and sherbet. By 1849 the only articles subject to Excise were spirits (or strong waters), malt, hops, paper, soap, hackney carriages, stage carriages, post horses, bricks, railway passengers, sugar (made and used in brewing) and British chicory.

Not surprisingly, therefore, the need was felt to rationalize the revenue services and to effect large-scale economies. The Office of Assessed Taxes and the Stamp Duties Office had already been united in 1834, and since union had proved successful, parliament decided to add the Excise to it. The Customs at this time was a relatively large department on its own and presumably it was felt that the organization would become unbalanced if it were amalgamated with the Excise. But in some ways such a union, even at this time, would have been more practical as both services still had many things in common; in particular, bonded warehouses, and a concern with spirit duties. In the event, there were staff savings at the higher levels, for Collectors of Excise were appointed Receivers of Taxes and, in due course, were also appointed Distributors of Stamps.

A commission of inquiry into the management of the Customs service appointed in 1848 recommended that the number of Customs commissioners should be reduced to seven. It also suggested that the number of cruisers should be reduced from seventy to forty-nine, and that the Land Guard be disbanded altogether.

In 1849 the Navigation Laws, which had existed in some form or other since the days of Elizabeth I, were finally repealed. The application of these laws, particularly with regard to Plantation shipping, had involved the Customs service in a great deal of non-revenue work. The registration of ships which had been a direct result of these laws did not itself come to an end when they were repealed.

A dispute between the Customs department and two London dock companies caused a considerable stir at this time. Acting on rumours that people were obtaining sugar and coffee from the docks without paying duty, a force of Customs officers searched St. Katherine's Dock and London Dock on 4th December 1849, the result being that informations were laid against the two dock companies. The penalties were very high, and a committee of London merchants, as well as a select committee of the House of Commons, were set up to deal with the matter. In the end, the case was settled by each company paying £100.

The Board came in for a good deal of criticism during the inquiries, and it was stated by the select committee, when considering the appointment of Commissioners, that 'such appointments ought to be made with a scrupulous regard to the possession of the requisite qualifications of ability and experience and not so much from political or personal considerations as has hitherto been too often the case'. Mr. Lushington had been appointed at the age of twenty-six, Mr. Spring Rice at twenty-four and Mr. Goulburn at twenty-seven and the committee remarked that all three were 'sons, brothers or relations of Chancellors of Exchequer or Lords of the Treasury'.

For a number of years the Customs service had been dealing with the work connected with passengers leaving the country. As a result, it was customary for passenger lists to be made out and sent to the medical officers in the plantations. An act of 1852 formally empowered Customs officers to act as Emigration officers, and although in the next century a new department, the Immigration Department, was formed from a nucleus of Customs officers, even today in every part of the country the Customs service carries out immigration duties.

When the Crimean War broke out in 1854, the work of the department was complicated by the numerous orders prohibiting the exportation of articles which might reach the enemy and be useful to him. In order to reduce the inconvenience to trade, however, permission was granted to merchants to export many of the prohibited articles to places remote from the war area, so long as they gave bond to the Customs to produce a certificate of the actual landing of the goods at their destination within a specified period of time. These were known as 'war-bonds', and in the two years of the war the number of bonds entered into in London was 15,200. The enforcement of the wartime prohibitions and restrictions placed a great strain on the truncated Customs service, since frequently investigations had to be made in doubtful cases, and legal proceedings sometimes instituted. This all involved a great deal of troublesome correspondence and complicated bookkeeping.

The Merchant Shipping Consolidation Act of 1854 was important as far as the Customs service was concerned since it made provision for the Board of Trade to take over the general superintendence of the registry of British ships. The Customs service, however, still continued to carry out the actual work of registry. The Office of Registrar-General of Shipping and Seamen was set up under the aegis of the Board of Trade, and Surveyors for the measurement of ships were appointed at various places. The existing transcripts of registers and the surviving muster-rolls were transferred to the Registrar-General, and the Chief Registrar's interest in registry was confined to the Port of London, although he acted as technical adviser to the registrars of the United Kingdom and of certain overseas territories.

The ancient office of Comptroller of the Port of London was also abolished in the same year, bringing to an end the long line of succession from Geoffrey Chaucer who had held that position from 1374 to 1386. It was the last of the original patent appointments of Customer, Comptroller and Searcher to survive from the early Customs period. Although the office of Searcher still exists in name today, the task now performed is a purely clerical one, in connection with export shipping documents. The title of Comptroller is also retained in the Office of Accountant and Comptroller General.

Light dues for the upkeep of lighthouses and other lights had long been collected by the Customs service but an act of 1855 made the Board of Trade responsible for the financial administration of these dues while the Customs Department remained responsible for the actual collection. As the Board's Report of 1857 pointed out, the intricacy of the calculations involved, and the amount collected, made the task an extremely laborious and responsible one. In 1855, nearly £400,000 was collected on behalf of the three corporations, the Trinity Corporation, the Dublin Corporation and the Commissioners of Northern Lighthouses.

An act of 1853/4 also required Customs officials to act as Shipping Masters. This involved the signing on, supervision and paying off of ships' crews, the registration of the names and characters of seamen, the settling of disputes between masters and crews, the arranging for the entry of apprentices on board ships, the examination of the sufficiency and quality of the provisions for outward voyages. Other tasks to be carried out in the interests of seamen, under the heading of Mercantile Marine duties, included the management of the Seamen's Savings Bank, the custody of the effects of deceased seamen and the checking of the seaworthiness of emigrant ships in ports where there were no regular emigrant agents. Many of these functions are still part of a Customs officer's duties.

Under the same act, Customs officers were called upon to act as Receivers of Wreck. This involved duties which were, and still are, very intricate and time-consuming. In cases of wreck, casualty and disputed salvage it was necessary, for example, to conduct all inquiries before magistrates. Officers were obliged to go in person to any vessel stranded or in distress and take whatever measures were considered necessary for the safety of the ship, crew and cargo; the same Act empowered them to demand any assistance they might need for this purpose. They were required to receive and take custody of all articles saved or washed ashore and to search for, and, if necessary, take by force, any goods which might have been plundered or concealed. They were also obliged to give notice to all parties who might have any claim on wreck, to send full particulars to Lloyd's within forty-eight hours of the occurrence, and to sell without delay all trivial and perishable articles which might, in their judgment, deteriorate by detention.

Other non-revenue functions which continued to be part of Customs work included the enforcement of quarantine regulations, control over the importation of animals to prevent the introduction of disease into native stock, the preparation of monthly and annual trade statistics, and the enforcement of the provisions of the Copyright Act for the protection of British authors against pirated editions published abroad.

Since the tariffs of 1842 and 1845 had introduced many reductions in duties, the number of principal articles liable to duty had dropped from 564 in 1841 to 153 in 1855, and yet the danger to the revenue from smuggling had not so greatly diminished. The pattern of smuggling had also changed, for ships were now normally too great in size to make successful 'runs', and the carrying of contraband ceased to be the primary object of a voyage. Smuggling was confined to a few articles subject to high duties, such as tobacco, spirits, watches and silk, and such contraband was usually concealed in vessels carrying legitimate cargo. The building of enclosed docks in the main ports, however, facilitated the prevention of smuggling, particularly as police were given authority to make seizures of uncustomed goods.

Consequently, fewer guards were needed than before, and the Board of Customs was able to suggest ways of improving the revenue protection and, at the same time, to introduce staff economies. Although passenger trade had greatly increased, personal smuggling was still comparatively infrequent. Nevertheless, the Board took steps to control this traffic, and in its first report referred to the thoughtless habit of 'packing dutiable articles within the folds of ladies' dresses as to answer the purpose, or at least to give the appearance, of fraudulent concealment', which prevailed among passengers arriving from abroad.

In 1859 the office of 'Jerquer' was finally abolished in the Customs service. However, the name survives in Customs 'jargon', for officers still send their files of papers in connection with ships and their 'Blue Books' to be 'jerqued', and the Inward Clearing Bill which is issued to a master of a ship on the final discharge of his cargo is still called a 'jerque note'.

In its report of 1857 the Board explained that as a result of the reductions and simplifications of the tariff, the examination and delivery of free and low duty goods had been transferred from the Landing Department to the Waterguard. The Treaty of Commerce with France in 1860 led to the abolition of many of the remaining duties and, on the 18th of April, the Board submitted to the Treasury plans for re-organizing the department in accordance with the new situation. As the duties of the Landing Officers were now considerably reduced, the integration of the Landing and Waterguard departments was proposed. It was estimated that this would result in a staff saving of 282, and a consequential reduction in expenditure of £42,000. The Treasury accepted these proposals, and their implementation resulted in the virtual extinction of the Old Waterguard, which had later become the Coastguard. The titles of Tide Waiter, Tide Surveyor, Landing Surveyor and Landing Waiter disappeared, and were replaced by the new ranks of Surveyor, Examining Officer and Outdoor Officer who would be responsible for both Waterguard and Landing duties.

Because of great increase in trade merchants were demanding extended facilities, and the Inland Bonding Act of 1860 authorized the appointment of Manchester, Birmingham, Leeds and Sheffield, and other such towns as might be thought fit, as warehousing places for the securing of Customs duties.

One of the results of the French Commercial Treaty was the imposition of graduated rates of duty on wine according to the degrees of proof spirit. The three categories established were fifteen, twenty-six, and forty degrees. In order to test the wine, laboratories were set up at the Customs House and at the London, Victoria and St. Katherine's Docks.

On the outbreak of civil war in the United States of America in 1861, a proclamation was issued on the 13th of May forbidding enlistment in this country into either the Confederate or the Federal Union army, and also the supplying of equipment to either side. The Customs service was concerned with the diplomatic repercussions of war since the Foreign Enlistment Act of 1819 involved it in a number of duties. The act made it illegal 'to equip, furnish, fit out, or arm, or knowingly aid, assist or be concerned in the equipping, furnishing, fitting out or arming of any ship or vessel with the intention in order that such ship or vessel shall be employed in the service of any foreign Prince, State or Potentate . . . with whom Her Majesty shall not then be at war . . .' However, Confederate representatives had found a loophole in the workings of the act, and had placed orders for a number of ships with British shipbuilding yards. They had consulted lawyers who concluded that the building of ships within British territory – whatever the intent of the parties – was not in itself an offence against the act, which prohibited merely the equipping of ships. Accordingly, the Confederate government made arrangements with various yards for ships to be built; the most famous of these was the *Alabama*, to be constructed by Messrs. William and John Laird of Birkenhead.

While the ship was still in the construction yard, the Ambassador of the United States in London, Charles Francis Adams, made numerous representations to the British authorities that this was a breach of international law. The '290', as the vessel was then called, was launched on 15th May 1862 and entered the graving dock for fitting. A month later she started trial runs, and Mr. Adams pressed hard for the British Government to take action to prevent her sailing. The Customs authorities at Liverpool were asked to report on the affair. The Surveyor stated that, although there was no attempt on the part of the builders to disguise what was apparent, that she was intended for a ship of war, they were unable to take any steps under the Act to prevent the departure of the vessel.

On 29th July the '290', now called the *Enrica*, sailed under an English master and crew, ostensibly on trials. On 31st July the Government sent a telegram to the Customs at Liverpool ordering the detention of the '290', only to receive a telegram by return saying she had already left. The sequel to this story is quite well known. The *Enrica* managed to evade the Federal warship, the *Tuscarora*, and made for the island of Terceira in the Azores where she took on stores and armaments. As the *Alabama*, she then commenced her activities as the greatest raider of all time, as she was later described. During the next two years she captured or sank over a hundred of the Federal ships, until she was herself finally destroyed by a more powerful vessel. After the civil war, the victorious Federal Government took action against Great Britain in the International Court, and in 1872 the Geneva Arbitration Tribunal made an award of £3,100,000 damages to be paid by Great Britain to the United States of America.

In 1861 one of the few remaining duties – the import duty on paper – was abolished. This duty, as well as the excise duty, had been frequently attacked, since many considered it a tax on knowledge. The question of repeal aroused a great deal of debate and controversy; when Gladstone first introduced the proposal in 1860 it was thrown out by the House of Lords although it had a successful passage in the Commons. The following year Gladstone raised the matter again, and this time the measure was passed by both houses.

One result of transferring the Coastguard to the Admiralty had been the truncation of the Customs department. In 1862 the government appointed a select committee to consider the practicability and advantages of consolidating any of the establishments of the Inland Revenue and Customs, or of uniting any portion of the duties performed by their officers. Sir Thomas Fremantle, the Chairman of the Board of Customs, gave evidence before this committee, and when asked how many officers the Board maintained for the prevention of smuggling, he replied that there were none, apart from officers employed in small ports and creeks along the coast. The Committee of Inquiry suggested that this was a waste of man-power, since Customs and Coastguard Officers were duplicating each other's jobs. But Sir Thomas explained that the Coastguard was responsible for keeping a general watch on the coast, while the Customs officer was employed merely on a local basis, to prevent smuggling vessels entering the creek or port where he was stationed.

In 1863 the Excise duty on playing cards was reduced from one shilling to threepence in an attempt to reduce the incidence of evasion. Previously, a revenue stamp had been affixed to the ace of spades in each pack, but since this gave great opportunity for cheating, it was discontinued. A wrapper was introduced in its place, without which the sale of the cards was illegal.

Passenger traffic on the railways was increasing enormously. In its report of 1857 the Board mentioned that passengers travelling by the night mail from Paris to London via Dover were commonly allowed the privilege of having their baggage examined at London Bridge railway terminus, instead of Dover. For some time, this service had also been extended to passengers arriving by 'tidal train' via Folkestone. In 1864 Charing Cross Station was opened, followed by Victoria in the following year, and in due course

Customs staff were provided at both these stations for the convenience of passengers.

The Excise Department undertook the collection of agricultural statistics in 1866 on behalf of the Board of Agriculture. This work, though not difficult in itself, was harassing as the farmers were not always particularly accommodating. Another task imposed on the Excise the following year was the collection of dog licences. This was originally entrusted to parish officials but it was felt that the Excise with its country-wide organization would be able to collect the duty more efficiently.

An event of great importance, both to the Customs and to the economy of the country as a whole, was the final repeal, in 1869, of the last duties on corn and corn products. This was the culmination of the work of the anti-corn law movement which had gathered force just after the Napoleonic wars and had already brought about the partial repeal of the corn laws in 1846. The view that protection should be given to British agriculture had lasted from the fourteenth century until the mid-nineteenth century, but had now given way to the belief that Britain should become the workshop of the world, and should buy her food in the cheapest markets.

From 1869 onwards there were a number of inquiries into the work of the Customs department, and subsequent reports resulted in certain changes. Among the branches examined were those of the Receiver-General of Customs and the Accountant-General. As a result, the office of Receiver-General, which dated back to 1671, was abolished, and the work of the two branches was integrated into a new branch called the Office of the Accountant and Comptroller General.

An investigation into the statistical services provided by the Customs department included those of the Examiner's Department concerned with the *Import and Export List* and the *Bill of Entry*. The latter was not, of course, an official department but a staff association, since the Customs Fund had purchased the patent to publish the *Bill of Entry* in 1816. As a result of this particular inquiry, the Statistical Office was set up, which later took over publication of the *Bill of Entry*.

The inquiry by the Treasury into Customs Statistics in 1870 had proposed that the Crown should take over publication of the *Bill of Entry* at an agreed price. A Committee which was appointed in 1878 to investigate official statistics came to a slightly different conclusion, recommending that the patent granted to the Customs Fund, which still had some years to run, should be allowed to lapse. No reference was made to payment, and publication was taken over by the Customs Department in 1881.

One of the duties performed by Customs officers in connection with the importation of livestock was the inspection of cattle to ascertain if any disease were present. Although in London officers were assisted in this task by veterinary surgeons, this was not the general practice elsewhere. In 1870, however, responsibility for inspection of imported cattle was transferred to the Privy Council. In the same year a radical change was made in the grading of the chief officials in the ports. From time immemorial the principal officer in a port had been called the Collector of Customs, although salaries were graded according to the importance of the port. The chief officer in smaller ports was now called 'Superintendent of Customs and Mercantile Marine'.

Another duty – on sugar – was repealed in 1869. It had always been difficult to rate liability for this, since payment was graded according to the degree of sweetening. At this time, colour was the determining factor. The Excise duty on racehorses, originally imposed in 1784, was also repealed at this time. An Act which affected the Customs Service in 1875 was the 'Sale of Food and Drugs Act', which was intended to prevent adulteration in food. Since one of the principal articles of food concerned was tea, Customs officials were required to test supplies coming from abroad.

In a review of the revenue position, the Commissioners of Customs referred to the apparent paradox that, although 1875 was 'almost without exception, a bad year in every trade and for every interest', the revenue from Customs duties increased in a greater ratio than in either of the two preceding years. The Board found difficulty in reconciling this fact with the theories of the best authorities on questions relating to the incidence of taxation, since they maintained that the bulk of Customs revenue, almost wholly derived at that time from tobacco, spirits, tea, dried fruit, coffee and cocoa, was paid by that portion of the population (the majority) dependent upon weekly wages, who would therefore be expected to have cut down on consumption. This theory is borne out by the yield from wine, which was consumed mainly by the well-to-do, and contributed less than nine per cent of the Customs revenue.

A civil service inquiry in 1875 considered methods of selecting personnel, and the possibilities of transfer from office to office and grading. It investigated the system of employing writers as unestablished clerks on an hourly basis. It recommended that service scales should be introduced instead of division into classes, but this was found to be inapplicable in the case of the Customs service because particular technical knowledge was needed. The Board therefore opposed the recommendation since no clerk, however efficient, would have been able to go beyond the clerical maximum of £200. A compromise was reached by forming a special grade of 'Customs Port Clerks' with the possibility of promotion to Collector, 'as merit and service record and service requirements might determine'.

The total amount of gold and silver bullion and specie imported into the United Kingdom in 1875 was £33,264,789 and the total amount exported £27,628,042, leaving an excess of imports over exports of £5,636,747. The Commissioners of Customs were concerned about the many inaccuracies discovered in the accounts of coin and bullion returned to the Statistical Department; persons dealing in coin and bullion seemed anxious to conceal the movements of precious metals, and large quantities were conveyed to the continent as personal luggage. Fines for irregularities had been imposed from time to time, but even so the Commissioners felt that the accounts must, to a certain extent be regarded as defective. Under 34/35 Vic.c.103 clearance of goods before shipment could have been legally enforced, but the stoppage of valuable goods of this kind would probably have led to much inconvenience. The total value of goods imported into the United Kingdom in 1875 reached a record amount of £373,939,577, but total exports had dropped considerably to £281,612,323. In the same year, the number of vessels entering inwards and clearing outwards in the Port of London was 19,915 with a tonnage of 8,882,630. The corresponding figures for the Port of Liverpool are 10,665 ships and 9,790,319 tons, and it is interesting to note that although almost twice as many vessels used the Port of London, the tonnage given for the two ports is almost equal.

In the following year the value of imports continued to rise and, although there was some increase in exports, the excess value of imports over exports attained the unprecedented figure of £125,968,263; or 44 per cent. The quantity of brandy and rum imported had increased, in the former case rising from 4,069,000 gallons in 1875 to 7,913,000 in 1876, and in the latter reaching a record figure of 10,395 gallons. On the other hand, the figures for Geneva and other plain spirit dropped by 14·4 per cent; probably because the failure of the potato and other crops in Germany had caused an increase in the price of spirit.

In 1876 a Customs Duties Consolidation Act and a Customs Laws Consolidation Act were passed. As a result some improvement was made in the position of the lower grades of the Customs service. The outdoor officers, constables, boatmen and so on were supplied with uniforms free of charge, and the lower grades generally were granted small annual increments instead of increases every five years. Examining officers and gaugers, however, were still required to purchase uniforms at their own expense. The Customs Building Act, which made provision for all Customs buildings to be transferred to H.M. Officer of Works, had important consequences for the service. The responsibility of deciding on the suitability of Customs accommodation now belonged to a department with a detached interest in the matter, and, by degrees, the service had to relinquish many of its fine buildings constructed in the heyday of Customs architecture. This was partly because the Office of Works was under compulsion to adjust its expenditure on an annual basis, and so preferred to rent often at high rates, rather than construct buildings for a particular purpose. Two years later another act applied the same procedure to the Inland Revenue.

Another event of great interest from the point of view of the Customs was the opening of the Royal Albert Dock in London. Circumstances had altered radically since the days of Elizabeth I, when twenty legal quays were appointed, and the completion of the Royal Albert Dock, eighty years after the laying of the foundation stone of the West India Docks, marked the end of a long period of dock-building in the nineteenth century. The aspect of the Thames dockland had completely changed. Where previously hundreds of ships had been moored in the Pool, loading and discharging overside into lighters, while countless more awaited their chance to enter, and riverside thieves plundered both ships and lighters, vessels were now accommodated in enclosed wet docks with plentiful quay space for their cargoes. This development had been made possible by the granting of permission to construct bonded warehouses, which not only had allowed importers to delay paying duty on their goods until they were sold, but had enabled London to become the greatest centre of the entrepot trade.

An act passed in 1880 re-introduced the beer duty, originally imposed when Excise was first introduced by the Long Parliament in 1643 and replaced by the duty on malt in 1830. This was, of course, simply another way of taxing beer, and the change was unpopular with many brewers, who objected to the presence of an Excise officer on their premises. One of the larger brewers, Mr. Bass, feared that the Excise officer would gain a knowledge of the brewers' trade secrets as a result. The re-introduced duty was to be based on the specific gravity of the wort, unless there were further objections to the standard gravity of 1055 which was proposed as an equivalent to the Malt Duty, another brewer, Mr. Watney, suggesting that it should be set at least at 1060. A compromise was reached at a standard gravity of 1057. At this time there were still a great many independent small brewers and inns and it was estimated that about 120,000 people brewed beer on their own premises. Consequently Excise officers were involved in a good deal of extra work trying to supervise the brewers in the interest of the Revenue. The new measure also affected the Customs service since it was required to look after the export of beer and arrange for drawback to be paid. This also involved the sampling and testing of beer to ensure that the claim to drawback was correct.

In the same year the Board published results of analyses carried out on tea samples in its laboratories. Out of 1,242 samples sent for analysis that year, only 16 were found to be unfit for human consumption. Other imported goods requiring analysis were spirit-based preparations. Such goods were liable by law to a duty equivalent to that charged on the same quantity of imported spirit, so that British manufacturers of similar goods who had had to use duty-paid spirits would not be at a disadvantage against foreign competitors. For example, in 1880 214 samples of transparent soap were analysed for this reason. The number of wine samples tested by distillation in the same year was 48,837. Beer analysis was far more complicated as the duty on imported beer was legally chargeable on the basis of the specific gravity of the worts before fermentation. This required an elaborate testing process which took three times as long to carry out as the method of testing wine. For this reason, the Board stipulated that all testing of imported foreign beer should be carried out in London by officers specially skilled in this work, and suggested that it would be simpler and more economical if the duties could be assessed according to the alcoholic strength of the beer.

In 1881 an act was passed making provision for the speedier landing of perishable goods which required no duty. It also prohibited the landing of any goods, except diamonds and bullion, lobsters and fresh fish caught by British fleets on Sundays or holidays, or between certain specified hours, or elsewhere than at legal quays or approved places, without the authority of the Commissioners.

In the same year, the Treasury set up an inquiry into bonded warehouses. In 1862 the problems facing merchants who had to carry out the regulations of two different boards in connection with their goods, were given consideration, and at the time the amalgamation, or partial amalgamation, of the two revenue services was proposed, but was not carried through. The new committee now had the task of deciding whether it would be possible to combine the regulations of the two Boards, while ensuring that each retained their respective warehouses. To achieve this, a code of Warehousing Regulations was produced, and the warehousing establishments in the Inland Bonding Towns were transferred from the Customs to the Inland Revenue. As a result of the same inquiry the establishments of a large number of the ancient ports, such as Rye, Lyme, Chepstow, Deal and Lancaster, were reduced by depriving them of their status as Head Ports, and placing them under minor officials. Four more ancient ports, Wells, Gainsborough, Woodbridge and Maldon, were demoted shortly afterwards because there had been a falling off in trade. On the other hand, the Customs outdoor establishments at Newport and Swansea were increased since the business of the ports was rapidly expanding, and the growth of the passenger and cargo trade to Cherbourg occasioned a similar development at Weymouth. At this time, the Board of Customs reported that the revision of the clerical staff in the Outports had been effected, and that many of the temporarily-employed copyists had been absorbed into the new establishment, thus securing to the Department the benefit of the experience they had already gained. As all clerks in the Outports were eligible for promotion to the rank of Collector – a position which required a thorough knowledge of the business of the Department – it was decided to form two classes of clerks. The lower class would supply vacancies in the first class and, when they had acquired the necessary experience in this post, would succeed to collectorships at the smaller ports and later, according to their fitness, to those at the more important ports.

Within six days after final clearance outwards of an exporting ship information about the cargo had, by law, to be given on an Export Specification, so that statistical Returns of Exports could be compiled as accurately as possible. However, delays or inaccuracies often occurred in returning this information, and so the Commissioners were forced to take stringent measures, and to inflict substantial fines for failure to furnish the necessary documents.

The Revenue Act of 1883 made new provisions to ensure the testing of all imported foreign plate. Under the previous law it had been provided that imported foreign plate should be assayed, stamped and marked in the same way as British plate, but with the addition of the letter 'F' to denote its origin. As sub-standard foreign plate was being offered for sale, a ruling was made that all foreign plate arriving in this country should be *actually or constructively* immediately warehoused, until it was removed to the assay office for testing. If found to be of standard quality, it was then cleared for home use on payment of duty. Otherwise it had to be re-exported within one month.

The second section of the same Act changed the regulations governing the admission of articles of foreign manufacture bearing British marks. Previously articles bearing any name, brand or mark of manufacturers resident in the United Kingdom, or the name of a place in the United Kingdom, unless there was some indication that the articles came from a similarly-named place abroad, were not allowed entry into this country. Under the new enactment, any articles bearing the name *and* address, or the name *and* trade mark, of a manufacturer of such articles in the United Kingdom, would be excluded in the absence of evidence that they were imported by him; but articles bearing a name only, or a mark only, would be passed unquestioned by the officers. The names of places in the United Kingdom on articles of foreign manufacture would not exclude them entrance, unless the names were those of places in some way noted for the production of such articles. When the duty on plate was repealed in 1890, the department still remained responsible for arranging the assay of imported plate.

The Sea Fisheries Act made it lawful for fishing boats of all nations to come into any port in the United Kingdom and sell their fish. Provision was made in the act for foreign sea-fishing boats to come under the laws and regulations of the Customs in all matters relating to their arrival, bringing to, examination, boarding of officers, protection of stores, report of cargo, etc. By another provision of the act, every Collector and principal officer of Customs in any place in the British Isles was appointed a British Sea-fishery officer for the purposes of the act.

A review of the work of the Department published in 1884 gives details of the tasks carried out by officers on behalf of the Board of Trade. In 1883 the number of Light Bills issued was 218,144, and the amount of dues received £470,982. The details given of mercantile marine work show that in the same year 26,064 men were shipped on board 3,567 vessels and 28,937 crew members were discharged from 3,903 ships; 896 orders were issued for the payment of wages and effects; 15,091 money orders were issued and 21,153 paid. The transactions of the Seamen's Saving Bank show 494 receipts and 475 payments. A total of £83,213 was received on account of mercantile marine transactions. Acting in their capacity as Receivers of Wreck, Customs officers reported 9,436 droits and sold 7,309; they took 13,686 depositions, and on account of wreck received £26,086. Acting as Registrars of British Ships they registered 24,601 ships of a tonnage amounting to 7,233,862. As Registrars of Royal Naval Reserve they had on their books a total of 15,815 men. In 1886 the Board again made special reference to the variety of work carried out by the department which was unconnected with, or formed no part of the collection of revenue. It pointed out that since these tasks were performed on behalf of other departments of State, officers were not generally credited with having carried them out, as would probably have been the case if their entire administration were assigned by law to the Customs department. These extra duties included the analysis of tea, the search for explosives, the collection of Light Dues, mercantile marine work, the administration of the Sea-fishing Boats Act and the registry of sea-fishing boats, the registry of shipping, wreck work, the enrolment of Royal Naval Reserve Volunteers, the collection of imports and exports, and shipping and navigation statistics, administration of the Bill of Entry, work in connection with the Contagious Diseases (Animals) Acts, the Quarantine Act, the Public Health Acts, the Foreign Enlistment Act, the Passengers' Acts, Foreshores, the payment of Army and Navy Pensioners, the search of imported goods to prevent the introduction of foreign reprints of British copyright works, of goods bearing British marks, and of indecent and obscene prints and articles.

Because of recent trouble in Ireland in 1884 extra precautions were taken to prevent dynamite and other explosives entering the country illegally. Officers were instructed to make a minute and vigorous examination of the baggage, and in suspicious cases the persons, of all passengers arriving from abroad. It was also considered necessary to exercise special vigilance over the traffic between British and Irish ports for the purpose of detecting packages or cases which might contain arms and explosives.

By a patent of 1887, the number of Commissioners of Customs was reduced to three, Sir Charles Du Cane, Chairman since 1878; Herbert Harley Murray, Deputy Chairman; and Horace Alfred Damer Seymour, Commissioner. By this time, a great deal of the work formerly performed by the Commissioners had been delegated to 'Committee Clerks' and members of the Secretariat.

There had been many developments since the introduction of the colonial and foreign parcels post in July 1885. It had been foreseen that this post would offer a ready means for the introduction of contraband and prohibited goods, and consequently Customs officers were required to be present at the General Post Office at all times of the day and night, and also on Sundays. From the date of the scheme's inception up to 31st March 1887, Customs officers had cleared 190,963 parcels of a value of £274,241. 658 of them were found to contain contraband articles, and 9,338 parcels contained dutiable goods which had not been declared.

A royal Commission was set up in 1887 to inquire into the Civil Establishments. One of the chief objects of the inquiry was to consider the possibility of amalgamating the Customs and Inland Revenue – a proposal supported by Gladstone as well as the Chairman of the Board of Inland Revenue. The scheme put forward involved selling the Custom House and removing the staff to premises on Tower Hill. However, the Commission decided against amalgamation, stating that, 'the *onus probandi* thus lying with the advocates of amalgamation, we are of the opinion that no case had been made out before us sufficient to justify so important an experiment'. In support of this view, the Commission added, 'Even if we were in favour of the amalgamation of the Boards, we could not endorse the suggestion that the united Board should sit at Somerset House, and the present Custom House buildings be sold, the Customs staff being accommodated in rooms now vacant at Tower Hill. We do not believe that the present work of the Customs Board could be done satisfactorily at Somerset House. The premises at Tower Hill are, we believe, inadequate and we are convinced that the removal of the controlling authority from the neighbourhood where it is at present located would meet with most strenuous opposition from the trading community of the Port of London who would be most seriously inconvenienced by it.'

On 1st January 1888 the Merchandise Marks Act came into operation. It was much wider in scope than any previous legislation dealing with the same subject, and consequently of great interest to the mercantile community. Particular sections of manufacturers expected the importation clauses to 'check unfair and untruthful marking of goods' since examinations by Customs officers would be thorough and exhaustive. However, to establish a foolproof system of examining imported goods would have involved large additional expenditure, as well as serious delay and inconvenience to merchants. The Board, therefore, had to find a way of giving reasonable effect to the intention of the act without appreciable cost to the taxpayer, and at the same time of preserving the advantages of a restricted tariff intended to facilitate the free movement of trade.

In the same year Parliament imposed an additional duty on wine imported in bottles. This chiefly affected only expensive wines, which were usually imported in this way, and was welcomed by the wine trade since it was calculated to assist the bottling industry in this country. However, representations were made by the wine trade in France and other quarters, as a result of which a subsequent act modified the earlier provisions and allowed a reduction of duty in cases where the market value of the wine did not exceed 15s. od. per gallon. This enactment caused some controversy, since traders considered the market value to be the price shown on the foreign shipper's invoice, and the Commissioners regarded it, within the meaning of the act, as the price obtainable on the home market.

Some changes were made in the prohibitions contained in Section 42 of the Customs Consolidation Act of 1876. As a result of the International Copyright Act of 1886 and the Copyright Convention of 1887, the literary and artistic works of copyright owners in the Contracting States had the same right of copyright protection in the United Kingdom as for works first produced in this country. This protection ran for the same period, but not longer, as in the country of origin. One of the most important privileges of copyright owners was that by giving notice of a particular copyright work to the Commissioners of Customs they could prevent copies of that work being imported into this country by any means.

Since 1873, masters of steamships had been required to furnish the Customs at clearance with an account of coal shipped for use during the voyage, but as ships merely calling for coal were not required to make clearance, no account was made of coal shipped in this way. The masters of such ships were now deemed to be 'exporters' within the meaning of the Customs Acts and were obliged to deliver a specification of the coal thus exported.

Under the Customs Consolidation Act of 1876 ships on which concealments of smuggled goods were found were liable to forfeiture. Shipowners protested strenuously against this penalty, and consequently in 1890 an Amending Act was passed by parliament which limited seizure to vessels of 250 tons or less, and gave power to impose a monetary fine in other cases.

The Outdoor staff of the Customs service had, for some years, made many energetic complaints about the inadequacy of their pay, their lack of prospects and conditions of service. Eventually in 1891, Goschen, the Chancellor of the Exchequer, undertook to conduct a personal inquiry into the matter, out of which the 'Goschen Minute' emerged. He recommended that the Water-guard service in all its branches should be re-established, thus reversing the policy of an earlier Board of Treasury which had stressed the desirability of making Customs officers interchange-able with the various classes of officer in the Outdoor service. The Minute also recommended certain salary improvements and some minor establishment changes.

In 1895 the Outport Clerical Service was re-organized, and a new class of 'Assistants of Customs' was formed to undertake the more responsible duties of the Outdoor officers. Watching and guarding work was assigned to a new grade of 'Watcher'. The precursors of the Watchers had been known for centuries as Glut-Waiters, Glut-Weighers and Glut-Lockers, and were extra men who were only employed in times of stress. In 1893 they were formed into a grade of 'Permanent Labourer of Customs', but even as Watchers they remained an unestablished class on weekly wages.

In 1894 the Merchant Shipping Act was passed, of great im-portance for the Customs since it consolidated all the existing shipping laws, and ran to 748 sections and 22 schedules. A few rules were relaxed to fit in with current conditions; in connection with Ships' Registry, for instance, provision was made for Dec-larations on behalf of Corporate Bodies to be made by the Sec-retary, or any other officer authorized for the purpose. This could now be done before any Registrar of British Ships, a Justice of the Peace, or a Commissioner for Oaths. Previously it was not un-known for the Secretary of a Corporate body in London to have to go to Scotland or Ireland, or even for a Secretary to travel from Australia or India to make a declaration with regard to a ship.

The Public Health Act of 1896 repealed the old quarantine laws and transferred the administration of quarantine from the Cus-toms to the local government boards. The old 'quarantine hulks' which had been used for the accommodation of patients suffering from plague and yellow fever had gradually disappeared, and at the time of the new act only two were in existence: the London Station at Stangate Creek at the mouth of the river Medway, and the Channel Ports Station at Motherbank off Ryde in the Isle of Wight. However, the responsibility for boarding vessels and questioning ships' masters about health remained with the Water guard department, and Customs officers were still required to detain vessels until they had been cleared by the local medical officer of health.

A Select Committee of the House of Commons which was appointed to inquire into the effects and operation of the Merchandise Marks Act reported in 1897 that they were, 'of the opinion that it is unnecessary and uncalled for by the Act to detain goods and insist upon a qualification, because they are marked with English words of description, unless such words are calculated to deceive the purchasers in regard to the country of origin'. The Commissioners commented that British consuls had for years insisted that English manufacturers should describe their goods in the language of the country to which they are exported for sale as a means of stimulating trade in British goods abroad, and the Committee's conclusion was only an application of this principle to foreign traders who manufactured for an English-speaking market.

An agency task on behalf of the Board of Agriculture was imposed upon the Customs service in 1897. As a result of the 'Dogs Order' of that year, the importation of dogs without licence was prohibited, and imported dogs were liable to go into quarantine for a period of six months. Needless to say, this regulation caused a good deal of heartache to passengers with pets and gave the officers a sometimes unpleasant job.

In 1898 the system of placing officials on board vessels at Gravesend to accompany them to their berths was discontinued. In earlier times tide waiters had performed this task, and were also required to tally the cargo out. A continuous patrol by steam launches was now employed to guard vessels on their way up the river.

When the Spanish-American War broke out in 1898 the Commissioners – no doubt with the *Alabama* affair in mind – ordered that special measures should be taken to ensure due observance of the provisions of the Foreign Enlistment Act. The following year Great Britain herself was at war against the Boers. As a result, the duties on certain goods inevitably increased, and their application involved the Customs service in a good deal of extra work.

In the same year the Sale of Food and Drugs Act placed on the Customs department the duties of public prosecution in connection with the illegal importation of margarine; adulterated or impoverished butter, milk or cream; condensed, separated and skimmed milk, or any other adulterated or impoverished article of food. There were special provisions about the taking of samples by Customs officers and proof of adulteration rested on the certificate of the principal chemist of the government laboratories.

THE PREVENTIVE WATERGUARD

In 1809 a new revenue force, called the Preventive Waterguard, was set up to close the gap in the overall efficiency of the Waterguard between the cruisers and the riding officers. The coast of England and Wales was divided into three districts, each of which was placed under an inspecting commander. The districts and complements were as follows:

London to Land's End   23 cruisers and 42 preventive boats

Land's End to Carlisle   10 cruisers and 13 preventive boats

London to Berwick   4 cruisers and 13 preventive boats

Like other branches of the Customs service, this branch gradually acquired responsibility for carrying out certain non-revenue functions. One of these was concerned with wreck and life-saving and a Customs Board's minute of 1819 provided for the setting-up of shipwreck stations with mortars for shooting lines to distressed vessels. Later these developed into Rocket Apparatus stations. In due course provision was made for the compulsory purchase of land along the coast to provide accommodation for the Preventive Waterguard. However, coastal landowners, possibly in league with smugglers, were reluctant to sell land for this purpose. A Customs Board's minute of 1820 ordered that the Preventive Waterguard should be extended to Ireland under the control of Lieutenant Dombrain, Deputy Comptroller General of the Preventive Waterguard of England.

Simply because there are no means of knowing what quantities of contraband are imported, it is impossible ever to compute how much is lost to the revenue by smuggling. It is reasonably certain, however, that smuggling continued unabated during the Napoleonic Wars, and possibly increased since so many of the revenue cruisers were assisting the Navy. The cessation of hostilities left many naval ships and seamen without employment, and the Admiralty put forward a plan, suggested by Captain McCulloch of HMS *Ganymede*, to establish a blockade of the coast between Dungeness and the North Foreland. It was adopted, and a force was assigned to Captain McCulloch under the orders of the Admiralty to take the place of the Preventive Service in the area.

At the same time control of the revenue cruisers was transferred to the Admiralty. In making the change, the Treasury pointed out that the declaration of peace had, by opening up the ports of Europe, restored to the smugglers the advantages they formerly possessed, and urgent action should be taken to stop the progress of the increasing evil, since many daring professional men, discharged from their occupation and averse to the daily labour of agricultural or mechanical employment, would he hardy enough to engage in smuggling. The Treasury also decided that, for the better discovery and punishment of offenders, it would be necessary to establish a system of discipline and vigilance over the revenue boats, and thought it would add greatly to the efficiency of their exertions if they were put under naval watchfulness and discipline.

THE COASTGUARD

It seems that these measures did not prove successful for in 1821 a Commission of Inquiry expressed the opinion that the efficacy of the vessels protecting the revenue was by no means proportionate to the expense of maintaining them. It recommended that the number be greatly reduced, and that they, as well as the Preventive Waterguard, be again placed under the control of the Customs, as 'such a course would not only tend to efficiency by placing all the different forces employed for the prevention of smuggling under one authority, but would also render it possible to make considerable reductions and effect substantial savings'.

It was also suggested that the title of Preventive Waterguard be changed to 'Coastguard' and that this body should form the principal force for the prevention of smuggling. The riding officers of the Preventive Mounted Guard should be auxiliary to it by land, and the small cruisers by sea. The Treasury accepted these regulations *en bloc*, and by a Minute of the 15th January 1822 the whole of the preventive staff in Great Britain, with the exception of the Coast Blockade, was placed under the Board of Customs.

At that time, the staff, excluding naval vessels, was made up of 157 riding officers, 1,738 officers and men of the Preventive Waterguard, 1,650 officers and men on the cruisers, and 1,276 officers and men on the coast blockade, a total of 4,821. There were 59 revenue cruisers employed on the coasts of England, Wales and Scotland, and 11 on the coast of Ireland. By 1823 the number of cruisers had been reduced to 49. The Coastguard force was placed under a Comptroller General, Captain W. Bowles, R.N., and the establishment continued to be partly naval and partly civilian. The crews of the cruisers were made up of commanders, mates, gunners, boatswains, stewards, carpenters, mariners and boys. The staff ashore consisted of chief officers, chief boatmen, Mounted Guard (formerly Riding Officers), commissioned boatmen and boatmen.

In 1831 it was decided to withdraw the coast blockade in Kent and Sussex, and to substitute the Coastguard. This change was intended to be carried out without increasing the Coastguard service, and a Committee of Special Inquiry recommended that the whole of the Coastguard should be withdrawn from Scotland where, it was alleged, there was now no systematic smuggling, not so much through the efforts of the Coastguard, as because the national taste had turned to whisky. Captain Bowles, the Comptroller, disagreed with this plan and suggested that only a few cruisers and some men be removed. He was supported by Sir James Graham, First Lord of the Admiralty, who said, 'the best naval authorities concur with Captain Bowles opinion that cruisers unaided by a force on shore at the ports most easy of access cannot secure the coast from the successful attempts of the smuggler who always chooses his wind, his weather, his place and his opportunity and that a small number of cruisers on a long line of coast with a few men on shore judiciously posted, forming as it were a double line, will be found always against the smuggler more efficacious than a much greater number of cruisers without the aid on shore, at best forming only a single line and that line constantly broken by adverse winds and tempestuous weather'.

Sir James Graham also suggested that the efficiency of the Coastguard be increased by 'rendering the service in all its branches essentially naval', pointing out that the Coastguard service 'composed of naval men may be rendered available for great national objects independent of the benefits it will confer by the protection of the Revenue'. In a Minute of the 10th May 1831, the Treasury concurred with his arguments, stating that they were entirely agreed that an appointment in the Coastguard service should in every case be held out as a reward for merit and zeal displayed in His Majesty's Naval Service.

A similar reorganization of the Mounted Guard in 1832 provided that recruitment should be made from volunteers in the cavalry regiments and that the whole of this service should be placed on day pay. By this means the Preventive service had become largely a military force.

A change in the system of revenue protection was introduced in the port of Liverpool from 1849. The practice had been to place a tide waiter on board a vessel on her arrival at the Boarding station. He would remain there until the vessel had reached her place of discharge and had completely discharged her cargo. Mr. Gardner, the Comptroller at Liverpool, suggested that when vessels were lying in enclosed docks, a system of regular patrol on shore might be substituted without risk to the revenue. The system proved successful at Liverpool and so it was gradually extended to other ports.

When the Crimean War broke out in 1854, in anticipation of the hostilities 3,000 men were transferred from the Coastguard to the navy. Two years later the whole of the Coastguard, including the revenue vessels, was transferred to the control of the Admiralty. This was a forseeable result of the measures introduced in 1831 at the instigation of Sir James Graham, to make the Coastguard into a naval reserve. The Board of Customs opposed this transfer and, in a report to the Treasury, pointed out that the measure could not fail to be productive of serious consequences to the revenue, since the experiment had been tried before at the time of the Coast Blockade and had been found far from satisfactory. It was urged that the duties of the Coastguard in protecting revenue of upwards of £23,000,000 required much local knowledge, experience and strict integrity and that harmony and co-operation should exist between them and other Customs Officers. It was pointed out that a naval committee of the highest character and experience had decided against the advisability of such a transfer from the naval point of view. The Board ended its report by referring to the heavy responsibility placed upon them as collectors of the public revenue, which would be greatly and unduly increased if they were to be deprived of all influence and control over the Coastguard, since they relied on it for assistance and co-operation in the discharge of an anxious, unpopular and difficult duty. In reply, the Treasury entirely exonerated the Board of Customs from all responsibility if any of the inconveniences they feared should arise, to the detriment of the public service.

In their first report of 1857, the Board again reminded the Treasury that they had taken the liberty of calling attention to the practical difficulties and confusions likely to arise from a divided authority, as well as the risk to the revenue and the probable unsatisfactory working of a system which severed the power from the responsibility, which assigned to one Board the task of doing the work and to another the duty of seeing that it was done. All these remonstrations had no effect on the Treasury's decision and the Customs service was left with the comparatively small force of land waiters and tide waiters. From this time the service was unarmed, although the Coastguard continued to be armed.

Chapter 8

SMUGGLING IN THE NINETEENTH CENTURY

There is no doubt that the Napoleonic Wars, during which both naval and revenue vessels were extensively employed on war duties, allowed full opportunity for the growth of smuggling activities. A number of references show the extent to which revenue cutters were used on naval work. On 10th September, 1801, the *Argus*, which had lost her shrouds off West Capple, was ordered by Nelson to refit and join him again. Captain Saunders consequently asked the Collector to order such necessaries to enable him 'to join his Lordship with the quickest despatch'. On the same day Captain Hawkins of the *Hound* cutter announced his arrival in Dover in order to obtain a new main-stay and sundry other articles 'agreeable to an order from Lord Nelson for that purpose', and on 16th September Captain Saunders informed the Collector that he intended to go to sea on the next high water 'to join his Lordship in the Downs'. Later in the month Captain Frazer of the *Ranger* cutter and Captain Case of the *Antelope* cutter told the Collector that they were having refits and repairs in the service of Lord Nelson.

It is impossible, therefore, to form a true picture of the extent of illicit traffic during this period. But it is apparent that methods of smuggling were changing, and that the smugglers no longer relied so much on their superior force to fight their way through, but rather on the speed of their vessels. Instead of boldly and defiantly landing their contraband and handing it over to the armed gangs, they were prepared to sink their goods near the shore when

threatened and to pick them up later in safety and at their convenience. Caves along the coast were used for storage, and contraband was often sent inland concealed inside bales of wool and
hops, and so forth. Vessels were increasing in size; and there was
a tendency for fewer ports to be used, and for the crew members
to attempt to conceal dutiable or prohibited goods in the cargo, or
in specially-made places of concealment.

Affrays of the old type still occurred between smugglers and
Customs men. In December 1801 a boat from the *Tartar* cutter
and one from the Excise cutter *Lively* gave chase to a lugger, the
Ned of Deal, in the Downs. As they approached the lugger, they
were warned to keep off or else be sunk and destroyed. The *Ned*
fired at them but the *Tartar*'s crew managed to climb aboard, although one of their men was wounded and another thrown into
the sea. The *Lively*'s boat crew then succeeded in boarding the
lugger on the other side and eventually drove the crew of the *Ned*
overboard. By this time, the lugger had run on to the beach near
Deal and the revenue men tried unsuccessfully to heave her off, so
they began to lighten her by transferring the cargo to the *Tartar*
which was riding in the roads. During this operation they were
attacked from the beach by a large number of people who 'kept
up a constant fire of musketry', and in the end the Customs officers
'were under the necessity of making a precipitate retreat'. Two of
their men were wounded, one fatally. There were 1,200 packages
of goods in the *Ned*, and of these the officers managed to secure
454 parcels of crepe, cambric, starch, spirits, tobacco and cards, as
well as 14 muskets and 2 swivel guns. The Commissioners of
Customs later offered a reward of £100 to any person discovering
and apprehending the persons concerned.

In 1805 the *Tartar* was again involved in an incident, once more
assisted by the *Lively*. They chased a lugger into Dungeness Bay,
but the smugglers ran aground and escaped. On boarding the
vessel, the revenue officers found 665 casks of brandy, 237 casks
of Geneva, 118 casks of rum, 119 bags of tobacco, 6 packages of
wine and 43 lbs. of tea. A party of people from Lydd and
Dungeness attempted to 'rescue' the goods, but a company of

the Lancashire militia, quartered nearby, advanced and cleared the beach, enabling the revenue officers to remove the goods to a safe place.

In a similar incident at Deal in 1806 Captain Haddock of the *Stag* sent two boats to intercept some luggers which were making for the port. One boat which succeeded in going alongside a lugger was greeted by a volley of fire, and several of the crew were badly wounded. The other luggers ran ashore, and the inhabitants of the town immediately assembled and carried off the cargo.

The Revenue officers were also hampered in their duties by the precautionary arming of all types of vessels and people in case of a French invasion. The Sea Fencibles were enrolled from among the fishermen in the area, and many of the Revenue officers themselves were members of this volunteer force. The Collector at Dover was obliged to ask the Commissioners whether the various armed vessels were to be regarded as belonging to the King's service, and consequently exempt from seizure. The Commander of the Sea Fencibles at Dover, Captain Ossington, also enquired whether he and his officers were entitled to the privilege of duty-free wine on board their vessel, in the same way as officers of H.M. Ships.

In November, 1807, John Pitts, Collector of Customs at Whitby, wrote to Lieutenant General Pye at his Beverley Headquarters, and explained the system of smuggling practised along the coast. Robin Hood's Bay, five miles to the south of Whitby, and Staithes, eight miles to the north, were the main places to which the large cutters and luggers engaged in smuggling resorted. On the expected arrival of one of these ships, their agents would send word to the different people concerned, who assembled at the landing places in great numbers. As soon as the smuggling vessels made their appearance, the cargo was taken ashore either in their own boats, assisted by fishing cobles, or in the cobles, to a more convenient landing place along the coast. From here a large part of it was immediately taken into the interior of the country by the numerous footpaths across the moors and hilly country. The remainder was secreted until there was an opportunity to dispose of it in small quantities among the inhabitants of the towns and villages along the coast. Pitts was of the opinion that, in order to prevent the illicit traffic, strong detachments of infantry should be stationed at Robin Hood's Bay and at Staithes, and that as soon as a smuggling vessel appeared a party of troops attended by a Customs officer acquainted with the by-roads should immediately be sent to prevent the landing of the goods, or to seize them on landing. He was convinced that, once the goods were landed and distributed, 'all exertions to stop them would be fruitless as the country will not admit of the service of Cavalry'. He also recommended frequent changes of troops so that they would not get to know the inhabitants too well.

A seizure made in interesting circumstances is described in the following letter:

August 2nd 1815   H.M. Ship Bellerophon
Plymouth Sound.

Sir, I have to represent to you that whil waiting on Lord Keath for the purpose of communicating information with which I was charged from Napoleon Bonaparte I sent my Gig on board the ship that the crew might get their dinner, with orders to return immediately and meet me at Mount Wise. After waiting two hours I received information that the boat had been seized by Custom House Officers at Stone House for having eight bottles of wine in her – As they were not put into the boat by my orders and I was totally ignorant of their being there as will appear by the orders my Coxswain had received, I request you will apply for the restoration of the boat which is my private property as well as that the gear which is all King's stores may be returned to the ship I command.

I remain, Sir,

Collector of the Customs.   Fredk. Maitland.

It was to be expected that at the end of the Napoleonic Wars many of the men discharged from the army and navy would turn to smuggling, and would not be averse to using firearms. To cope with such a situation the Coast Blockade was established on the coasts of Kent and Sussex in 1817, and the Preventive Water-guard withdrawn from this area. Violence reached an unprecedented level. Smuggling gangs were formed once again, and smugglers and Coast Blockaders became involved in pitched battles, with lives lost on both sides. Some of these 'affairs' have been graphically described by Neville Williams in *Contraband Cargoes*, and details of many of the smuggling incidents are recounted by Atton & Holland in *The King's Customs*. Many of the smugglers were captured, many sentenced to death or transportation, and by degrees the large-scale running of contraband began to decline. The more severe anti-smuggling laws, the harsher penalties, and the better organization of the revenue protection services were having their effect. The system was, however, an expensive one, and in 1822 control of the Preventive Waterguard, including the cruisers, was revested in the Board of Customs. The Coast Blockade, however, survived until 1831 when the Coastguard took over responsibility for the entire revenue protection.

In 1827 two Italians purchased a large quantity of coral warehoused at the London Docks for export which they sent to Rotterdam and re-imported concealed in kegs of butter. All would no doubt have gone well if, while the Customs officers were weighing the butter, one keg had not fallen and burst open, revealing the coral. The following year thirty tin cases containing spirits were found in the double bottom and double sides of the *Mary* of Dover, and in the same year officers of the revenue cutter *Vigilant* found 1,045 tubs of spirits hidden under wooden hoops on the barge *Alfred* which was voyaging along the coast from Arundel to London. In 1828 the Coast Blockade at Shoreham seized 1,245 gallons of spirits and 1,950 lbs. of tobacco from one boat, while their colleagues at Arundel arrested two boats loaded with 1,117 gallons of spirits, 54 lbs. of tea and 2,183 lbs. of tobacco.

There were reliable reports of several large runs the following year; for example, one at Lydd on 20th March, in twelve carts escorted by eighty armed smugglers, and another at Winchelsea on 5th June when seventy to eighty men carrying two tubs each were seen going through the town. On the same night ninety tubs were floated up the Breda Channel to Winchelsea Sluice.

Many seizures were made from passengers' baggage examined at Dover. These consisted mostly of articles of clothing and adornment, including silk stockings, handkerchiefs, cravats, gloves, buttons, earrings, beads, necklaces, fans, eardrops, glass beads, shawls, petticoats and lace. There were also musical boxes, playing cards, musical snuff boxes, eau-de-Cologne, silk umbrellas, forks and tea. Larger seizures included one of 55 lbs. of vulture feathers, one of 44 yards of silk riband, 2,170 'porcelain teeth', 300 human teeth and 1 bracelet, and another of 16 silk dresses, 24 pieces of trimming, 4 silk tippets, 26 embroidered caps, 37 embroidered tippets, 42 pieces of embroidery, 1 embroidered dress and 8 bonnets.

In 1830 a number of large seizures were made by the Coast Blockade. At Hastings, 1,706 lbs. of tobacco and 487 lbs. of snuff were taken from the *Mary* on 22nd March, and 2,971 lbs. of tobacco and 1,389 lbs. of snuff from the *Neptune* on 31st March; at Margate 2,439 yards of figured silk, 1,265 yards of black silk, 3,667 yards of coloured silk, 35 yards of silk gauze and 4,607 yards of Petersham gauze were seized on 29th May; and in the Rochester area, 1,850 gallons of spirits, 2,688 lbs. of tea and 41,110 yards of silk gauze were found on 23rd June. Again, in the Rochester area, 1,974 gallons of spirits and 1,203 lbs. of tea were seized from the sloop *William* on 22nd September. In the last two cases the goods had been loaded at sea.

The result of an incident at Weymouth in 1832 showed that the attitude of the populace towards the Customs Service had altered. Two officers, Carter and Lovell, intercepted a boat towing tubs of spirits near the old Sluice at Weymouth but the smugglers escaped. Afterwards a number of men armed with sticks came along and attempted a 'rescue'. Lovell's cutlass was knocked from his hand and Carter was attacked whereupon he opened fire with his pistol. The smugglers dispersed, carrying off many of the tubs but leaving two of their number dead. At an inquest held on the deaths of the two smugglers, the jury returned a verdict that the deceased 'came by their deaths by being shot with pistols balls by some officers in the Service of the Coastguard in the execution of their duty, for the preservation of themselves and to prevent the rescuing of contraband goods which they had seized in the king's name'.

In 1832 it was decided at Falmouth to institute a special search of the postal packet *Messenger* from Gibraltar. The following concealed goods were found: 414 lbs. of leaf tobacco under the planking of the coal hole; 60 lbs. of cigars under the engine-room plates; 15 lbs. of cigars under cinders in the smith's forge on deck; 2½ lbs. of cigars in the starboard paddlebox; 2¼ lbs. of cigars under sails in the sail room; 16 lbs. of leaf tobacco under firewood in the forehold; 12 glass tumblers under a false sill in the engine room. At Plymouth in 1833 Customs officers discovered 211 tubs of spirits beneath a cargo of limestone on the coasting barge *Rebecca*. An act of 1836 relaxed the regulations governing the size of packages in which spirits and tobacco could be legally imported. Spirits could not be imported in casks of not less than 20 gallons, and tobacco or snuff in packages not weighing less than 300 lbs. The legal size for ships importing goods was also reduced to 60 tons. The same act also empowered magistrates to deal with minor smuggling offences without special authority from the Commissioners of Customs.

The *Sylvia* revenue cruiser made two large seizures in the Penzance district in 1837. On 14th March the following spirits were found on the *Good Intent* schooner: 26 tubs in a false lining, 138 tubs in a double bulkhead, 26 tubs in the coal locker, 148 tubs in a double bulkhead between forepeak and hold, and 21 tubs under the flooring of the forepeak.

A London merchant managed to perpetrate an ingenious fraud when importing casks of brandy. These casks were normally gauged by officers who inserted a graduated rod diagonally into the bunghole so that the fluted end fitted into the bung of the cask and the content in gallons was read on the upper end of the rod. The defaulting merchant artificially shortened the diagonal of the casks in which he imported his brandy.

Between 1842 and 1850 there was an enormous amount of smuggling, particularly of tobacco, and large seizures were made. In London 11,280 lbs. of tobacco was taken on one occasion, and similar seizures took place throughout the country: 7,047 lbs. at Holyhead, 11,482 lbs. at Goole, 7,222 lbs. at Harwich, 5,918 lbs. at Stockton (Yarm), 9,471 lbs. at Exeter, 5,922 lbs. at Southampton, 2,063 lbs. at Kirkcaldy, 28, 620 lbs. at Waterford, and 8,788 lbs. at Tynemouth. Tobacco smuggling, consequently, was not confined to any particular locality and it was obviously an organized business. Even established tobacco concerns were tempted to join in the illicit trade, if only to stay in business. Most of the tobacco came from near continental ports, and no doubt a very large portion of it had been exported from this country on payment of drawback and then illicitly re-imported. A good deal of spirits was also smuggled, but on a reduced scale. Many of the tricks and stratagems resorted to during this period have been described in detail, and it is obvious that for quite a long period the Customs and Excise officers could not cope with large-scale smuggling of this kind.

In the second half of the century smuggling tended to ease off, although some very large seizures were still made from time to time, and one must assume, therefore, that an even larger quantity was successfully smuggled. Atton and Holland (see bibliography) describe many of these cases and only the more remarkable of them need be briefly mentioned here. In 1852 the *Marie* of Dunkirk was intercepted by two Excise officers, acting on information received, just as she was about to run 6,000 lbs. of tobacco near Ramsgate. In March the following year a policeman near Woodbridge seized three horses and two carts loaded with 1,231 lbs. of tobacco and 2,541 lbs. of tobacco stalks. The goods had been landed from a vessel called the *Susan*, which was seized, and the master and crew arrested. As a result of evidence given by one member of the crew, the rest were convicted and imprisoned. In April, 1853, a Coastguard officer seized 5,165 lbs. of tobacco near Whitby from the *John and Susannah* of Lowestoft. The master of the ship was so distraught that he tried to drown himself. At

Lowestoft in September of that year, Coastguards in a steam tug chased and captured a French lugger, *L'Abondance*, which was hovering off the coast. There were 7,380 lbs. of tobacco on board, and in his statement the captain said that he had brought it for an Englishman who was to pay him 500 francs for his trouble. In May 1854, 2,481 lbs. of tobacco were found by the Coastguard in an oyster boat in the river Medway and the following year, Excise officers searching the premises of a well-known smuggler at Wenhaston in East Anglia, discovered 1,400 lb. of tobacco.

A different form of smuggling is referred to in the Commissioners of Customs' First Report of 1857. From about 1850 to 1856 a London dealer, Lucien Marchand, was engaged in the large-scale smuggling of Swiss watches, employing members of the crews of cross-Channel boats to bring them illicitly into England for him. In 1852 one of these men was caught on the *City of Boulogne* with a number of watches and a corset to conceal them in. Ultimately Marchand was implicated, but was not finally brought to trial for receiving until 1856, when he was fined £3,510.

In 1858 a report of the Board of Customs drew attention to the increasing incidences of petty smuggling by passengers from abroad and pointed out with some degree of moral highmindedness, that notwithstanding the generally low rate of duties, and 'notwithstanding also the liberal construction now placed by our officers on the amount of new articles of apparel which may be allowed to pass free, there are not wanting some gentlemen, many ladies, and more ladies' maids, who are still silly and perverse enough to risk pounds that they may save pence, and both incur and inflict endless trouble and annoyance for the tremulous and vulgar joy of cheating the revenue and evading the vigilance of the officers charged with its collection'.

The failure of the wine crop in France accounted for the virtual cessation of brandy smuggling during this period. The only recorded tobacco run at this time was one of 890 lbs. from a vessel called the *Telegraph* on the Lincolnshire coast. It was intercepted by the Coastguard, however, and the tobacco was seized. Ingenious methods of concealment were frequently resorted to. Customs officers in Galway discovered 1,000 lbs. of tobacco hidden in tin cases which had been inserted into tierces of pickled pork. On another occasion, also in Galway, 1,300 lbs. of snuff was found distributed through ten casks of flour.

During 1860 a number of seizures of tobacco and spirits were made. At Leith, 746 lbs. of tobacco was discovered concealed inside some bundles of willows, and another 700 lbs. came to light under an old boat at Innishowen Head. Sixty tubs of spirits were seized at Arundel, in Hampshire and forty-five in Kingstown Harbour (Dun Laoghaire). A large seizure of 1,981 lbs. of un-manufactured tobacco was made by the Hampshire police in June. The police often gave assistance to the Customs by intercepting contraband which had evaded the revenue controls in the ports and on the coast. They were empowered to seize goods and this seems to have had some preventive effect and they thus assumed the former function of the Riding Officer. The employment of Admiralty police in the Royal dockyards similarly checked the amount of smuggling from naval vessels.

In May, the crew of the cutter *Fly* seized a cargo of 4,100 lbs. of tobacco stalks in Portlelet Bay, Jersey, which was probably intended to be run near Dublin. The owner escaped, but was subsequently caught and convicted.

In March the following year 769 lbs. of tobacco were found in an outhouse near Grouville Bay, in Jersey, and in April another 300 lbs. were discovered on board the lugger *Arage*. The only notable seizure of spirits in 1861 was 42 tubs which were recovered on the Dorsetshire coast in November. The owner was never traced.

In April 1863 an attempt was made to smuggle 262 lbs. of tobacco from the *Baron Osy* of Antwerp by the simple device of lowering it from a cabin window to a boat which had put off on a preconcerted signal. Unfortunately for the smugglers, the *Fly* revenue cruiser was in the vicinity and was watching the manoeuvre. As a result, two watermen and the ship's steward were prosecuted and convicted. The vessel was also detained and finally released on payment of a fine of £200. The following month, 327 pounds of tobacco were found concealed on board the *Magnet* from Rotterdam. The goods were packed in such a way, attached to ropes, to suggest that the tobacco was to be thrown overboard on the way up the Thames. In August, a case of furniture from Hamburg was sent to the Queen's Warehouse to await clearance. On examination, it was found to contain a sofa and seven chairs stuffed with tobacco and cigars.

By this time very few articles were liable to duty, and the Commissioners felt it necessary, for the better protection of the Revenue to return to a stricter examination of free goods imported from countries where tobacco was unrestricted and could be bought cheaply.

In 1864 they were able to report that there had been, to their knowledge, no organized smuggling nor any attempted runs during the past year. Their opinion was that smuggling by this time was confined almost entirely to the concealment of small amounts of spirits and tobacco on board ships. Four examples of such cases were quoted: 105 lbs. of tobacco on a ship at Liverpool, 118 lbs. at Shields, 200½ lbs. at Sunderland and 110 lbs. at Ardrossan. Although these amounts must have seemed small compared with the contraband cargoes of the previous century, the Customs Service of today would certainly not regard smuggling on this scale with complacency.

In 1865 two cases of 'old style' smuggling were foiled. The Coastguard at Deal seized a fishing boat, the *Providence*, on the beach. It was found to have 66 gallons of foreign spirits concealed on board. When the *Jane* of Cowes was seized in Petit Bot Bay in the Isle of Guernsey, 4,680 lbs. of tobacco stalks were discovered, apparently intended for running on the Irish coast.

Eighteen convictions for smuggling in London in 1866 involved quantities of tobacco of ten pounds or more, and of two gallons or more of spirits. A further 111 cases were summarily dealt with by magistrates. The only large quantity of tobacco seized in London was 267 lbs., found concealed on a ship belonging to the General Steam Navigation Company. There were 744 seizures in the outports that year; in two cases the quantity of tobacco exceeded 100 lbs. Smuggling increased slightly the following year, and the number of tobacco seizures rose by twenty-three.

One or two attempts at evasion are of particular interest. On the Dutch vessel *Maas*, which arrived in London from Gustermunde in February 1867, 131 lbs. of tobacco and cigars were found concealed in a hollow beam in the engine-room. On another occasion, two casks purporting to contain duty-free camomile flowers were imported in the *Saxon* from Stettin. On examination, 129 lbs. of cigars packed within the flowers were discovered. Another consignment of camomile flowers, this time from Hamburg, was found to contain 129 lbs. of cigars. Again in 1867, the coastguard at Portsmouth seized a boat drifting towards the shore with a cargo of 4,609 lbs. of snuff. At Liverpool 1,100 cigars were found in a cargo of glue which had been entered as duty-free goods. There were also one or two large seizures of spirits: forty tubs containing 116 gallons were taken on the beach at Small Hope; twenty tubs at Totland Coastguard Station; forty-four tubs (105 gallons) at the South Yarmouth station.

Smuggling declined considerably in 1868, as compared with the previous year. One of the more ingenious attempts was foiled when 600 lbs. of tobacco were found concealed in six bales of hops on board the *Holland* from Ostend. In this case the miscreant was prosecuted, convicted and sentenced to imprisonment. Smugglers also managed to land seventy-two casks of brandy (205 gallons) at South Yarmouth in the Isle of Wight, but they escaped in the dark, leaving their cargo behind. A substantial seizure of tobacco (97 lbs. was also made on board HMS *Speedy*, an Oyster Fishery Protection vessel stationed at Jersey. The two largest hauls of the year were both in Ireland. In Londonderry, 630 lbs. of unmanufactured tobacco were found concealed in the pump case of the *Minnehaha* from New York, and at Tralee, 948 lbs. of leaf tobacco, together with two horses and two carts, were seized by officers.

A common method of smuggling tobacco after the introduction of free trade was by concealing it inside free goods. A particularly interesting case started at Bradford in 1877 when a tobacco dealer there informed the Excise that a paper dealer had offered him tobacco at a price lower than the duty. Arrangements were made for the tobacco dealer to purchase some tobacco from the paper dealer and the dealer was eventually arrested. The premises of a retailer in the town were also searched where 500 lbs. of tobacco were found and in another shop at Leeds a further 746 lbs. concealed in reams of paper. In June the vessel *Fairy* arrived from Hamburg with a consignment of 57 reams of paper addressed to the paper dealer's accomplice in Leeds. The officers allowed them to go to Leeds where they examined them and found them to con-852 lbs. of tobacco. The total quantity of tobacco seized in this case was 2,601 lbs. Similarly at Goole 127 lbs. of tobacco were found in two cases consigned from Hamburg as apples. They were allowed to go forward to their destination, Halifax, and seized when the consignees took delivery. Likewise at West Hartlepool 218 lbs. of tobacco were found in two consignments of onions which were allowed to go on to Newcastle until claimed. A consignment of bran which was placed on the railway at Londonderry for shipment to Enniskillen was found to contain tobacco but the Customs allowed it to go forward and it was seized at Enniskillen. At the time a large trading barque which had arrived from America was lying in the port of Londonderry and a search of this vessel resulted in the discovery of 961 lbs. of tobacco concealed in the sail cabin and 1,438 lbs. in the main mast. The master, two mates, and four other men were tried and convicted.

The Royal Navy had long had the privilege of being able to purchase tobacco duty free for consumption on board ship or within certain shore establishments and it was customary to serve out this tobacco in the leaf and unstripped from the stalk. The consumers would then make up the tobacco according to their own fancy and usually in the so-called 'perique' form. The naval authorities did not, however, make any provision for the collection or destruction of stalks, and this fact tempted sailors to sell them ashore for purposes of manufacture or adulteration, or for conversion into snuff. The extent to which this illegal traffic had grown is shown by a return of the quantities of tobacco stalks seized at Portsmouth on H.M. Ships or in or about the dockyard; 259 lbs. in 1877, 577 lbs. in 1878 and 1,664 lbs. in 1879. In the latter year 343 lbs. were also seized at Plymouth. The Board of Customs considered that some restrictive regulations should be imposed to obviate or reduce this risk to the revenue. The Board were able to report in 1881 that this traffic had been checked and arrangements made with the Admiralty to issue tobacco from which the stalks were removed.

Tobacco smuggling at this period posed considerable problems for the Customs and seizures of quite large quantities were made in all parts of the country. Although there was a reduction in the total quantities of tobacco and spirits seized, the following figures for 1879 give some idea of the scale of some of the operations. In London, 84 lbs. were found in the ceiling plate of the shaft tunnel of a steamer from Hamburg; at Hull, 298 lbs. in a specially constructed compartment between the frames of a ship from Harlingen. Also found on board ship were 158 lbs. at Bristol, 122 lbs. at Liverpool, 101 at North Shields, 68 lbs. at Sunderland. 100lbs. of tobacco stalks were found on shore at Bristol, 21 lbs. of tobacco goods in a public house at Cowes, 58 lbs. carried by a man on Deal beach, 34 lbs. on New Brighton beach near Liverpool, 100 lbs. in process of being illegally hawked at Cullercoats near North Shields and 88 lbs. at Ramsgate. The largest seizure of spirits was made at Skeld in Shetland, by the crew of a revenue cruiser, from a fishing vessel from Iceland and Faroe. It consisted of 34 gallons of brandy in kegs and casks, 28 lbs. of tobacco were seized at the same time.

There seemed to be something of a resurgence of large-scale tobacco smuggling in the 1880s, particularly in the Hull area. Over 6,700 lbs. were found on a vessel lying in the Hull River, 3,141 lbs. and some spirits on a tobacconist's premises at the village of Cottingham, 154 lbs. on premises belonging to the same owner in Hull and 2,190 lbs. in a hut on the banks of the Humber near Hessle. This tobacco had apparently come from a large boat lying off Hessle, in the search of which 82 lbs. of cigars were found. The boat was seized and a man prosecuted and convicted. An even larger haul of tobacco, this time in London, took place as a result of information received from Holland that some men in Rotterdam were engaged in packing tobacco and cigars into two large iron boilers and a drum. In due course these were imported and allowed to go to their destination in London. The two boilers were examined at Stepney and found to contain more than 10,000 lbs. of tobacco and cigars and the drum which was examined in Gray's Inn Road contained nearly 4,000 lbs. The men who were engaged in unpacking the boilers were arrested, two of them belonging to the gang which had packed the tobacco abroad. On an afternoon in May officers saw a boat leave a cutter which had anchored off Brighton pier. On reaching the shore they were interrogated and asked to return to the cutter. The master of the cutter admitted that he had tobacco on board and a thorough search of the vessel was organized which resulted in 290 lbs. of tobacco being found on board. The ship's papers showed that she was ostensibly on a voyage from Ostend to Dieppe and a shipping bill showed that 440 lbs. of tobacco had been taken on board. When the case was brought before the magistrates the prisoners claimed that the cutter was engaged in a *bona fide* voyage from Ostend to Dieppe but this plea was not admitted and the master and men were convicted. As the construction of the vessel was such that she was unsuitable either for legitimate trade or for use as a pleasure craft, it was concluded that she had been specially built or adapted for the contraband trade and she was seized as forfeit.

By 1890 the number of seizures of smuggled goods had risen to 5,518 as compared with 1,391 in 1881. By this time smuggling was almost wholly confined to tobacco and spirits, yet the quantity of tobacco seized in 1890 amounted to 18,084 lbs. as compared with 21,473 lbs. in 1881. Likewise the quantity of spirits seized had fallen from 197 gallons in 1881 to 187 gallons in 1890. The figures led to the assumption that the tendency now was for a much larger number of people to smuggle in smaller quantities. It was also realized that a great deal of the contraband was concealed in engine-rooms of steamships and landed by boats. Steps were therefore taken to increase the number of steam launches in order to ensure more effective supervision of the numerous small craft plying in the busier rivers such as the Thames, and also to extend the detective service. The measures taken seem to have had some effect – although the number of seizures increased, their average size was smaller. However, some large seizures, including one of nearly a ton of tobacco, were made in the Hull area during the early years of the last decade of the century, and a Customs operation off the south of Ireland, when a force of Customs and Coastguard officers was landed on an island from a revenue cruiser, resulted in the seizure of 490 lbs. of tobacco, 31 lbs. of cigars and 39 gallons of spirits.

The steady fall in the number of seizures, and of the quantities seized, continued up to the end of the century. By 1900, seizures had fallen from 5,842 in 1891 to 3,778; the quantity of tobacco from 16,756 to 6,784 lbs., and of spirits from 239 gallons to 101 gallons.

Chapter 9

THE BEGINNING OF THE
TWENTIETH CENTURY

When the new century opened, Britain was still at war in South
Africa. Parliament had taken steps to prevent arms and ammunition, naval and military stores and other strategic goods which
might prove helpful to the enemy from being exported to certain
places, and the Customs was responsible for enforcing the prohibitions. Revenue had increased since traders were anxious to fore-
stall an expected rise in duties to meet the costs of the war.
Between 1892 and 1901 the gross receipts of the Customs had
risen from over £23 million to over £31 million, but the cost of
collecting the duties had actually decreased; from a percentage
rate of £3 16s. 7d. in 1892 to £2 16s. 7d. in 1901. The duties on
tobacco and snuff now provided more than one-third of the total
revenue, and tea duty about one-fifth. The duty on spirit also
accounted for a large part of the total.

The Customs department now carried out an immense amount
of agency work for other government departments. On behalf of
the Admiralty, the department continued to enrol and pay members of the Royal Naval Reserve, and also supplied funds to pay-
masters of Coastguard district ships. Further services to the
Admiralty included making special returns for exported war
materials, and circulating and posting notices for the Hydro-
graphic Office. The Contagious Diseases (Animals) Act provided
that the department should control the import of animals on behalf of the Board of Agriculture. The requirements of the Board
of Trade involved the Customs in a great variety of duties es-

pecially in connection with mercantile marine work: the engagement and discharge of ships' crews, the taking and recording of depositions, the recording of casualty returns, the custody of wrecked property, the sale of droits and the payment and accounting for of all money received for, or by, salvors, or on behalf of lords of manors. The collection of Light Dues still formed an essential part of Customs work, and a great deal of time was still taken up with the registering of ships, dealing with aliens and collecting certain harbour dues. In addition to collecting pilotage dues for Trinity House, the Customs service also disseminated information for the benefit of shipping regarding derelicts, buoys and the shifting of lightships.

Monthly and annual returns of trade figures, statistical abstracts and special returns for the Board of Trade Journal had to be made, and restrictions on the exporting of salmon entered. Assistance was given to the Colonial Office, particularly over tariff matters and the registration of ships. The Customs department also collected some duty for the Inland Revenue and in the financial year ended in March 1901 over £7 million was thus collected, mainly from spirits. Beer and spirit duties were also collected on behalf of the local government boards of England, Ireland and Scotland.

On behalf of the Foreign Office, Customs officers ensured that the provisions of the Foreign Enlistment Act were applied. Advice was given about tariff matters in relation to foreign countries, and reports furnished about British emigrants. Gold and silver plate was detained for assay on behalf of the Goldsmiths' Hall, vessels were arrested and released on behalf of the High Court of the Admiralty, the importing of explosives was controlled for the Home Office, and public health regulations concerning the entry of persons and import of goods carried out for local government boards.

In April 1901, parliament imposed an export duty of one shilling per ton on coal, exempting coal shipped for bunkers. The effect of the duty was to reduce the quantity of coal exported from 45,153,000 tons in the year ended March 1901 to 44,064,889 in the year ended March 1902, largely because shipowners, in order to escape the duty, now carried sufficient bunker coal for the voyage out and home, instead of bunkering at coaling stations abroad. The Finance Act of 1901 also levied duty on sugar, molasses and other goods containing sweetening matter. The duties were graduated according to the percentage of sweetening matter contained, this being ascertained by a polariscopic test. The yield for the first year after the duty was imposed amounted to £6,399,328 and thus, after tobacco, contributed most to the total yield. The revenue from wine continued to decrease and there was a marked tendency to prefer wines of the lower ranges of alcoholic strength. Although the yield from the duty on coffee fell appreciably in the same year, the drawback paid on re-exporting it increased, mainly because large quantities were shipped by traders to South Africa for the use of the British troops there.

A significant change was made in the law dealing with the liability of composite goods. Under the Act of 1876, goods containing any dutiable ingredient or ingredients were liable to the full duty at the highest rate, but this provision was considered unduly harsh and had not been fully applied for some time. Consequently, when sugar – a basic ingredient of numerous imported articles – became liable to duty, some sort of modification in the law was felt necessary. While the existing power to absorb the lesser duty in the higher was retained, provision was made for each component part to bear its own rate of duty.

The duty on sugar prompted another legal change. Attempts had been made to evade the duty, which was widely expected to be imposed, by importing and landing large quantities of sugar before the act was passed. Under the 1876 act, imported goods still remaining on board ship or deposited in a warehouse were liable, on being entered for home consumption, only to the duty in force at the time of their being imported. The same act laid down that goods should be considered as 'imported' from the moment when the ship carrying them actually came within the limits of the port where it would in due course be reported. Consequently, to prevent these large consignments of sugar escaping the new duty, the Finance Act provided that in this case, and in every other case of the first levying of a new duty, goods should not be considered to be actually 'imported' until they had been cleared. It was thought only just and right to make the same principle apply to the repeal of a duty as well.

The revenue from the coal duty continued to rise, and in the financial year 1903 to 1904 the gross receipts amounted to £2,317,874. This was, to a certain extent, due to a considerable increase in the shipments to China and Japan as a result of the Russo-Japanese war, and the total tonnage exported in that year reached the record amount of 63,877,735. There was also a slight increase in the receipts of the coffee duty although the consumpsumption per head of population was gradually diminishing, from 1·11 lbs. per head in 1863 to 0·71 lbs. per head in 1903. The consumption of tea, on the other hand, had risen to 5·17 lbs. per head in 1903.

The number of detentions made under the Merchandise Marks Act rose from 1,744 in the year ended March 1905 to 1,818 in the year ended March 1906. Among the articles forfeited were consignments of German and Dutch spirits in bottles labelled 'Finest Old Scotch Whisky', 'Vieux Cognac', 'Fine Champagne', 'Fine Old Jamaica Rum'; sewing machines from the United States marked British; cutlery from Belgium marked 'Sheffield'; and tooth brushes of French manufacture marked 'London', consigned to Norway.

The Customs Commissioners issued an order to the Service in 1906 stating that entries for wine described as 'port' from countries other than Portugal should not be accepted for import unless qualified by an unmistakable indication of the country in which the wine was produced, e.g. Spanish Port, French Port. Wines described as 'sherry' from countries other than Spain were to be similarly dealt with.

The analysis of foodstuffs under the Sale of Food and Drugs Act now involved the Customs service in a great deal of work, and in the year ended March 1906 the following samples were drawn by Customs officers and analysed under the Sale of Food and Drugs Acts: tea, 2,906; butter, 1,875; margarine, 92; cheese,

88; fresh and sterilized milk, 50; condensed milk, 131; and cream, 83. In connection with butter there were twenty cases in which the importers were prosecuted and fines imposed and in connection with margarine proceedings were successfully taken in ten cases. Proceedings were also successfully taken in one instance of importation of fresh and sterilized milk and in three instances of importations of condensed milk. As far as cream is concerned, proceedings were taken in four cases but no conviction was secured. When tea was found to be unfit for human consumption, it was allowed to be re-exported or used in the manufacture of caffeine.

In September 1905, there was an interesting case concerning 220 oz. of imported antique silverware. Exemption from assay was claimed on the grounds that the goods were ornamented plate of foreign manufacture made prior to 1600. Samples were submitted to the Goldsmiths' Company who judged that they were not genuine antiques manufactured before 1800. Since the importers could not produce proof when called upon to do so, the goods were eventually returned to the continent.

The Customs service was still responsible for the enforcement of the law concerning imported 'copyright' works and large quantities of foreign reprints were regularly confiscated. Previously all such works had been destroyed, but now, with the consent of the copyright owners, it was arranged to present them to Trinity House for use on light-ships and in light-houses.

Under the provisions of the Obscenity Act of 1876, Customs officers were empowered to seize indecent prints, paintings, books, photographs and so on. The introduction of the 'picture postcard' greatly increased the work of the department in this respect. In the year ended March 1906 three London dealers were prosecuted and convicted for procuring and selling obscene books, and two of them received prison sentences. In the ten years before March 1908 Customs officers seized 208,544 postcards, 25,248 pictures, 14,720 books and periodicals and 18,000 toys.

From time to time there were 'plague scares', either in Britain or on the continent, and Customs officers boarding vessels had to be especially careful to ensure that the provisions of the Public

Health Acts were carried out. It was particularly important that the Customs officer should know whether or not the vessel was 'infected'; that is, whether she had or had had on board during the voyage any case of cholera, yellow fever or plague. If so, the vessel was detained pending an examination by the Port Medical Officer. In 1905, a vessel arriving at an east coast port with a suspected case of cholera on board was accordingly detained. It turned out, however, that the unfortunate victim was in fact suffering from the effects of excessive drinking.

In September 1907 revised health regulations were issued by the local government boards for England, Wales and Scotland. These required the detention not only of 'infected' ships, but also of 'suspected' ships; that is, ships which had had during the voyage a case of cholera, yellow fever or plague, but had not had a fresh case of the disease within a period of eighteen days prior to the time of the arrival of the vessel from a foreign port.

As a result of the Aliens Act of 1905, which came into force in January 1906, the Customs department acquired new responsibilities. The object of the act was to prevent 'undesirable immigrants' landing in this country, and Customs men were appointed Immigration Officers for this purpose. Masters of ships taking on or putting down passengers were required to furnish a return of all aliens on board.

A considerable amount of extra work devolved upon Customs officers as a result of the act. A report of 1907 shows that during that year 609,926 alien passengers landed and 574,972 embarked in the United Kingdom. Customs officers were required to investigate the character, means and health of incoming alien steerage passengers, other than transmigrants and those specially exempted. 41,430 aliens were inspected during the year, and of these 975 were refused permission to land. The landing, transit and reembarkation for overseas destinations of alien transmigrants were also under the control of the Customs officers employed on immigration work. During the year this applied to 172,488 persons.

Certain provisions of the Merchant Shipping Act of 1906 relating to load-lines and the loading of ships with grain cargoes affected the Customs department to some extent. The Workmen's Compensation Act of 1906, which provided for the payment of compensation to servants, was applicable to certain persons employed by the Customs service, and one section of the act contained a provision relating to claims against the owners of a ship. By this, an Order of Court could be made directing any Customs officer to detain a ship until compensation was paid or secured.

In 1906 the export duty on coal was repealed. During the five and a half years of its existence it had brought in a net revenue of over £11 million. In the financial year ended 1907 the total exports of coal, including bunker coal, had risen to 77,491,475 tons.

A number of changes were made in 1907 to the regulations governing the importing of animals. Under the acts of 1894 and 1896, 'foreign animals' – that is, ruminating animals and swine – were only allowed to be landed at certain places. The landing of animals from one or two particular countries was absolutely prohibited. The Customs Service was responsible for seeing that these requirements were carried out, and it also had to ensure that dogs were not imported without a licence. The landing of horses, asses and mules was also controlled by Customs officers under the Glanders or Farcy Order of 1907 which, with certain exceptions, prohibited the landing of such animals unless a permit from the department of agriculture was produced.

Under the Destructive Insects and Pests Acts of 1877 and 1907, officers also played a part in preventing the introduction of the Colorado Beetle into the United Kingdom, and detained for inspection imported gooseberry and currant bushes. The importing of hay and straw from certain countries was also prohibited under the Foreign Hay and Straw Order of 1908.

Under the Public Health (Foreign Meat) Regulations of 1906, Customs officers were required to detain for examination by a Medical Officer of Health any boneless scrap meat (not cooked or manufactured ready for human consumption); tongues, kidneys and tripe imported in barrels in an unfrozen state; meat of any description that appeared manifestly unsound; unlabelled pork or other edible parts of the carcasses of pigs (not being bacon or ham); and, on the written request of the medical officer, pig carcasses and meat of any description.

AMALGAMATION OF CUSTOMS AND EXCISE

A most important change was introduced in 1908 by the Finance Act which provided that the management of the duties of Excise should be transferred from the Commissioners of Inland Revenue to the Commissioners of Customs, who should now be styled 'Commissioners of Customs and Excise'. It was decided by Order in Council that the transfer should take place on 3 December 1909.

The possible amalgamation of the Customs and the Inland Revenue had been considered as early as 1862, that is thirteen years after the formation of the Inland Revenue Department, but the Inland Revenue Board, supported by Gladstone, had argued against the merger. In 1869 the Ridley Commission took evidence and reported on the question of amalgamation. At this time the Customs Board was strongly against, and the Inland Revenue Board strongly for it. Gladstone gave evidence to the Ridley Commission, and stated that although in 1862 he had not thought the time was ripe for it, he now inclined to the opinion that amalgamation was desirable. However, the main recommendation of the Ridley Commission's report was that at present it would be inexpedient.

In December 1899 the Chairman of the Board of Customs reported on the question of a transfer of business, mainly concerned with warehousing, between the Inland Revenue and the Customs. Although the warehouses of the Excise might with advantage be transferred to the Customs, a transfer of the Excise to the Customs was impractical. In February, the Chairman of the Board of Inland Revenue made a similar report and agreed cordially with the conclusions of the Chairman of the Board of Customs. He thought that the Ridley Commission was unquestionably right in rejecting amalgamation, but there was something to be said for a fusion of

Customs and Excise. However, the disadvantages of such a merger far outweighed the advantages.

After this date nothing further appears to have been done about the matter until, on the 8th of May 1908, Asquith, then Prime Minister, announced, 'Another and more far-reaching change which I propose to take power to make by Order in Council, if and when the time arises, is the transfer of the Excise Department from the Inland Revenue to the Customs. From the point of view of administration, economy and efficiency, I think, and my opinion is shared by almost all those distinguished officials who have had the closest experience of the inner working of both offices, a substantial gain will result to the Public Services for that change though it will have no effect on the finances of the present year.'

It seems that when Sir Thomas Pittar was about to retire as Chairman of the Board of Customs in 1908, the Prime Minister asked him whether there were any measures of reform or change in the Customs he considered desirable in the interests of good administration. Sir Thomas emphatically informed Asquith that in his view it would be a decided improvement to place Customs and Excise under one Board, and that he regarded the findings of the Ridley Commission as arguments for inaction because no harm would arise from inaction, not as arguments against change because change would be bad.

The amount of work involved in implementing the amalgamation was immense. The whole business had been sprung on the service without warning, and neither the official side nor the staff had had time to ponder the allocation of work and the welding together of the staff. In the event, the actual amalgamation of the staffs did not begin until August 1911. The Chancellor of the Exchequer had appointed a Committee to deal with the matter.

One of the main difficulties was the difference in staff structure between the two branches. Apart from the Waterguard, there were three classes of Customs officers and three classes of Excise officers with greatly differing salary scales, and on the clerical side there were the Customs Port Clerks 1st and 2nd class and the

Excise Clerks Upper and Lower Sections. The Committee proposed that all these grades, with the exception of the 1st Class Examining Officers and the Port Clerks 1st Class, should be merged to form one grade of officer on a single salary scale. A new grade of Surveyor was introduced and the higher grades were made up of Collectors and Inspectors, 1st and 2nd Class according to the importance of the Collections. At the head of the Outdoor Service was a Chief Inspector assisted by two Deputy Chief Inspectors and nine Superintending Inspectors. In general, the amalgamation was unpopular with the Excise officers who felt that they did not do so well from it as their Customs colleagues, and that their opportunities for promotion were impaired.

It was customary for Customs officials dealing with the public to wear uniform, and in spite of staff representations it was decided that it should continue to be worn. Surveyors and officers employed on the quays were supplied with a uniform cap and badge and a suit of blue serge.

Conditions of work offered another difficulty. Customs officers normally worked a regular day and received overtime for any excess attendance, but Excise officers by the nature of their work had to put in appearances at all times of the day and night. Visits to distilleries and breweries had to be made to suit the traders' convenience and surreptitious visits made at other times. No payments were normally made for excess attendance and it was customary for the officers to make their attendance suit the varying pattern of the work. However, these difficulties were gradually overcome, and by the time war broke out in 1914 the newly integrated Service was working relatively smoothly and geared to meet the extraordinary demands placed upon it during the national emergency.

Another landmark occurred in the year of the amalgamation, this time in the history of technical progress. On 25th July 1909, Louis Bleriot, the French airman, made his historic flight across the English Channel and landed in a field near Dover. Although it was not realized at the time, this was the beginning of a new age. The

Customs Commissioners were informed of his feat in a letter from the Surveyor at Dover, which ran as follows:

Honourable Sirs,

I have to report that M. Bleriot with his monoplane, successfully crossed the Channel from Calais this morning, and landed in a meadow at the East side of Dover Castle, about 2 miles from our Watchhouse shortly after 5 a.m., having occupied 33 minutes in crossing.

Surveyor, H.M. Customs. Dover.

Included with this letter was a report from another officer to the Collector.

Sir,

On the arrival of the Monoplane from Calais, the Preventive Man in charge interviewed M. Bleriot and issued to him a Quarantine Certificate, thereby treating it as a yacht, and the aviator as Master and Owner.

Your obedient Servant,

J. M. Johnson.

The interesting thing about the second report from the point of view of the Customs is that a precedent was created in regarding an aeroplane as a yacht, and as subject, therefore, to the regulations governing the treatment of yachts.

On the same day Mr. Williams, the Collector, reported to the Board that he had himself visited the scene of the landing and had got into conversation with a bystander whose interest was in the Wright aeroplane. He gave it as his opinion that 'although airships will never come into commercial use, there are great possibilities in store for them'. The Collector went on to say that he thought himself that a time might come when the department would have to treat the arrival of aircraft seriously, and take steps to ensure that no opportunity be given for revenue interests to suffer through indiscriminate landings of airships in this country.

At the end of the first financial year after the amalgamation of Customs and Excise the amounts paid into the Exchequer by the two sections were almost equal. £30,122,583 was paid in on account of Customs and £30,541,917 on account of Excise. The largest contribution to the Excise revenue came from the spirits duty which amounted to £14,565,272, followed by the beer duty with £12,531,620. The revenue from licences amounted to £2,700,467, and the only other considerable items were the railway passenger duty which brought in £322,132 and the medicine stamp duty with £313,114. So far as Customs duties are concerned, the tobacco duty still provided the largest single source of revenue, amounting to £15,680,906. The next most considerable item was the tea duty which contributed £5,677,790, followed by the spirits duty which amounted to £3,293,100. The sugar duties brought in £2,960,202, the wine duties £1,123,152, and the new duty on imported motor spirit, £312,881.

The motor spirit duty was imposed on imported motor spirit from 30th April, 1909, and on home-made motor spirit from 1st June, 1909, at a rate of 3d. per gallon. Section 84 of the Finance Act of 1909 defined motor spirit as 'any inflammable hydrocarbon (including any mixture of hydrocarbons and any liquid containing hydrocarbon) which is capable of being used for providing reasonably efficient motive power for a motor car'. Under the act, any person using motor spirit for purposes other than supplying motive power for motor cars was entitled to an allowance or repayment of the duty paid, and any person using motor spirit 'for the purpose of supplying motive power to a motor car used solely for the conveyance of goods or to a motor cab, omnibus or other vehicle being a hackney cab or to a motor car used by a duly qualified medical practitioner for the purposes of his profession' was entitled to an allowance or repayment.

Among the duties which had been transferred to the Customs and Excise were those from medicine stamps and playing cards. Excise licences were numerous by this time and included licences to brewers, distillers, rectifiers and compounders. There were also licences for dogs, guns, game, game dealers, male servants, carriages – including hackney carriages and motors or vehicles drawn by motors – armorial bearings, appraisers, auctioneers, house agents, hawkers, plate dealers and pawnbrokers. From 1st January 1909, the job of collecting some of these licence duties was handed over to the County and County Borough Councils. In the financial year ended in March 1910 the greatest number of licences issued were those to tobacco dealers, which numbered 383,700. 232,915 licences were issued for male servants, 42,413 to patent medicine makers, and 40,795 gun licences.

The same act of 1908 which had brought about the amalgamation of the Customs and Excise had also introduced old age pensions, and the appointment of Excise officers to act as Pensions Officers throughout the country put a great strain on the staff and on the administration. The Pensions Officer had to examine claims and, in the event of an appeal, start investigations under the statutory regulations before it went to the Pension Committee or the Local Government Board for consideration. He had to give effect to the decisions of the boards, whether granting, revoking, or altering the rate of a pension, and to ensure that the pensioner had the means of drawing his pension so long as he remained entitled to it. It was up to the Pensions Officer to see that the pensioner received his Pension Order Book, and periodically to visit him in his home for the purposes of review. The number of pensions in force on 31st March 1910 was 699,352.

The Old Age Pensions Act of 1911 introduced a number of changes, the most important being the method of assessing the means of a married couple. Previously husband and wife had been dealt with separately, and this usually meant that the husband's pension, if any, was less than the wife's. Now, however, the means of both husband and wife were taken to be half the total means of the couple, and each, if qualified, could receive the full pension. A woman who had lost her British nationality by marriage to an alien, but was otherwise qualified for a pension, could now be granted a pension if her husband was dead or the marriage dissolved or annulled, or if she had been legally separated from, or deserted by, her husband for at least two years.

The National Insurance Act of 1911 affected the Customs and Excise Service, since officers were made responsible for carrying

out investigations into claims for exemption under Section 2 of
the Act. They were given no powers of decision on claims, their
function being to collect the relevant information and transmit it
to the Insurance Commissioners.

As a result of the Finance Act of 1910 changes were made in the
duties on licences granted for the sale of intoxicating liquors, and
these took into account the increasing number of clubs where
liquors could be supplied without liability for the licence duty.
The main features of the changes thus introduced were the establishment of uniform descriptions of licences at the same rates of
duty throughout the United Kingdom, a minimum rate of duty
for public houses and beer houses, according to the population of
the locality where they were situated, and uniform rates of duty
according to the full annual value of such establishments. Four
differential rates of duty were imposed for off-licences selling
beer, spirits and wine, and for on-licences selling wine, sweets and
cider, according to the annual value of the licensed premises. At
the same time, the secretary of every registered club in the country
was required to deliver to the Commissioners of Customs and
Excise each January a statement of all intoxicating liquor purchased in the preceding calendar year, and was charged Excise
duty of sixpence in the pound on it. The duty paid by an hotel or
restaurant was based on the estimated annual value of the premises
so far as they were used for the purpose of selling liquors, and the
same act laid down the method of determining this value. However,
as the result of a legal decision in December 1910, it was altered in
the Revenue Act of 1911. In future, the annual value for determining
licence duties was to be the same as that declared in assessments
for Inhabited House Duty or for Income Tax purposes.

The prohibition against growing tobacco in England and Scotland, which had existed in England since 1660 and in Scotland
since 1782, was repealed. This had already been done in Ireland in
1908. As a result, any person taking out a five shilling Excise
licence could now cultivate tobacco in any part of the United
Kingdom, subject to the payment of a duty on the tobacco grown
and to certain Customs and Excise regulations.

The outbreak of war in August 1914 led to inevitable increases in duty. That on tea was increased from 5d. to 6d. per lb., and the Excise duty on beer from 7s. 9d. to 23s. per barrel at the standard gravity of 1,055 degrees; corresponding increases were made in the Customs duties and drawbacks. In March 1915 there was a surplus of over £7 million, partly as a result of increased duties and partly because of forestallments, especially in spirits, tea, sugar and tobacco. Increased consumption due to higher wages earned by greater numbers, and to the large consumption of dutiable goods by troops under training, also accounted for some of the surplus. Understandably, wine duties suffered heavily as a result of the war, but the receipts for coffee and chicory duties increased considerably. The striking increase in the quantity of chicory was put down to the demand for it from Belgian and French refugees domiciled in this country. The sugar duties were greatly affected by the war; in the three years before 1914 the United Kingdom had obtained 53 per cent of its sugar from Germany and Austria–Hungary. The price of sugar rose rapidly and soon doubled, but the government intervened to fix a maximum retail price.

Many prohibitions were introduced as a result of the war, and the Customs and Excise department was called upon to put them into operation, as well as the provisions of many emergency wartime acts, such as the Aliens Restriction Act and the Trading with the Enemy Act of 1914, and the various Defence of the Realm Acts. A budget introduced on 21st September 1915 led to further increases in existing duties, and proposed new Customs duties at $33\frac{1}{3}$ per cent ad valorem on certain other articles, including imported motor cars and cycles, clocks and watches, and musical instruments. As a result, the Customs and Excise receipts for the financial year for the first time exceeded £100 million. Indeed, the total amount was £120,783,000 which showed a surplus of more than £17 million over the September estimate.

This surplus was largely thought to be the result of the high earnings of large sections of the working classes and the absorption into industry of considerable numbers of people who had previously earned little or nothing. The continued growth of the armies in training had also helped to maintain the consumption of many dutiable articles, particularly of tobacco. A 100 per cent increase in the yield from the duty on cocoa was also attributable to a remarkable rise in the consumption of chocolate by members of the armies at home and abroad.

In spite of the war conditions the quantities of dried fruit imported actually increased. Figs and raisins, which in normal times had been imported from Turkey, were now obtained from other countries – figs from Greece, Spain and the United States of America, and raisins from Italy, Greece, the United States of America and India.

The introduction of a new influence into the life of the community was marked by the imposition of certain specific duties on cinematograph films. We also find gramophones and phonographs classified as musical instruments.

It is noticeable that during the first year of the war the number of wrecks reported leapt from 5,349 in 1914 to 9,935 in 1915. Much of this was probably due to enemy action. As the war continued, more and more work was allocated to the already overburdened Customs and Excise staff. In addition to the new duties already mentioned, others were imposed on matches, mechanical lighters, cider, perry and table waters. A new Excise duty on entertainments was imposed in May 1916, and the collection of this tax and the administration of the statutory exemptions required the setting up of entirely new machinery. The receipts from this tax at the end of the first financial year it was in force amounted to £3,001,000.

Special concessions with regard to dutiable goods imported for hospitals, overseas contingents of troops, etc., had to be applied, and special arrangements made to safeguard the revenue in connection with the despatch of dutiable articles in parcels sent to prisoners of war. In addition, over £100 million in income tax was collected or received on behalf of the Inland Revenue.

Non-revenue tasks also had to be carried out, of course, and work in connection with importing, exporting and removing goods coastwise was considerably increased as a result of wartime controls. All imported goods had to be examined, and control exercised over bunker coal, oil fuel and all stores shipped.

The job of checking up on aliens, carried out on behalf of the Home Office, was obviously more stringently performed in wartime. Forty officers were seconded for service at the approved ports, and Customs officers generally were responsible for assisting the naval, military and police authorities in preventing the landing and embarkation of alien passengers, and in controlling the movements of alien masters and crews.

The department was also required to give the Foreign Office details of cargoes carried by diverted and calling ships, to search ships and cargoes for concealed contraband, and to control transhipment goods in order to prevent trade to and from enemy countries through the United Kingdom. The importing of arms and ammunition from abroad was strictly controlled under the Defence of the Realm regulations, and important and confidential duties were carried out for the Admiralty in connection with the movements of shipping and the control of wireless telegraphy on vessels in port in the United Kingdom. Even in peacetime, Customs officers acted as Admiralty Marshall Substitutes and as such were able to arrest ships and seize cargoes. In wartime, the working of securing and disposing of contraband cargoes seized as prize was very heavy.

A good deal of extra work occurred in connection with old age pensions when the government allocated additional allowances to those suffering special hardship from the rise in the cost of living. 669,574 applications for these benefits were received in 1916, and after investigation 528,374 were allowed. Pension Officers were also called upon to investigate claims for separation allowances from the dependents of unmarried soldiers, and these required patient and careful consideration. By March 1916, Pension Officers had already received 1,700,000 claims and had, on appeal, reinvestigated a further 72,000 cases.

In spite of further increases in duties, the Customs and Excise revenue for 1917–18 fell short of that for 1916–17 by over £18 million. This was largely a result of drastic restrictions on the output of beer and the clearance of spirits and wine. Reductions had been made in the supply of tea, sugar, dried fruits and motor spirit, and prohibitions placed on the importing of certain articles, such as matches, motor cars and motor cycles. At one period during 1917–18, tea was rationed to civilians at 1½ oz. per head per week. The number of reports of wrecked property continued to rise; in 1917 there were 29,175 – a sure reflection of the stepping-up of the U-boat campaign against British shipping.

Chapter 10

THE AFTERMATH OF THE
FIRST WORLD WAR

At the end of the first financial year after the war the Customs and Excise revenue showed a substantial surplus of £15,429,000 above the estimates. These, of course, were based on the assumption that the war would continue throughout the financial year, and that supplies of many dutiable articles would remain restricted. When hostilities ceased in November 1918, improved supplies of spirits, tobacco and motor spirit became available, and as the troops returned the number of consumers in the country increased.

After the Armistice many of the non-revenue duties which had accumulated during the war were gradually relaxed; in particular, those concerned with trading with the enemy, export restrictions and navigation instructions. Furthermore, the continuous day and night attendance at the Custom House was ended in March 1919. Wreck work was still very heavy, however, and there were over 20,000 reports of wrecked property.

During the war, aircraft had been used for the first time and there was rapid development in this field. One of the early acts after the war was the Air Navigation Act of 1919 which made provision for the licensing, inspection and regulation of aerodromes, and stipulated the conditions under which aircraft could be used for carrying goods, mails and passengers. On 15th June, 1919, Alcock and Brown completed their epoch-making flight across the Atlantic.

Many Excise licence duties were increased immediately after

the war, and the budget estimate for the Customs and Excise amounted to £237,500,000. However, a further estimate of £276 million was made in October 1919 taking into account the great and unforeseen increases in receipts during the first six months of the year. In the event, the actual receipts amounted to £283,336,000, a surplus of over £7 million. This was primarily due to the rapid re-absorption of the armed forces into the community, the payment of war gratuities, and the rise in wages which took place in 1919–20, all of which greatly increased the spending power of the public. At the same time there were much larger supplies of important dutiable articles available. The greatest surplus was in the revenue on spirits, which exceeded the estimate by over £6 million.

Another landmark in the history of the Customs and Excise was introduced by Section 8 of the Finance Act of 1919. This was Imperial Preference and it came into force on 2nd June that year. It took the form of an additional duty on non-Empire spirits, and a reduction of duty on other articles produced in and consigned from the Empire. In the case of tea, cocoa, coffee, chicory, sugar, tobacco and motor spirit the reduction was one-sixth, and in the case of films, clocks, watches, cars and musical instruments it was one-third. Excise duties on chicory, sugar and tobacco were lowered correspondingly. Naturally, Preference brought with it the need for special documentation such as Certificates of Origin, and particular vigilance had to be exercised with regard to cargo and passengers' effects to ensure that foreign goods were not passed off as Empire goods in order to take advantage of the lower rates.

An act of 1919 which added to the burdens of the Customs and Excise was the Anthrax Prevention Act which prohibited goods infected or likely to be infected with anthrax from entering the country. One result of this enactment was that Customs officers were required to ban all shaving brushes manufactured in or exported from Japan.

The Finance Act of 1920 introduced substantial increases in the duty on spirits, beer and wine. The same act repealed the Customs duty on imported motor spirit, the duties on motor spirit dealers' licences and the duties on motor car and motor cycle licences. These were replaced by a new scale of duties on mechanically-propelled vehicles, the proceeds of which did not form part of the Customs and Excise revenue.

In 1920 a separate Immigration Branch of the Home Office was formed. This was an important break with the past, although the nucleus of the new Immigration Service was made up of existing immigration officers attached to the Customs and Excise, who were then transferred to the Home Office.

The Customs Service had been responsible for controlling immigration and emigration from early times, and in 1719 had been given the task of preventing the 'seducing of artificers in the manufactures of certain goods into foreign parts'. In the middle of the nineteenth century, when mass emigration to the Colonies was taking place, Customs officers were made responsible for furnishing details of emigrants and were empowered by statute to act as Emigration Officers. When the control of immigrants into this country was tightened up by the Aliens Act of 1905, the Commissioners of Customs had designated certain of their officers to act as 'immigration officers' under the authority of the Home Office in the performance of these duties, in the same way as the Customs Registrars of British Ships and Receivers of Wreck were responsible to the Board of Trade.

It was obvious, however, that it would have been a wasteful duplication of personnel if immigration officers were placed in every port or place where foreign passengers or seamen might arrive. Provision was made, therefore, for Customs officers throughout the country to continue to act as immigration officers.

Two other acts passed in the same year were of immediate concern to the Customs and Excise. The Firearms Act required every person manufacturing or selling firearms or ammunition by way of trade or business to keep a register of transactions which should be produced for inspection by any officer of Customs and Excise. The Dangerous Drugs Act prohibited the importing or exporting of raw or prepared opium, morphine, cocaine, ecgonine, diamorphine (heroin), their respective salts, and medicinal opium. Provision was made for a Secretary of State to grant import and export licences for raw opium at certain ports to be approved by the Commissioners of Customs and Excise. Other prohibitions were introduced by the Dyestuffs (Importation Regulation) Act of 1920 which banned all synthetic organic dyestuffs, colours and colouring matters, and all organic intermediate products used in their manufacture coming from abroad.

There was a deficit of nearly £15 million in the year ended 31st March 1921, mainly attributable to the severe trade depression which had recently set in. As a result, a most important act – the Safeguarding of Industries Act – was passed in 1921. This introduced key industry duties, and made provision for the imposition of a duty on 'dumped' goods, or goods affected by a depreciated currency.

When the Excise staff were transferred to the new Customs and Excise service, they brought with them a great number of licence duties in addition to their newly acquired pensions work. In 1888 acts had been passed directing that the proceeds of certain Excise licence duties should be paid into the Local Taxation Accounts for England and Scotland. In 1890 the Customs and Inland Revenue Act directed that such portion of the existing duty on beer as amounted to 3d. per barrel, and an additional duty of 6d. per gallon on spirits, were to be paid by the revenue departments into the Local Taxation Accounts for England (80 per cent), Scotland (11 per cent), and Ireland (9 per cent). In 1907, however, it was directed that from 1907–8 the proceeds of all these duties on beer, spirits, and Excise licences should be paid into the Exchequer instead of into the Local Taxation Accounts and that an equivalent amount should be issued to those accounts out of the Consolidated Fund. In 1908 the power to levy the duties on certain local taxation licences in England and Wales was transferred, as from 1st January 1909, to the County and County Borough Councils. Payments out of the Consolidated Fund in respect of such licences then ceased, except for an annual sum of £40,000 to be distributed among the Councils.

The Finance Act of 1920 imposed new scales of licence duty on mechanically propelled vehicles and directed that all licence duties on road vehicles should be levied throughout the United Kingdom by County Councils, subject to the general direction of the Minister of Transport, and paid into the Exchequer. The Road Fund was set up and was responsible for bearing the expenses incurred by the Councils in levying the duties. As from 1st January 1921 the Commissioners of Customs and Excise ceased to be concerned in the collection and disposal of any of the revenue from road vehicle licences.

Another act of 1921 of direct interest to the Customs and Excise was the Importation of Plumage (Prohibition) Act which prohibited the importing of the plumage of any birds except those imported alive, those ordinarily used in the United Kingdom as articles of diet, and those included in the schedule to the act. The schedule included African ostriches and eider ducks but could be varied by the Board of Trade on the recommendation of an advisory committee set up under the act. Plumage imported as part of the wearing apparel of a passenger was also excepted if, in the opinion of the Commissioners, it was intended and was reasonably required for the personal use of the passenger.

The Government of Ireland Act of 1920 was put into operation in respect of Northern Ireland from November 1921, and so far as the Customs and Excise was concerned, involved the transfer to the government of Northern Ireland of Northern Irish old age pensions, entertainments duty and a number of Excise licence duties. Although the British Government had transferred all administrative functions in the Irish Free State to that State as from 1st April 1922, the Customs and Excise duties continued to be assessed, levied and collected as previously, and it was not until the 6th December 1922 that the Free State Government assumed direct control of Customs and Excise.

Another great change carried through in 1923 in the area of revenue protection was the final disbanding of the Coastguard, and its replacement by a new force, the Coast Preventive Service, entirely under the administration of Customs and Excise. As has been mentioned in an earlier chapter, the Admiralty had taken over responsibility for the Coastguard in 1856 for reasons of defence, and especially to ensure the ready manning of the fleet in the event of a national emergency. But the position with regard to naval resources had altered radically in seventy years, and a committee was set up to examine the situation. This found that the maintenance of such a large force in peacetime was no longer justified, and while the Admiralty should retain a 'Naval Signalling Section', other departments should absorb the various duties of the Coastguard. Thus it recommended that the Board of Trade should establish a 'Coast Watching Force' to carry out work in connection with life-saving, the salvage of wreck, the administration of the foreshores, etc., and that a 'Coast Preventive Force' should be formed under the control of the Board of Customs and Excise to supplement the existing Waterguard staff responsible for revenue protection work.

The Board therefore took steps to set up such a force, proposing to draw recruits from the existing Coastguard Force and from pensioners of the Royal Navy. Notices were issued to this effect, and instructions issued to the new service describing the work they would be called upon to do. According to these, the Chief Preventive Man was to be responsible for guarding a particular stretch of coastline or estuarial water, and was required to visit all harbours, coves, landing places and other places on his station. He was to board vessels from abroad, see that the health regulations were adhered to, seal stores, deal with any animals on board, and search for contraband. He had to keep a general watch on shipping and fishing boats in order to prevent the illegal landing of dutiable and prohibited goods. He was further required to board any Coasting vessels, examine their log-books and transires and satisfy himself that the cargo agreed with the description on these documents. A record of arrivals and sailings, and a pocket journal were to be kept. He was also to keep a look-out for any wreck or foreshore encroachments, and report them to the Coast Watching Force and the Receiver of Wreck.

The transitional arrangements which had been made between

this country and the Irish Free State with regard to dutiable articles and the allocation of revenue came to an end on 31st March 1923. After that date, trade with the Free State by sea, or across the land boundary with Northern Ireland, was designated as foreign trade, and a Customs land frontier was established along the boundary.

The setting up of a customs staff in Northern Ireland posed quite a new problem for the department. There had been no land frontier within the United Kingdom since the Act of Union with Scotland in 1707, although an Excise force continued to be stationed on the Scottish border for more than one hundred years afterwards to deal with certain excisable articles.

The land boundary between the Irish Free State and the Six Counties was about 250 miles in length and did not follow a natural line of demarcation. A Customs cordon was set up to control imports and exports for revenue and other purposes. The movement across the boundary of merchandise other than farm produce was prohibited, except along certain approved roads and by the railways.

A Customs Station was set up on each approved road as close as possible to the boundary, staffed by Customs officers supervised by a Surveyor. Additional Customs stations were established behind the boundary to prevent the unloading of goods at intermediate points, and a Boundary Post, staffed by Preventive Officers and Land Preventive Men, was situated almost on the boundary so that imports and exports could be observed as they actually crossed it, and to make sure that nothing escaped examination at the Customs Station. Arrangements were made for a mobile force of the Ulster Constabulary to patrol the boundary to prevent smuggling and the conveyance of merchandise on unapproved roads.

When De Valera became Prime Minister of the Irish Free State in 1932, he proceeded to take steps to break away completely from Great Britain. This precipitated a tariff war and under the Irish Free State (Special Duties) Act a duty of 20 per cent was placed on goods coming from the Free State; later this was increased to 30 per cent, and 40 per cent on live animals.

A number of acts affecting taxation were passed in the next few years. The so-called McKenna Duties on motor cars, musical instruments, clocks and watches, originally imposed in 1915, lapsed on 2nd August 1924 and were not immediately renewed. Certain other duties which had been levied under the Safeguarding of Industries Act were also discontinued, and some reductions and exemptions were made to the Entertainments Duty.

These changes in taxation resulted in a decline in the revenue yield of over £32 million and the following year a Finance Act reimposed the McKenna Duties. The same act imposed Customs duties on silk and artificial silk in all forms, and Excise duties on British produced artificial silk, making provision for export drawbacks. These new duties brought the department into contact with trades with which it had had no previous experience, and occasioned a considerable amount of additional work. The Finance Act also imposed Safeguarding Duties on cutlery, gloves and incandescent mantles.

In the same year pensions were granted to widows, dependent children and orphans, and the work of investigating and reporting claims was carried out by Pension Officers. The need for extra staff to cope with it was met by increasing the number of women Pension Officers and temporary clerks.

The Finance Act of 1926 introduced an Excise duty on betting, to be charged on every bet made with a bookmaker on every kind of event. This kind of duty was entirely new to the department and led to a considerable increase in the numbers of Headquarters and Outdoor staff, as well as the appointment of a special Betting Duty staff. The imposition of a new Customs duty on packing and wrapping paper posed a number of problems for the department and substantially increased its work. The 1926 Finance Act also made reference to imported antiques by providing that all goods, other than spirits or wines, manufactured or produced more than one hundred years before the date of import should be exempt from Customs duties.

The General Strike of 1926 had a marked effect on the revenue yield from the Customs and Excise, which showed a deficit of

£9¾ million. Most of this was undoubtedly directly attributable to industrial disturbances. The following year Customs duties were imposed on articles made of translucent or vitrified pottery used for serving food and drink, and an Excise licence duty was imposed on moneylenders for the use of premises to carry on their business. The duties on wine, tobacco and matches were all increased but in spite of these measures, the revenue yield again showed a substantial deficit.

The implementation of the provisions of the Public Health (Preservatives in Food) Regulations of 1925 were involving the department in a good deal of extra work. The regulations prohibited the importing of food and drink containing more than a stipulated amount of preservatives and, in addition to the samples of dutiable goods already being taken for revenue purposes, samples now had to be taken from free goods. The Therapeutic Substances Regulations of 1927 prohibited the importation of vaccines, sera and so on, unless covered by licences issued by a health authority in the United Kingdom. Once more, the job of enforcing these regulations was laid at the door of the Customs and Excise.

In 1928 the Finance Act imposed a duty of fourpence per gallon on imported hydrocarbon oils, making provision for drawbacks in the usual way. Hydrocarbon oils were defined as 'petroleum oils, coal tar and oils produced from coal, shale or peat'. The yield from this duty for the first year, 1928–9, amounted to £13·1 million. Rebates were allowed in order to free heavy oils from the tax. Although this duty obviously entailed extra work for the department, it was a cheap duty to collect in view of its total yield. The same act levied import duties on certain buttons and certain wrought enamelled hollow ware, and imposed a Customs and Excise duty of sixpence each on mechanical lighters. But the revenue once again fell short of the estimate, this time by £8·6 million.

The department had to take account of developments in international aviation to make arrangements for dealing with this new contingency. In 1929, for instance, Imperial Airways, which had been set up in 1924, began a regular weekly service to India.

The duty on tea was repealed in April 1929, but imports still remained subject to inspection by Customs officers under the Sale of Food and Drugs Acts. Two other duties were repealed by the Finance Act; the long-established Railway Passenger Duty, and the more recently imposed Betting Duty. In the last complete year of its imposition, 1928–9, the former tax had produced £366,967, and the latter £2,245,117.

Orders in Council referring to the Merchandise Marks Act of 1926 had brought a number of additional articles under its control, including oat products, eggs, currants, sultanas and raisins, cutlery, ball and roller bearings, scientific glassware and raw tomatoes. In the year 1929–30 1,498 consignments of such goods were detained for examination. 323 of these were allowed to be exported or returned to the port of shipment, one was seized, and the remainder delivered on being satisfactorily marked.

By 1930 the effects of the Great Depression, precipitated by the Wall Street crash of 1929, were beginning to make themselves felt. The revenue for the financial year ended March 1931 once again fell short of the estimates, this time by £6·5 million, as the high level of unemployment severely reduced the purchasing power of the nation. One telling illustration of this is provided by the beer revenue, which fell by £1½ million although the duty had been increased by three shillings per standard barrel.

A new prohibition was introduced in 1930 by the Parrots (Prohibition of Import) Order by which the importation of parrots was prohibited with a view to preventing the spread of the infectious disease, psittacosis. For many years Customs officers had to cope with ingenious attempts to smuggle these birds, which were frequently doped, or packed in such a way as to cause suffocation.

The financial position had become very serious and the Chancellor, Philip Snowden, a former Excise Officer, had the difficult task of balancing the budget in 1931. The principal measure affecting the revenue was the increase of duty on hydrocarbon oils. The Labour Government fell in August 1931, and the new National Government introduced a second Finance Act which raised the duties on beer and tobacco, and made a further increase in the duty on hydrocarbon oils. This alone produced a surplus of £13·4 million, and there was a net revenue surplus of £2·2 million.

New scales were laid down for the Entertainment Duty, introducing a much wider range of payments and causing a fifty per cent increase in the number of claims for exemption. The Arms Export Prohibition Order of 1931 added such items as aircraft, aircraft engines, tanks, bayonets, swords and lances to the list of prohibited goods.

A reorganization of the Customs Waterguard Services resulted in the establishment of a new grade of Waterguard Surveyor and the substitution of one grade of Chief Preventive Officer for the two existing grades.

Free trade finally came to an end when a comprehensive Customs tariff was introduced under the Import Duties Act of 1932. A general ad valorem duty of 10 per cent was imposed on all goods imported into the United Kingdom. Although the duties on certain goods were repealed, they became liable to the general ad valorem duties, but certain goods already chargeable were exempted from the new impost.

The Customs and Excise revenue in 1932–3, the first complete year that the Import Duties Act was in force, amounted to £287·7 million, against £255·2 million in 1931–2. The new duties made necessary a large increase in staff to cope with the extra work they caused. This was achieved, partly by transferring staff from other government departments, partly by recruiting in open competition, and partly by employing temporary workers.

An Imperial Economic Conference met in Ottawa in the summer of 1932 from which deliberation emerged the Ottawa Agreements Act, intended to promote imperial free trade. Provision was also made for the imposition of tariffs on certain goods imported from non-Commonwealth countries. An Import Duties Advisory Committee was set up in Great Britain to advise and assist the Treasury. It was expected to consider the question of restricting imports into the United Kingdom, as well as safeguarding commercial and industrial interests.

During the year ended 31st March 1933 there were 7,725 seizures of smuggled goods. 4,093 of these were seizures of tobacco and spirits, there being 5,237 lbs. of tobacco and 199 gallons of spirits.

The following year the government introduced measures to protect the home match industry by increasing the duty on imported matches; the Customs and Excise duties on mechanical lighters were also raised, and discriminated in favour of the home-produced article. Heavy hydrocarbon oils were now made subject to a duty of one penny per gallon, and the Excise duty on British sparkling wines was increased. In order to implement a trade agreement with Germany in April 1933, the Customs duties on certain musical instruments and on certain clocks and clock movements were reduced.

A number of other restrictions came into force in 1933–4. Under the Wheat Act of 1932, every importer of flour was obliged, in addition to paying Customs duties, to furnish the Customs and Excise office at the port of importation with a receipt from the Wheat Commission showing that the prescribed quota payment had been made. The Bacon (Import Regulation) Order of 1933 prohibited the importation, except under licence or quota certificate, of bacon produced in certain foreign countries. The Ottawa Agreements (Importation of Meat) Order banned unlicensed imports of frozen mutton and lamb, and frozen and chilled beef not produced in the British Empire. Similarly, the Sea-Fishing Industry (Regulation of Landing) Order of 1933, prohibited the landing, without licence, of any sea fish unless caught in fishing boats registered in the United Kingdom, or any part of the Empire, so long as the catch had not previously been landed in any country outside the United Kingdom.

Two new prohibitions were implemented by the department during the course of the year: the Potato (Import Regulation) Order which banned the importing of potatoes grown outside the Empire or the Irish Free State, and the Pork (Import Regulation) Order which made a similar prohibition, but omitted reference to the Irish Free State. The Finance Act took steps to strengthen the law preventing smuggling across the land boundary from the Free State. Numerous orders were issued in 1934-5 under the Import Duties Act, imposing or varying additional duties on selected classes or descriptions of goods and adding to or modifying the list of articles previously exempt under the act.

The growing numbers of diesel-engined vehicles used in road transport had a detrimental effect on the revenue, since they were powered by heavy oils dutiable at one penny per gallon, instead of petrol at a rate of eightpence per gallon. It was estimated that in 1934-5 the Exchequer lost about £1·3 million on account of it. But the following year this duty, too, was raised to eightpence, and the oil revenue as a whole rose by £2·1 million.

The Customs and Excise receipts for 1935-6 gave signs of an economic recovery, showing a substantial increase of £13·9 million over the previous year. The expansion in the purchasing power of the people was indicated by an increase of £4·3 million from the tobacco duties, which represented a rise in consumption of over six per cent compared with an average annual rise of about two per cent in the previous decade. The beer revenue showed a sharp increase of £2·1 million, representing a rise in consumption from three per cent to four per cent. Tea consumption rose by a similar amount, with a revenue increase of £148,000, and the revenue from cocoa (and cocoa preparations) went up by twenty-five per cent to 208,000. Inexplicably, however, the revenue from sugar declined by £136,000, and as the result of a reduction in duty, the revenue from entertainments also fell. But the Jubilee celebrations of King George V, combined with the hot summer of 1935, reinforced the general impression of improving prosperity.

This improvement was maintained, and the following year Customs and Excise receipts rose by more than £16 million. Spirits revenue increased by over £1¼ million, and beer by £1·9 million, showing a rise in consumption of over five per cent and three per cent respectively. The Customs duties on tea were increased all round by twopence per lb.

So far as the revenue was concerned, the immediate result of the Spanish Civil War which broke out in July 1936, was a rise of over £1½ million in the receipts from the duty on wine. This was because wine merchants, fearing that supplies from Spain would be interrupted, had built up their stocks. In order to comply with the terms of the International Agreement, special steps were taken to prevent arms being exported to Spanish territory. This included aircraft leaving under their own power.

The Diseases of Fish Act, passed in 1937, prohibited the introduction of any live fish or the live eggs of any fish belonging to the salmon family into Great Britain and, except under licence, of any live freshwater fish or live eggs of freshwater fish. The Quail Protection Act of the same year banned the imports of live quail during the period between 14th February and 1st July in any year, and included them in the prohibitions under the Customs Consolidation Act of 1876.

The net receipt from the Customs and Excise continued to grow, and in 1937–8 rose to £335·6 million, the highest figure yet reached, and an increase of about four per cent on the previous year. Beer consumption once again leapt up by five and a half per cent, producing a revenue of over £65 million, a rise of over £3 million.

The yield from tobacco rose by nearly £5½ million, which indicated an increased consumption of over six and a half per cent. The total revenue from tobacco was now more than £82¾ million, and oil receipts exceeded £50 million. In the following year, the yield from the Customs and Excise increased by £4·9 million, but comparison with the previous year is difficult because of budgetary disturbances. The duties on oil and tea were increased in April, and a new duty on power alcohol was imposed on 2nd May. On the other hand, the revenue from spirits, beer, silk and also from the McKenna duties (now replaced by equivalent duties under the Import Duties Act) decreased. Duties on goods from Eire came to an end on 19th May and there were a number of reductions of duty in fulfilment of the Trade Agreement with the United States of America. These may have had some effect on the fall in revenue but there was no doubt that it was mainly due to the trade recession. An enactment at this time that air raid protection works should be left out of the account in the determining of the annual value of premises for the purpose of the Excise licence duty gave an ominous hint of things to come.

In 1938–9 the net receipt from Customs and Excise duties rose to £340·55 million. The receipts from the entertainment duty attained £8,154,000, and a breakdown of the contributing sources is of interest. Cinemas provided by far the greater part, with a yield of £5,610,000, followed by theatres and music halls (£1,050,000), football matches (£470,000), horse-racing (£240,000), other kinds of racing (£270,000), cricket matches (£30,000), and other entertainments (£180,000).

Chapter 11

THE SECOND WORLD WAR
AND POST-WAR PERIOD

Immediately following the outbreak of war in September 1939 a first War Budget was introduced, the second budget of that financial year. It increased the duties on spirits, beer, wine, British wine, sugar and tobacco. The receipts exceeded the estimates and amounted to over £400 million in spite of the fact that certain goods – sugar and petrol for example – were now rationed. The duties imposed under the Import Duties Act, Ottawa Agreements Act and the Finance Acts were adapted to the exigencies of war time by the Import Duties (Emergency Provisions) Act of 1939.

The Customs and Excise department became responsible for certain special work in connection with the war emergency. Many imports were controlled in the interests of saving foreign exchange and conserving shipping space, and were only permitted to enter under Board of Trade licence. In the same way, many exports were controlled in order to prevent valuable commodities coming under enemy control. In connection with contraband control, the department was responsible for reporting to the Ministry of Economic Warfare information about calling ships, transhipment cargoes, and diverted and arrested ships. Officers were required to release ships or prize-court goods and carry out search for concealed contraband. Collectors acting as Admiralty Marshal Substitutes were responsible for the custody and disposal of cargoes which had been prize-courted.

Under the Trading with the Enemy Act of 1939 the department was required to stop the import or export of goods consigned from or to firms in hostile territory, and an increased supervision had to be exercised over coastwise and transhipment cargo with a view to controlling the passage of goods between neutral and enemy countries. A strict watch also had to be kept on bunkers, deck and engine stores, and rationed foodstuffs for use on ships. The department was required to collaborate with the Admiralty, the Ministry of Shipping and other departments in implementing the government's policy regarding the movements of shipping and the control of wireless telegraphy in ports of the United Kingdom.

Members of the department acting as immigration officers were responsible for ensuring that no passengers landed or embarked without the permission of the Home Office District Inspector, and for controlling the shore leave of alien seamen. They co-operated with the censorship authorities in controlling written, printed and pictorial matter, and assisted in preventing the smuggling of currency outwards and pigeons inwards and outwards. Under the Exchange Control regulations, the department also had to check on the proper use of allotments of foreign currency or transfers of sterling for the purchase of imported goods and the full surrender of the foreign exchange proceeds of exports to certain countries.

A great deal of emergency legislation was passed in connection with these duties, and enactments adapted existing legislation to the circumstances. The Prize Act of 1939, for instance, applied existing prize law to aircraft, and special provision was made by the Liability for War Damage (Miscellaneous Provisions) Act 1939 to provide relief for goods chargeable with Customs or Excise duty which were lost or damaged by wartime activity before the duty was paid.

There were two war budgets during the next financial year. In April, further increases were made in the duties on spirits, beer, tobacco, matches and mechanical lighters, and in July on beer, tobacco, wine and entertainments. The most important item, however, was a completely new tax, purchase tax, which was imposed by the July budget, and brought into operation on 21st October 1940 by the Purchase Tax (Commencement) Order 1940.

The Customs and Excise receipts for 1939–40 rose to over £532 million, and the increase in yield from the principal items was headed by beer with over £60 million, tobacco with over £55 million, purchase tax with over £26 million, spirits with nearly £5 million and wine with over £2 million. The increase from the entertainments duty and the tea duty was in each case a little over £1,700,000. The effects of the war were most immediately apparent in the great falling-off in the receipts from the Ottawa duties. The Budget had estimated these at £7 million, but actual receipts only amounted to £1,816,000.

On the outbreak of war, the yearly output of home-made beer was restricted to a maximum of about 19 million barrels. Gravities were later reduced, and a substantial fall in the output of standard barrels was expected. The demand for beer was so strong, however, that consumption actually increased.

The rationing of tea to 2 oz. per head per week for civilians was largely responsible for reducing the revenue from this commodity, against an increase in the yield from both cocoa and coffee. Sugar was also rationed, and the quantity retained for consumption fell by about 25 per cent.

As the war continued, carrying with it the danger of invasion, many of the emergency duties carried out by the department were added to or had to be intensified. Security measures were taken in connection with both foreign and coasting ships to prevent the introduction of enemy agents or arms or instruments for use in sabotage. It was known that during the occupation of France and other territories the enemy had succeeded in acquiring large amounts of United Kingdom currency, and special efforts had to be made to prevent the illegal importation of bank notes and also the exportation of sterling bearer securities by people apprehensive about the outcome of the war.

In 1941–2 the net receipts from Customs and Excise rose to over £700 million, exceeding the estimates by £126·21 million. The yield from purchase tax increased by over £72 million, from tobacco by over £48 million, and from beer by about £25½ million. Other receipts were affected by the exemption of a range of goods and materials predominantly imported for government use from Key Industry and General Ad Valorem duty. It is interesting to note that the quantity of non-dutiable spirits received for use in arts, manufactures and science had increased from over 25 million proof gallons in 1938–9 to over 57 million proof gallons in 1941–2.

The largest single contributor to the revenue was the duty from tobacco, which yielded about £220½ million; then came beer with about £164½ million. Purchase tax furnished over £98 million, hydrocarbon oils nearly £55 million, sugar and molasses over £31 million, Import Duties Act receipts over £26 million and the entertainments duty nearly £16 million, exceeding the Budget estimade by £5 million. The receipts from cincmas alone accounted for nearly £14 million. In making the estimate, allowance had been made for air-raids, but in actual fact there were comparatively few air-raids after May 1941.

When the rationing of clothing and footwear was introduced on 1st June 1941, the department was required to assist in issuing supplementary coupons for essential clothing and footwear to people who had suffered loss as a result of war damage, civil damage (including theft) or accident, or to people, such as immigrants, coming within the scheme for the first time.

The Budget estimate for 1942–3 was £805 million, but the net receipts in fact exceeded £886 million. The increase was mainly due to further duties imposed by the 1942 Finance Act on spirits, beer, wine, tobacco and entertainments and a rise in the purchase tax on certain articles. The Budget did, however, exempt utility garments, footwear, headgear, gloves and utility cloth from purchase tax. There was a substantial fall in the revenue from sugar, molasses, etc. This was possibly due to the extension of the sugar ration (in force since 1940) to confectionery in 1942. The yield from this source fell to a little over £26 million. On the other hand, receipts from the hydrocarbon oil duty rose from nearly £55 million in 1941–2 to nearly £56 million in 1942–3, although oil for civilian use had been severely rationed since September 1939, and the basic ration for motor cars had ceased as from July 1942. In addition, oil for use in road vehicles had been restricted to specific quantities allowed for special purposes.

The difficulty of making revenue estimates under wartime conditions was once again evident in the year ended 31st March 1944. War restrictions had stopped the supply of many commodities, and because shipping and foreign exchange was short, most of the goods liable to Customs duties could only be imported under licence. In other cases, and particularly where goods liable to purchase tax were concerned, the manufacturers or wholesalers were limited to a percentage quota of their turnover in a basic period. Other commodities, such as tea and sugar, were subject to rationing.

Under these circumstances it was reasonable to assume that if duties were left at their existing level, the revenue would have been considerably less than in the previous year. Accordingly, duty increases were imposed on spirits, beer, wine, tobacco and entertainments, and also in the higher rate of purchase tax. The total estimate amounted to £975½ million, but the net receipts turned out to be £1,044 million. The duties on tobacco, beer, oil, entertainments and spirits all yielded more than the previous year, but there was a drop of more than £18 million in the revenue from purchase tax.

15,528 seizures of smuggled goods were made during the year, 9,594 of which were tobacco and spirits. Convictions were obtained in over 1,970 cases. In England and Wales 27 cases of illicit distillation were detected, 2 in Scotland and 24 in Northern Ireland. Many of the smuggling cases referred to attempted evasion, including 970 cases of evasion of duty, 590 of wartime prohibitions and restrictions, 160 of purchase tax, 29 of liquor licences, 140 of other excise licences, and 12 of entertainments duty.

The following year the Customs and Excise receipts were again in surplus of the Budget estimates, and attained £1,076·3 million. The Chancellor of the Exchequer explained that this was largely due to a substantial rise in the home consumption of beer. The cost of collecting the revenue was about £5,953,000, or 0·55 per cent of the net receipts, which also covered the considerable non-revenue work of the department. It was achieved, furthermore, with a staff which had been reduced from 15,217 on 31st March 1939 to 9,634 on 31st March 1945.

Throughout the war the consumption of beer had been maintained at approximately the pre-war level in terms of standard barrels. This had been achieved by reducing the gravity so that in actual fact consumption increased by about twenty-five per cent in terms of bulk barrels. In order to meet increased demands from the limited amounts of materials available, the Ministry of Food had arranged for the gravity reductions to be made, and the officers of the department co-operated in ensuring that the brewers conformed with the arrangement.

Wine had been subject to import licensing from June 1940, but after March 1941 no licences for ordinary trade importations were granted. The Ministry of Food did, however, arrange for 'concession' imports to be distributed through ordinary trade channels. The total imports of wine in 1944 were only seven and a half per cent of the yearly average between 1936 and 1938. British wines suffered from the lack of the materials normally used, and by 1944 supplies of wine must have fallen to under one-seventh of the pre-war figure. Table waters had been subject to Ministry control from 1942, and to save transport, production had been diverted from bottled mineral waters ready for drinking to squashes and other concentrated drinks.

Most of the tea supplies continued to come from India and Ceylon, but the Ministry of Food made large bulk purchases from the Dutch East Indies. However, this source of supply was ended by the Japanese occupation. All the same, the ordinary civilian ration of tea remained at 2 oz. per week.

The supply and consumption of sugar had been regulated since the beginning of 1940, and as a result the total quantity of sugar retained for consumption fell from 44 million cwt. in 1939–40 to 29 million cwt. in 1944–5. The use of saccharin, on the other hand, was greatly increased, and the duty-paid quantity rose from 1 million oz. in 1938–9 to $8\frac{1}{2}$ million oz. in 1944–5.

The German occupation of Greece and the closing of the Mediterranean to commercial shipping greatly affected imports of dried and preserved fruits to this country, as before the war 65 per cent of supplies had come from this area. However, in 1941–2 increased supplies from the United States of America brought the total imports to over 4 million cwt., exceeding the figure for 1938–9 by 2·3 million cwt.

In 1938–9 the total quantity of tobacco cleared for home consumption amounted to 192 million lbs., and at the outbreak of war there were sufficient stocks of tobacco in bond to provide for two years' normal consumption. Deliveries for home consumption were at first restricted, but the demand was so far in excess of supplies that the restrictions were relaxed. Following the arrival of the Lend-Lease supplies from the United States of America the quantity duty-paid for home consumption rose to 236 million lbs., and in 1944–5 amounted to 219 million lbs. A larger outturn of manufactured tobacco from a given quantity of leaf had been obtained by limiting the quantity of waste tobacco rejected for manufacture to six per cent of the duty-paid weight of unmanufactured tobacco.

In 1938–9 the supply of mechanical lighters was just under two million, of which more than half were home-produced, Imports were restricted and eventually dwindled to negligible amounts. Home production also fell heavily, but owing to a shortage of matches and lighters, accentuated by increased smoking, the Board of Trade sponsored and licensed the manufacture of Utility lighters, and the quantity on which duty was paid increased from less than half a million in 1941–2 to over five and a half million in 1944–5.

The yield from the entertainments duty had increased enormously from £8·2 million in 1938–9 to £45·9 million in 1944–5. This was partly attributable to increased rates of duty, but even more so to a growth in cinema and theatre attendances. The government-regulated hours of opening, particularly in central London, the prolonged air raids of 1940–1, and the flying-bomb raids of the summer of 1944, caused periodic slumps in attendances and, in certain areas, where there was a threat of German invasion, houses were adversely affected. There was no comparable rise in the receipts from sport, other than greyhound racing.

The Ottawa duties felt the full force of wartime conditions, since they were imposed mainly on foodstuffs, and shortage of shipping caused a restriction in the quantity which was allowed to be imported. Two items, however, condensed and dried milk, were increasingly imported as supplies of home-produced milk were insufficient to meet demand. In spite of the dislocation produced by wartime controls, 4·7 million proof gallons of spirit were exported, of which 2·2 million went to the United States of America. This compared with a total export of 7·7 million in 1938.

THE POST-WAR PERIOD

The increased yield of the Customs and Excise duties in 1945–6, amounting to about £1,111 million, was mainly attributable to a rise in consumption of the chief dutiable commodities, beer and tobacco. The April Budget did not make any great change, but the 'interim' Peace Budget in the following October exempted a number of domestic and heating appliances from purchase tax. During the course of the year, the return of troops to this country swelled the demand for beer, tobacco and entertainment, and the taxation yield in respect of each of them reached a record level; tobacco exceeding £400 million, beer £300 million, and entertainments £50 million. As tea and sugar continued to be rationed, there were no great changes in the yield from these items.

In 1945 the Ministry of Food had allowed the production of whisky to be increased and had licensed the distillers to use sufficient barley and rye to produce forty-three per cent of the quantity of spirits produced in the year ended 30th September 1939. In January 1947, however, a world shortage of cereals prevented the further allocation of supplies to the spirits industry. At the end of the war, imports of certain spirits, such as brandy, increased to some extent, and imports of rum exceeded the pre-war level. Imports of whiskey from Eire, which had been subject to quota restrictions, were now restored to about the pre-war level. It was probably too soon for the yield on some commodities to be materially affected by the peace, but it was noticeable that the receipts under the Import Duties Act decreased slightly, while the revenue from purchase tax rose to over £118 million, compared with about £98½ million in the previous year.

As might have been expected, the Customs and Excise receipts for 1946–7, the first complete year of peace, rose to a record figure of £1,184, more than three times the amount in 1938–9. Although there was a marked increase in the yield from tobacco, purchase tax, wine, spirits and 'tariff' duties, there was a substantial decline in the revenue from beer. This was due to the restriction of output because of the shortage of cereals. A slight decline was also apparent in the receipts from the hydrocarbon oil duty, since increased civilian consumption had not been sufficient to make up for the drop in service consumption. The severe weather in February 1947, and the difficulty of maintaining supplies of fuel, had an adverse effect on trade and industry, and the principal revenues all suffered to a certain extent. It is difficult to ascertain the damage in such cases but it was estimated that the total loss on this account was in the region of £15 million.

The most important change in the work of the department was in the non-revenue field. Work in connection with old age pensions, which had been carried out by Pension Officers attached to the department since 1909, was now transferred to the Assistance Board from 31st of March 1947. Women Pension Officers and Surveyors were also transferred to the same Board.

There were two Budgets in the course of the next financial year, both introducing a number of changes. In April, the tobacco duty was increased and a number of changes were made to purchase tax rates. The duties on most categories of heavy oil were repealed, as well as the Excise duty on artificial silk. In November, the duties on beer, spirits and wine went up, purchase tax rates were increased generally, and a new duty on pool betting was introduced. The continued growth in the output of consumer goods was reflected in the substantial increase in the yield from purchase tax, which reached the record figure of £246,248,894.

During the post-war years the department felt the need to adapt itself to technical changes in industry and commerce, and made a number of changes in methods of assessing and collecting taxes. The full effect of the taxation increases in November 1947 was only felt in the financial year 1948–9 but the increase in the revenue paid into the Exchequer of £136 million which brought the total up to £1,557 million, was also due to the greater supplies and the higher consumption of goods liable to taxation. Most of the emergency war duties had been relinquished by the end of 1948, although some control over imports and exports and over currency was still exercised. The revision of the purchase tax schedule, introduced by the Chancellor of the Exchequer in his Budget speech in April 1948, added considerably to the work of the department. The effect of this measure was to reduce the taxes on the more necessary articles of personal and domestic use and increase those on other articles. The net result was a reduction of £39 million in the year.

Signs of a recession were apparent in 1949–50 when, for the first time since the war, the Customs and Excise revenue fell below that of the previous year. Some reductions in duty had of course been made in the 1949 budget, but receipts were also affected by a slackening-off in demand. This was particularly the case in connection with beer and entertainments, and lent support to the view that better supplies of consumer goods such as clothing and household equipment cause money to be diverted in this direction from other forms of consumer expenditure. The end of rationing also helped to change the pattern of revenue receipts. It was noticeable, for example, that the de-rationing of clothing helped to increase purchase tax receipts, while the de-rationing of sugar no doubt diverted some expenditure to this commodity from other dutiable articles.

The great increase in the post-war tourist traffic and the need to increase the nation's invisible earnings, led to the introduction of more rapid methods of passenger clearance and to increased duty-free concessions. The member countries of the Organization for European Economic Co-operation met to discuss and align their concessions to travellers, and changes were made in order to effect this. Another arrangement calculated to encourage foreign visitors and help exports was the introduction of the personal export scheme, whereby an overseas visitor could make purchases in this country free of purchase tax for delivery direct to the ship or aircraft in which he was travelling. In connection with this scheme, certain relaxations of exchange control and export licensing requirements were made.

The retention of licensing controls of imports and exports, together with the granting of relaxations, had resulted in a good deal of extra work for the department, which was responsible for deciding whether or not goods were admissible under general licence. Balance of payment difficulties caused the exchange control measures to be kept in operation, and the department continued to enforce the prohibition on unauthorized imports and exports of bank notes and securities, and the export of foreign currency notes. Although there was some reduction in the number of seizures under this heading, the number of prosecutions involved was almost as great as in the previous year.

The war in Korea, which began in June 1950, led to dislocations in the flow of trade, with effect on the revenue. The Customs duty on imported hydrocarbon oil was doubled, and an Excise duty of ninepence per gallon was imposed on hydrocarbons produced in the United Kingdom from substances other than imported hydrocarbon oils. Towards the end of May, petrol rationing was abolished and consumption rose accordingly. As a result, the revenue from this source in 1950–1 exceeded all expectations, amounting to almost £139 million compared with £62·5 million in the previous year. The outbreak of hostilities in the Far East caused an increase in commodity prices and, consequentially, in the yield from the ad valorem duties. Furthermore, the possibility of rises in retail prices led to an upsurge in public spending in the period just before Christmas, and this affected purchase tax receipts. The prospect of the war developing, accompanied by increased duties, also led to some forestalling by traders.

During the year a great deal of work was carried out on a

revision of Customs Laws, the intention being to consolidate and modernize the existing laws. In order to simplify them so as to bring them into conformity with the requirements of modern practice and conditions, it was found necessary to repeal, amend or change about 1,000 sections of acts and numerous statutory rules and orders.

The Customs and Excise Bill received the royal assent on 1st August 1952, and came into operation on 1st January 1953. The new act repealed in whole or in part some 200 acts of parliament passed during the previous 150 years. The act, did however, contain a general provision whereby orders, regulations and other instruments made under previous acts were continued in force.

The revenue remained buoyant in 1951-2, rising to £1,752 million. This accounted for more than forty per cent of all central government taxation. The most spectacular increase in yield was that from the Import Duties Act, which rose from £57 million to £93 million; an increase reflecting the larger volume and mounting prices of imports. Higher prices were also indicated by the inflated receipts from purchase tax, which rose to £338 million.

For some years the revenue from the beer duty had been falling, and in 1951-2 there was a further decline of nearly £3 million, this being due to a steady decline in consumption which had been continuing from the early part of the century (interrupted only by the war), and appeared to indicate a gradual change in social behaviour. There was a slight fall in the revenue from wine, but the quantity retained for home consumption rose to the highest level for ten years. There was also a fall of over £17 million in the yield from spirits. Exports of spirits continued to grow, and attained a record figure of over 13 million gallons.

The Finance Act of 1951 had doubled the purchase tax on cars, televisions and wireless sets, and on refrigerators, washing machines and vacuum cleaners. These changes were made in the interest of the export programme, and in order to encourage the transfer of resources away from production for the home market. In spite of these measures, the trade in such goods continued on the same level as, or even higher than, the previous year, although there was a recession in other industries, such as textiles.

Receipts from most branches of the Customs and Excise revenue declined in 1952–3, as the combined result of measures taken in 1952 to restore the balance of payments position and to check inflation, and of the downward trend in the price-level of many imported goods during the year. In spite of this, the total yield from the revenue exceeded that of the previous year. This was almost wholly due to large increases in the receipts from hydrocarbon oils resulting from an additional duty of $7\frac{1}{2}$d. per gallon imposed in the 1952 budget. The yield from the tobacco duty soared to £616¼ million, the highest yet recorded, being £3 million more than in the previous year. Despite reductions in certain rates, the purchase tax revenue from certain consumer goods decreased yet again. This was particularly true of textiles, thus reflecting the recession in demand, and the declining level of prices on the world market. The slight fall in receipts from the entertainment duty was partly attributable to reduced rates of duty, but principally to the general economic situation which limited marginal expenditure and had a particularly marked effect on attendances at race meetings, greyhound racing and football matches, which fell by about ten per cent, whereas the decline in cinema audiences was only about five per cent.

Towards the end of the financial year for 1952–3 a recovery in demand and business activity had begun to make itself felt and this continued progressively during 1953–4. Production continued to expand, and the terms of trade between the United Kingdom and the rest of the world continued to improve. Considerable relaxations in purchase tax were made under the Finance Act of 1953. Purchase tax rates which had previously stood at 100 per cent, 66⅔ per cent and 33⅓ per cent of the wholesale value were now reduced to 75 per cent, 50 per cent and 25 per cent respectively, some goods were subject to an even greater reduction, and some entirely exempted. Nevertheless, the total yield from the Customs and Excise was again higher than in the previous year, due mainly to increased revenues from tobacco, spirits and wine.

The import restrictions imposed in 1951 and 1952 were gradually withdrawn in 1953–4, and yet there was a considerable decline in receipts under the Import Duties Act. This was apparently due to the fall in the average price of imported goods which, of course, reduced the amount of ad valorem duty payable.

In October 1951 a committee had been appointed to review the organization of the Customs and Excise department and this produced its report in September 1953. As a result of its examination, the Committee said that in its view the general structure and organization of the department was sound, and that it had no fundamental criticism to offer. It did, however, make a number of recommendations and observations on particular aspects of the organization.

The budget of 1954 introduced only one significant revenue change in the revenue from indirect taxation; a reduction in the entertainments duty rates. The result was a fall of about £3 million in the revenue from this source as attendance at all types of dutiable entertainment continued to decline. The yield from purchase tax went up remarkably, reaching the record figure of £341·8 million. The largest increases were from gas and electric household appliances, radio and television sets and motor cars. The withdrawal of hire-purchase restrictions in July 1954 helped to maintain the high level of consumption. The total revenue of the department for 1954–5 rose by £97 million, and in 1955–6 exceeded £2,000 million. This last was an increase of over £120 million, and was the result of the continued high level of consumer demand in spite of the Bank Rate increase in February 1955 and renewed restrictions on hire purchase. Further attempts were made to arrest this tendency by imposing credit restrictions and restricting hire purchase even more tightly. In October, a second budget increased purchase and profits tax rates, reductions were made in public expenditure and in February 1956 even further restrictions were applied to hire purchase, the Bank Rate being raised to 5½ per cent, and food subsidies reduced.

The high level of consumer expenditure was particularly reflected in the increased yield from purchase tax, which rose by

£77 million, most of it from cars and durable consumer goods. The hydrocarbon oil duties also showed a substantial increase of £17 million, and the yield from tobacco rose by £19 million. The exceptionally fine summer tended to depress the revenue from the entertainments duty, but augmented that from drinks, in particular from beer.

The principal fiscal change affecting the Customs and Excise in 1956–7 was an increase of three shillings per lb. in the tobacco duty. In spite of counter-inflationary measures introduced in the previous financial year, the total yield now reached £2,108·4 million. A slackening in demand was, however, noticeable in the first half of the year, and the impact on the revenue was most pronounced in the receipts from purchase tax on durable consumer goods and motor cars. Later in the year, a new strain on the economy was imposed by the troubles in the Middle East, which resulted in the closing of the Suez Canal. The consequential interruption in oil supplies led to the rationing of this commodity for use in road vehicles, and in order to guard against a loss of revenue, a temporary increase in the hydrocarbon oil duties was imposed in December 1956.

The Finance Act of 1957 exempted from entertainments duty all admissions to entertainments other than cinematograph and television shows, and imposed a new duty on television receiving licences of £1 per annum. The same act reduced purchase tax from 30 per cent to 15 per cent on a wide range of household goods. In the early part of the financial year, the effects of the Suez Crisis were still reducing oil supplies and raising import prices, but in May, 1957, petrol rationing ended and the demand for motor cars revived. An important piece of legislation, so far as the Customs and Excise were concerned, was introduced by the Import Duties Act of 1958 which integrated protective duties into a single structure, and contained the authority for the introduction of an entirely new tariff classification based on the Brussels Nomenclature.

During 1958–9 restraints which had been imposed on the economy to check inflation were gradually removed, and this was reflected in the higher receipts from purchase tax, although the

Finance Act of 1958 had reduced the rate of tax on a considerable range of goods. Receipts from the duties on tobacco, football matches, pool-betting, and from the protective tariff duties, also responded to the upward trend, but expenditure on alcoholic drinks fell and the consumption of beer was reduced substantially. The revenue from beer dropped by nearly £8 million and in the budget the following year the duty was reduced, the total revenue receipts for 1959–60 rising by £94 million to £2,282·6 million. Tobacco still led the field by producing £788·5 million, purchase tax drew in £501·5 million, hydrocarbon oils £381 million, beer £218·9 million, spirits £145·5 million, and the protective duties £136·5 million.

In recent years, duties and taxes have been increased in order to reduce domestic demand for certain products so that the balance of payments position might be improved. In 1966 the regular surcharge of 10 per cent was applied to the duties on spirits, beer, wine, hydrocarbon oils and purchase tax. The surcharge was withdrawn in the 1967 budget, but the substantive rates of duty were increased to the surcharge-inclusive level, and a temporary charge on imports which came into effect in October 1964 was withdrawn on 30th November 1966.

The use of hydrocarbon oils in both road transport and in industry continued to increase rapidly, and arrangements were made from time to time for further facilities to be given for industrial use. Provision was made for the use of rebated fuel oil in works trucks used on and near the works site, and also for the duty-free oils used as materials or solvents in the manufacture of other articles. Trade interests were consulted and a scheme was evolved whereby the duty-free delivery of oils would be allowed to authorized users who were prepared to enter into a bond covering such use. The misuse of rebated kerosene in road vehicles is still causing concern, and many vehicles have been detected using gas oil which had been marked with chemical tracers to discourage the practice.

In order to encourage exports, the government introduced an export rebates scheme which gave manufacturers relief from certain indirect taxes affecting production costs of exported goods manufactured in the United Kingdom, such as hydrocarbon oil duty, vehicle excise licence duty and purchase tax. Under the scheme, exporters received rebates calculated as percentages of the value of goods exported. In order to expedite the settling of export rebate claims, a mechanized central unit was set up at Lytham St. Annes. Subsequently, as a result of recommendations by the Geddes Shipbuilding Inquiry Committee, these rebates were extended to ships built in the United Kingdom for British owners as well as to those sold on the export market. The export rebates on all goods, other than ships built in the United Kingdom, were abolished in 1968.

In 1966 the department shed its probate responsibilities, a branch of work which had accompanied the Excise when it was amalgamated with the Customs in 1909. This had entailed the handling of applications for grants of probate or letters of administration in England and Wales, and for confirmation in Scotland, in the case of estates of small value. The Administration of Estates (Small Payments) Act of 1965, and the raising of the limit of liability, caused a great reduction in the number of cases to be dealt with by the department. A Committee was appointed by the President of the Probate, Divorce and Admiralty Division of the High Court to consider the position and it was recommended that additional probate offices should be provided throughout the country, and that probate work performed by the Customs and Excise department should be transferred to these offices.

More and more of the departmental work which can be adapted to automatic data processing is being transferred to the department's computer at Southend-on-Sea, and has included the Overseas Trade Accounts, the payment of pensioners and the departmental warehousing accounts. The implementation of the recommendations of a working party appointed to review the 'open' warehousing systems has also resulted in economies both for the traders and the department, a joint scheme is being developed by the Customs and the leading airlines for carrying out the documentation and control of imports at Heathrow London Airport by the most modern computer techniques.

Frequent attempts are made to smuggle substantial quantities of cannabis resin, and a number of cases involving stimulant drugs have recently occurred including one case of 100,000 tablets, while indecent and obscene books are also seized in increasing numbers.

A General Betting Duty of 2½ per cent on all bets with book-makers and totalisators was introduced in October 1966 and a licence duty was imposed on premises where gaming took place. These duties, together with those on football pools and fixed odds coupon betting, virtually covered all forms of organized gambling.

On 8th June 1966, the Queen formally opened the new east wing of the London Custom House. This part of the historic building had been destroyed in 1940, and had been most skilfully and tastefully restored so that the façade of the new portion blended perfectly with the older part of the building, and yet the interior was laid out and equipped in accordance with the most modern standards.

For the last hundred years the tobacco duty had led the field as a revenue producer for the department, but at length its hegemony has come to an end, and its yield has been exceeded by the hydro-carbon oil duty.

REVENUE EVASION IN THE TWENTIETH CENTURY

The evasion of Customs and Excise duties in the early part of the twentieth century was confined principally to the smuggling of tobacco goods, spirits and saccharin, and although there were some instances of large seizures of tobacco and spirits – for example, when 209 lbs. and 6 gallons of spirits were seized from two Dutch 'coopers' – the quantities in general appeared to be small compared with the previous century. A certain amount of illicit distillation still took place but seemed to be slight, apart from Ireland. Even here, the many illicit operations which were detected were usually carried on in a very small way.

The quantity of tobacco goods seized rose from 8,723 lbs. in 1905 to 12,372 lbs. in 1906, more than 5,000 lbs. of tobacco and cigars being seized from two Dutch 'coopers', the *Nordster* and the *Active*, which were captured by HMS *Argus* inside the three mile limit off the River Humber. Apparently a fleet of seven Dutch coopers was carrying on a flourishing business by shipping cargoes of tobacco and spirits in Holland and selling them to the crews of the fishing fleets at various places round the coast during the herring fishing season. The Board had attempted to prevent the smuggling of goods obtained from these ships by stationing extra preventive staff at certain fishing stations during the season, and Admiralty cruisers responsible for fishing vessels also kept a watch on the coast for unlawful landings.

Two large seizures of saccharin were made at this time. One package of 150 lbs. was found in London by the Customs detective service and another of 61 lbs. imported from Boulogne, was found at Folkestone concealed in casks containing earthenware.

An incident which occurred at Harwich in 1905 provides a typical example of the type of smuggling practised. A Customs officer, examining the baggage of a passenger from Antwerp, found 14 lbs. of tobacco hidden in the lining of a portmanteau. He then searched the passenger and discovered a further 13 lbs. concealed around his body in the fashion of a life-jacket. The offender was charged in the magistrates' court and the Customs officer who was giving evidence was somewhat non-plussed when one of the magistrates asked him it if was not possible that the accused was wearing the tobacco band on medical advice, as he had known of such a thing. The magistrates found the case proved, however, and the defendant was duly sentenced. An attempt of a different kind was foiled at Hull in the same year when two firemen from a Dutch steamer from Amsterdam tried to smuggle fifty-two lbs. of compressed tobacco by concealing it under ashes in the ship's stokehold. In Bristol at about the same time the steward of a Dutch ship was convicted for smuggling twenty-two lbs. of tobacco and two lbs. cigars which he had hidden in various parts of the ship. Thirteen lbs. of the tobacco were found underneath some biscuits in a tin box in the storeroom, a further nine lbs. and one lb. of cigars in a potato locker on deck, and the remainder of the cigars in the casing of a closet.

In North Shields in 1906, Customs officers found thirty-six bottles of brandy and four casks of Geneva concealed beneath a steward's bed on board the Belgian steamer, *Levinia*, and at about the same time at Middlesbrough, the second engineer of the German ship *Consul Poppe* was convicted of an attempt to smuggle 8 lbs. of tobacco and 9 lbs. of cigars which a Customs officer had found hidden behind woodwork in the ship. It had been cut free, and the small screws then removed and cleverly covered up with beading. The Collector of Customs, who was prosecuting, told the court that in all his experience he had never seen a smarter piece of work.

Another ingenious concealment of tobacco and cigars was detected by Customs officers on the steamer *Teal* in London. The goods were discovered in a hollowed-out cavity in the carpenter's bench, and it was stated in the Thames Court that the bench had apparently been used before for this purpose. Indeed, the carpenter seemed quite proud of his work. In sentencing him, the magistrate said he thought the carpenter might be 'proud' to pay the fine.

A considerable seizure of tobacco was made at Blyth when Customs officers found 699 lbs. hidden underneath some potatoes in the hold of the steamer *Ragusa*. As a result, the second and third mates and the cook of the vessel were jointly charged with attempted smuggling. They claimed that the tobacco was not intended for Blyth, but for Messina, but nevertheless they were heavily fined.

In May 1907 a Dutch cooper, the *Cosmopoliet*, was captured by HMS *Skipjack* within the three mile limit, off Cape Clear on the south-west coast of Ireland. It was found to be carrying a contraband cargo consisting mainly of tobacco, and the vessel and the goods, amounting to 3,592 lbs., were seized. The Board, however, failed to secure a conviction before the Justices of Skibbereen. The owners of the cooper appealed against the seizure, and the Board instituted proceedings in the High Court of Justice at Dublin for the condemnation of the ship and her cargo. Eventually the Lord Chief Baron gave judgment that the ship and her cargo should remain forfeited.

In many cases crew members were intercepted as they attempted to land contraband goods, and frequently suspected offenders were followed and premises searched. A large quantity of smuggled saccharin was, for instance, discovered by Preventive Inspectors of the Inland Revenue in the house of a mineral water manufacturer. Much of the saccharin was found in a bath, but some of it had been formed into discs made to look like table-tops. A number of empty discs were found. They had been imported as table-tops and were so well got up as to deceive anybody.

Another smuggling incident occurred at Queenborough Pier, involving a passenger, his wife, and baby. On disembarking from the *Engeland* from Flushing, the passenger's wife and children were passed unchallenged and took their seats in a railway carriage. The passenger himself, however, was found to be carrying some undeclared tobacco and cigars, and 4½ lbs. of tobacco and some cigars were discovered stuffed in a pillow. The officers then went to the train and questioned the passenger's wife. It turned out that a further 4 lbs. of tobacco and 1½ lbs. of cigars had been hidden underneath the baby. The passenger was charged, convicted, and fined.

A large seizure of tobacco was discovered at Hull on the SS *Mellifont* from Antwerp. As a result, a fireman was charged with smuggling 136 lbs. of compressed tobacco and 10 lbs. of Cavendish tobacco. These goods had been ingeniously concealed in the forced draught chamber leading from the engine-room to the boiler space.

One of the tasks of the Excise, now the responsibility of the amalgamated services, was the prevention of illicit distillation. Apart from Ireland, the problem seemed well under control. In the year ended March 1910 there were no seizures of illicit plant in England, and only four in Scotland. However, in Ireland there were 1,099 such seizures by the Royal Irish Constabulary, but this was considerably less than in 1901 when there were 2,008. In the same year several large seizures of tobacco were made, including one of 260 lbs. of tobacco and 116 lbs. of cigars at Hull, and one of 86 lbs. at London. 385 lbs. of saccharin were also found in two houses in London.

During the first financial year of the war, the number of seizures of smuggled goods dropped considerably; from 7,694 in the year ended 31st March 1914, to 3,637 in 1915, although large quantities of tobacco including 97 lbs. in London, and 227 lbs. and 313 lbs. at Grimsby, were confiscated. Only 13 lbs. of saccharin was seized during the same period. But the pattern was reversed the following year, when the number of seizures made rose sharply to 5,241. There was an extraordinary increase in the quantity of foreign spirits seized, which rose from 75 gallons to 351 gallons. The McKenna duties on motor cars, cycles, clocks and watches, and musical instruments had been introduced in 1915 and other duties had later been imposed on matches and mechanical lighters. From the beginning some attempts were made to evade these duties, but it was not until the war ended, when supplies became available abroad, that smuggling occurred on any significant scale. Detected smuggling continued at much the same level for the rest of the war and in 1918 there were 7,080 seizures of tobacco, cigars (6,489 lbs.) and foreign spirits (136 gallons). Immediately after the war there was a great change. In 1919 over 10,380 seizures were made of tobacco goods and spirits. The quantity of tobacco involved rose to 10,117 lbs. and of spirits to 170 gallons. Oddly enough, the number of persons fined for smuggling dropped from 3,496 to 3,290.

In 1921 the introduction of the Key Industry duties and the prohibition placed on importing certain types of plumage enlarged the field to be covered by the Customs and Excise service. An interesting attempt to evade the latter prohibition occurred in 1923. An officer in a South Coast port was dealing with the consignment of cases supposed to contain imported eggs. One can judge of his surprise when he opened one of them and found it full of dead, legless birds. They were not of a kind he recognized, having brightly-coloured plumage, and he therefore sent them to the Natural History Museum for identification. The experts there were also puzzled, for although the birds obviously belonged to the Bird of Paradise family, they were unable to decide on the exact grouping or habitat of this particular variety; in other words, it was an unknown species. Extensive enquiries were made, and it eventually transpired that the species was only found in the Fly River area of New Guinea where the natives customarily cut off the legs on capture; this custom had apparently given rise to the assumption that the birds were born legless.

THE INVESTIGATION BRANCH

The introduction of the Import Duties Act in 1932 meant that many investigations had to be made in connection with the under-valuation of consignments of imported goods. A great deal of this work was carried out by what was then called the Special Inquiry Staff, which might be described as the detective branch of the Customs and Excise. This service had been built up gradually in the early part of the century from a nucleus of officers known as the Special Service Staff, which had itself been formed from three separate bodies; a small Customs unit of Special Duty officers which had functioned from about 1887, a detective crew of Preventive officers, and an Excise Detective service which had also begun to function in 1887. The Excise unit had been replaced by a detective branch under a Detective Inspector in 1895. When the Special Service Staff was established on the amalgamation of Customs and Excise in 1909, Alfred W. Cope became the Preventive Inspector of the combined unit and remained in this position until 1913, when he entered the office of the Chief Inspector of Customs and Excise. Cope, later Sir Alfred Cope, subsequently became Assistant Under-Secretary for Ireland and Clerk of the Irish Privy Council, and from 1922 to 1924 was General Secretary of the National Liberal Organization.

The type of work in which this staff was involved before the first world war was mainly confined to detecting illicit distillations, collecting information in connection with attempts to defraud the revenue, and co-operating with the Landing and Waterguard departments in following up 'referred' cases; that is, cases which were considered to require further investigation. After the war, the branch extended its attention to the problems of under-valuation in connection with the importation of ad valorem goods, and there was a great deal of work to be done in preventing illicit imports of many goods previously in short supply. The return of the armed forces to this country also led to a sharp increase in smuggling and, for the first few years after the Armistice, the quantities of seized tobacco and spirits rose sharply.

During the thirties, the duty on hydrocarbon oils was increased by degrees and, at the same time, road transport was rapidly expanding. The Special Service Staff had therefore to expend a great deal of time and effort in the difficult task of discovering whether hydrocarbon oil which had been exempted from duty for particular purposes, such as agricultural use, was not, in fact, being used as road transport fuel. The development of the aircraft industry also added to the revenue risks. Although legislation had been passed to prevent aircraft from abroad from landing goods at unauthorized places, it was very difficult to detect such landings. A great deal of reliance had to be placed on information received from the police and from other sources. At this time smuggling by air was obviously only profitable if confined to small articles of high value, such as saccharin and cigars.

The introduction of the Import Duties Act, which imposed an ad valorem duty on most classes of imported goods, loaded an enormous amount of extra work on the Special Inquiry Staff, as the service was now called, in dealing with under-valuation. The staff consequently had to be expanded to cope with the new situation. Customs officers responsible for examining and clearing cargoes would refer any cases of suspected fraud to the Special Inquiry staff, and the Inquiry officers themselves initiated investigations into the type of trade where fraud might be expected. Information was regularly received, anonymously or otherwise, and this had to be followed up. Investigation work now also involved the examination of business accounts and invoices, and this called for some knowledge of commercial and accountancy procedures.

The regular smuggling of tobacco goods and spirits continued, and a profitable trade had also sprung up in contraband mechanical lighters. Many of these found their way into the United Kingdom via the Irish Free State, where the import duty on lighters was much less than it was in this country. At the same time, the tariff war between the United Kingdom and the Irish Free State, which began in 1932 when this country placed a twenty per cent duty on all goods from the Free State, called for a much stricter investigation of the traffic between the two countries. The smuggling of greyhounds and the false declaration of the value of horses were among the items which had to be dealt with.

In the last financial year before the outbreak of the second world war seizures of smuggled goods numbered 9,611, of which only 3,671 consisted of tobacco and spirits. The quantity of tobacco seized amounted to 2,025 lbs., and of spirits to 175 gallons. There was an enormous increase in the number of detected smuggling attempts in the early years of the war. Seizures rose from 6,757 in 1940–1 to 15,634 in 1941–2, and the number of persons convicted in those years numbered 2,595 and 5,329 respectively.

The raising of duty on light hydrocarbon oil used in motor vehicles to eightpence per gallon, while the duty on heavy oils remained at one penny per gallon, obviously provided opportunities for fraud. Petrol garages frequently sold adulterated petrol which had been mixed with paraffin oils. More and more commercial vehicles now tended to run on diesel oil, so the duty on heavy oil was raised to eightpence per gallon when used as fuel in road vehicles. However, as farm tractors, stationary engines, and so forth, were still able to use oil at the penny per gallon rate, it was soon obvious that farmers and others were tempted to use the low duty oil in road vehicles. Frequent checks were therefore made of the records which users were now compelled to keep of the oil they purchased and the mileage covered. During the second world war, the effect of petrol rationing was to increase the incidence of fraud by using exempted oils as road fuel.

The measure which probably had the greatest impact on the

Special Inquiry staff at this time, however, was the introduction of purchase tax in 1940. When the tax was in its infancy, many of the traders who now became liable to it felt that evasion would not be difficult by falsifying the quarterly returns they were required to make. This led to a large number of prosecutions, but, as time went on, traders became more sophisticated in their methods and the task of detecting fraud was rendered more difficult.

By the end of March 1945, seizures of smuggled goods had leapt to 19,694, and over 14,000 of these were of tobacco and spirits. Liquor licence evasions rose to 110 in the same period. After the war, however, revenue frauds of all kinds were perpetrated on an ever-increasing scale. The war had restricted trade in most articles, and others had been almost impossible to obtain. Nylon stockings and watches were now being smuggled on a commercial scale, mainly because of their scarcity value, but in the latter case also because of the duty and purchase tax to which they were subject. In the first year after the war there were 344 detected attempts to evade wartime prohibitions, 148 purchase tax cases, 103 liquor licence cases and 23 attempts to evade the entertainment duty.

Tobacco goods and spirits were still regularly smuggled, and of over 22,000 seizures of contraband made in the financial year ending in 1947, two-thirds consisted of these commodities. Other goods in short supply or subject to restriction were smuggled on a large scale, and these included foodstuffs, combs, hair-grips and cosmetics. The quantities involved were often so great as to suggest they were in fact commercial consignments.

There was an almost ceaseless flow of contraband nylon stockings from the United States, brought over mainly by seamen. Large numbers of watches were irregularly imported by both passengers and seamen, who used ingenious devices, old and new, to escape detection: double-bottomed suitcases, pockets sewn inside specially-made waistcoats or corsets, and skilfully-constructed hiding places in motor cars. Hollowed-out books were used to conceal small articles of high value, such as watches and jewellery, and hollowed-out shoe soles to carry gold and currency. In 1950–1, nearly 60,000 watches were seized, compared to 40,000 in the previous financial year. A certain amount of drug smuggling took place after the war; it was confined mainly to opium, but quantities of cannabis (hashish) were beginning to appear.

A large number of fast naval motor torpedo boats were sold off after the war as navy surplus stores, and some people seized the opportunity they offered for making contraband 'runs'. One such craft was the *Dawn Approach*. This former naval MTB was used by its enterprising owner to make twenty-three successful 'runs', in the first instance smuggling pearls, then nylon stockings, and finally limiting its operations to watches. The owner constantly changed the place where the contraband was landed and at one time or another the vessel called at Ipswich, Weymouth, Yarmouth, Ramsgate, Dover, Newhaven, Scarborough, Shoreham and the Helford River. In due course Customs officers began to take some interest in this craft, and in Newhaven she was subjected to a rigorous search, but neither contraband nor hiding-places were discovered. On her twenty-fourth trip, the *Dawn Approach* loaded watches at Cherbourg and made for Beaumaris in the Menai Straits, where successful landings had been made previously. But a Customs investigation officer had observed the operations at Cherbourg, and other investigation officers were keeping watch on the car which was known to collect the watches and take them to London. The car was followed from London to Anglesey, and when the *Dawn Approach* arrived, a load of watches was transferred to it from the vessel. The investigation officers trailed the car back to London hoping to discover the organizers of the racket, but in the event they were forced to intercept the car in London. More than 13,000 watches were found inside it. In the course of their inquiries officers discovered some papers from which they were able to reconstruct the whole story. The watches had apparently been concealed in a space between the engine-room bulkhead and a cabin. Access to the hiding-place could only be obtained by removing a bathroom cabinet in the ladies' washplace. Later the *Dawn Approach* was seized as forfeit.

Investigations in connection with evasion of import and export licensing controls also provided plenty of work for the investigation staff. Painstaking examination of masses of documents was frequently necessary in order to establish proof of fraud. An unusual deception was uncovered when an attempt was made to import a large consignment of butter by describing it as 'sweetfat'. New methods of defrauding the revenue were increasingly practised, in addition to what might be termed the more orthodox smuggling of tobacco goods and spirits. Revenue was evaded by the false declaration of value of imported goods, and false returns were made to avoid purchase tax on goods such as stationery, radio equipment and toys.

The Investigation Branch, as the Inquiry staff had been renamed in 1948, also had to deal with a spate of watch smuggling in cars arriving in the passenger ports. In this they co-operated with the Waterguard department, but much detective work had to be done behind the scenes. Sometimes watches were concealed in the upholstery, sometimes in hollow parts of the chassis, and sometimes in specially-made compartments, particularly in the petrol tank.

Watch smuggling on a commercial scale continued long after the war, 7,000 being seized in 1956-7 and seventeen people being convicted of such offences. This form of smuggling only really began to abate once the EFTA reductions in duty were gradually introduced. By the middle of 1966, when the duty on EFTA watches and all quota restrictions had been removed, the large-scale smuggling of watches had virtually ended. However, since the import deposit scheme was introduced, there have been signs of a revival; 2,800 watches were recently found concealed inside a car. It is probable that purchase tax, together with the import deposit payment, has made watch smuggling a profitable business once again.

Tobacco and cigar smuggling also seems to be on the increase. Vessels have been shipping excessive stores of tobacco goods on the continent and then off-loading them into fishing boats at sea for landing in this country. Recently there was a seizure in Dartmouth of about 4 million cigarettes which had been exported from the United Kingdom to Tangiers and then re-imported. The organizer of the 'run' was fined £25,000 and sentenced to twelve months' imprisonment, and the captain of the smuggling vessel was sentenced to nine months' imprisonment.

In recent years the Investigation Branch has had to deal with serious cases of purchase tax conspiracy and fraud, as well as many valuation frauds, particularly in connection with the importation of amusement machines. Fraudulent attempts to import many other articles, such as watches, sewing machines, cameras, jewellery, mechanical lighters and currency, have also occupied the time of the Branch. Investigation of large-scale gold exports has resulted in the conviction of offenders, who were punished with long terms of imprisonment, and a number of currency offences have been discovered, including an attempt to export £30,000 in Bank of England notes. The offender in this case was fined £25,000.

Hydrocarbon oil frauds in connection with road transport have demanded the attention of the Branch from time to time, but after 1960, when an efficient method of 'marking' low duty heavy oil was found, Customs Road Fuel Testing Units were set up so that fuel used in road vehicles could be examined at any time and the constant checking of documents could be relaxed. Hydrocarbon oil frauds still occur, however, and recently there have been a number of important prosecutions in this connection. The drive against offences of this kind has been intensified, and the Investigation Branch and Outdoor Service are co-operating closely in the struggle.

In recent years a changing pattern has appeared in the smuggling of dangerous drugs. The trade in opium has almost ceased, but the smuggling of other drugs has increased, and some very large seizures have been made. One of the largest consisted of half-a-ton of cannabis resin, which was concealed inside trade consignments of pickles and similar goods from Pakistan. Investigations into the manufacture of the drug LSD have also been carried out. Eventually one of the carriers of this drug to the USA was arrested and subsequently sentenced to eighteen months' imprisonment. The quantity involved was the largest consignment of this particular drug yet seized at that time. Increased immigration from certain Commonwealth countries in recent years has led to a growth in illicit distillation, but the quantities do not appear to be great and the circulation of the spirit has, in general, been confined to the community producing it.

WATERGUARD DEPARTMENT

During the post-war period the Waterguard department has had to deal with an infinite variety of smuggling offences. Immediately after the end of the war the emphasis was on the smuggling of goods in short supply. Apart from the orthodox smuggling of tobacco, cigarettes and spirits, there were numerous attempts throughout the country to import articles such as foodstuffs, combs, cycle covers and tubes, watches, birdseed, lipsticks and other cosmetics, hair-grips, currency, arms and ammunition, fountain pens, opium, jewellery, cameras and accessories, gramophone records, saccharin, razor blades, wallpaper and nylon stockings. By 1951, supplies were much more easily obtainable, but large quantities of foodstuffs and nylon stockings were still being illicitly imported. The greatest danger to the revenue, however, came from the increased smuggling of watches, particularly at London Airport and Dover. The smuggling of cameras, jewellery and dangerous drugs also rose significantly, and it is noticeable that while opium smuggling seemed to be on the decrease, the smuggling of cannabis resin (hashish) was much greater than ever before. An interesting phenomenon of this period was the great upsurge in the export smuggling of coffee by the crews of vessels bound for coffee-drinking countries in Europe, where it had become a medium of barter.

The manning of the Irish land boundary led to some staff difficulties in 1951 when the Royal Ulster Constabulary, by agreement, relinquished its part in the patrolling and preventive work. The department gradually took over full responsibility, and was consequently obliged to employ considerable extra staff and established a system of mobile patrols. The revenue protection problem in this area was considerable, as organized gangs of smugglers, often violent, were running large cargoes of contraband across the border by car and lorry. In order to cope with the situation, it was decided that all Customs patrol cars should be equipped with wireless to enable them to call for assistance when required. The Customs force, unlike its predecessor, remained unarmed, and although there were difficulties, this policy seems to have proved itself as there have been few acts of violence. The smuggling of cigarettes, nevertheless, continued unabated and in one instance, two specially adapted cars were intercepted carrying nearly 200,000 cigarettes.

In more recent years there has again been a change of pattern. The variety of goods smuggled is not so great, but the quantities involved remain as large as ever. In places like London Airport and Dover smugglers seem to concentrate on high-value articles such as cameras, watches and jewellery. In the Port of London the emphasis is on cigarettes, spirits, cameras, lighters and clocks and watches; in Southampton, on cameras, lighters and watches; while in Cardiff the traffic is mainly confined to cigarettes and lighters. In Liverpool substantial quantities of the following goods have been smuggled in recent years: tobacco, cigarettes, spirits, cameras, nylon hose, optical goods, mechanical lighters and watches. In Manchester, lighters and watches, while in Belfast, the illicit trade seems mainly to be in tobacco and cigarettes. In the Glasgow area, cigarettes and lighters, and in Leith, cigarettes, lighters and watches. The same articles are smuggled in the Newcastle area; in Hull the emphasis is on tobacco, cigarettes, spirits, lighters and watches, and in Harwich on cigarettes, cameras, optical instruments and watches.

As a result of co-operation between the Investigation Branch and the Waterguard, a seizure of 11,294 watches was made from a Jaguar car arriving from Harwich. The watches were concealed in welded compartments behind the rear seat. Smuggling by aircraft became more common in the sixties, and on one occasion at Lulsgate (Bristol) Airport a quantity of tobacco, cigarettes, spirits and cigars was smuggled in hidden under the floor-boards of the aircraft. A passenger from Tangier at London Airport concealed 8¾ lbs. of cannabis resin in the linings of her coat and hand-bag and inside a torch from which the batteries had been removed. In many packet ports and airports significant quantities of watches have been smuggled in body belts. At Manchester Airport in September 1963 a passenger from Paris tried to smuggle as many as 539 in this manner. A passenger at London Airport concealed 500 watches in a girdle round her waist, and on a different occasion a man disguised as a clergyman attempted to smuggle 300 watches by the same method. A female accomplice was carrying 100 watches. At Gatwick Airport a Pakistani passenger arriving from Geneva failed to declare three ruby necklaces valued at £2,720.

In 1963 in Glasgow, after the police had seized a quantity of cigarettes, Customs officers searched a Danish ship and found over 37,000 cigarettes, 20 lbs. of tobacco and nearly five gallons of spirits in a false compartment and a cabin lining. At Middlesbrough 6,200 cigarettes and 4½ gallons of brandy were found beneath the cargo, in spaces between the side of the ship and a tank, and under boards in the ship's tunnel. In Liverpool in 1964, 380,000 cigarettes were found concealed on a Danish vessel, and a haul of 74,000 cigarettes was made as they were being landed from a fishing vessel at Teignmouth in August of the same year. At Rochester in 1966, officers intercepted the crew of a Finnish ship in process of landing 67,400 cigarettes, as well as some tobacco and spirits, all of which had been concealed in the ship's hold.

Throughout the sixties regular seizures of cannabis resin have been made. One consignment of over 70 lbs. was found in the baggage of a United States passenger bound for New York. Other dangerous drugs seized include opium and amphetamine sulphate tablets, 8,750 of which were found on a Swedish steamer in 1965. They were packed in a plastic bag concealed at the bottom of a tin of 'Foamite'. In the same year, 310 of these tablets were found on another Swedish vessel behind a storage tank in the engine-room, and in a toilet roll in the engine-room store-room.

There have been many outward seizures of currency, particularly at packet ports and airports. £1,190 in sterling notes was taken at London Airport in May, 1966, £1,465 at the same airport in September, and £970 at Dover. A seizure of as much as £30,000 was made at London Airport in December of that year. More recently, a passenger at the same airport bound for Malaga had £2,645 in sterling notes and five pieces of jewellery valued at £2,245 concealed in personal baggage.

Attempts to evade the revenue on cameras are frequently made by falsely declaring the period of possession abroad or by producing false receipts to support the alleged value. Attempts are also made to import cars illegally by making false claims for temporary import facilities. In May 1969, an attempt was made to introduce four Mercedes Benz cars in this manner. Obscene books and photographs are seized from time to time. Recently 1,050 obscene books were found at Harwich concealed in the door lining of a passenger's car, and in the back of the driver's seat. On the Belfast land boundary at Newry police and Customs officers co-operated in seizing 2,250,000 (one ton) of Irish Sweepstake tickets, worth about £2¼ million.

To sum up, there does not seem to have been any let-up in attempts to defraud the revenue or to evade import and export control and prohibitions, but certain general tendencies are noticeable. The swing towards the smuggling of cigars has already been referred to, and the move away from the smuggling of opium. However, the great increase in the smuggling of cannabis and more sophisticated drugs has more than made up for the latter tendency. Watches for a time ceased to attract smugglers but, as has already been mentioned, there are signs that the introduction of import deposits has provided an incentive for the renewal of this traffic.

INTERNATIONAL CUSTOMS CO-OPERATION

One of the outstanding features of the post-war era is the growth of international co-operation in Customs matters. The war-time alliances, followed by peace-time associations for defensive purposes, no doubt helped to foster the idea of international co-operation in other fields, and on 30th October 1947 the General Agreement on Tariffs and Trade was concluded at Geneva. As a result of United Kingdom participation, the British rates of duty on many articles were reduced or 'bound' against increase, principally those falling under the Import Duties Act, but also some Ottawa and Key Industry duties.

The following year some further changes in rates of duty were made, arising from the United Nations Conferences on Trade and Employment, which were held at Geneva and Havana. The possibility of creating a European Customs Union was also investigated at about this time, and work was begun on the formation of a common tariff nomenclature. In spite of the intricacy of such an operation, the first version of the draft nomenclature was ready towards the end of 1948. A study was undertaken with the aim of achieving greater tariff uniformity among the European countries, and the principles of Customs valuation and general procedure were also considered. Members of the Customs and Excise department participated in the discussions on civil aviation at the meetings of the International Civil Aviation Organization. The rapid development of international road transport in the post-war years posed new problems in this field, and an International Working Party on Customs procedure relating to road transport was set up. Conventions were drawn up covering the treatment of touring vehicles, vessels and aircraft, commercial road vehicles and the international transport of goods.

Interest in the promotion of international tourist traffic led to a general examination of duty-free concessions to travellers by the Organization for European Economic Co-operation. As a result, recommended practice was urged upon member countries of the OEEC in an attempt to bring these concessions into alignment.

The New York Convention on tourist allowances was concluded in 1954.

In the fifties, international customs co-operation continued, and two more international committees were convened under the auspices of UNESCO in order to formulate action which could be taken to reduce barriers to the free flow of educational scientific and cultural materials. This resulted in the drawing up of two Agreements providing for the free importation of such materials. Further consideration was also given to the question of a common tariff nomenclature and to the rules for valuation which had been prepared by the European Customs Union Study Group. An International Conference took place at Torquay in 1950, when all the existing tariff concessions under the General Agreement of Tariffs and Trade were reviewed, and further reductions in some United Kingdom tariffs were conceded.

During the next few years, discussions were held on the question of collaboration between European Customs administrations against smuggling and other offences. The department was also represented at Geneva in 1952 at a meeting on the Customs treatment of lift-van containers and similar transport equipment.

Three international Conventions were drawn up in Brussels, providing for the adoption by participating countries of a common classification of goods for their Customs tariffs, a common definition of value as a basis for Customs ad valorem duties, and the setting up of a Customs Co-operation Council. The United Kingdom adhered to all these Conventions. The Convention establishing the Customs Co-operation Council (CCC) came into force in 1952, and the first session was held in Brussels in January 1953. Under the Convention, the Council was required to make recommentations to ensure the uniform interpretation and application of the Conventions on nomenclature and valuation, to perform such functions as were expressly assigned to it in those Conventions, and to act in a conciliatory capacity in any disputes arising. The Council had the further tasks of studying questions relating to co-operation in Customs matters, examining the technical aspects of Customs systems with a view to proposing practical means of attaining the utmost harmony and uniformity, furnishing information to member states, and co-operating with other international organizations. A United Kingdom Customs delegation was permanently maintained at Brussels on the nomenclature work, and in June 1956, the Deputy Chairman of the Board of Customs and Excise was elected Chairman of the Council.

The work of the CCC was actively continued in the sixties, the number of member states increasing considerably. In May, 1960, the Nomenclature Committee replaced the interim committee previously responsible for matters concerning the Brussels tariff nomenclature and held several meetings during which a large number of questions on the classification of goods were dealt with. The Committee also prepared a correlation between the Brussels Nomenclature and the United Nations Standard International Trade Classification (SITC), and had the assistance of a committee of experts to advice upon technical questions involving chemicals.

The Permanent Technical Committee of the CCC considered the facilities for the temporary importation of packings and certain equipment necessary to persons travelling abroad in the exercise of their calling or profession. As a result of their deliberations, a Customs Convention on Packings and a Convention on the Temporary Importation of Professional Equipment were drawn up and discussed with representatives of GATT (General Agreement on Tariffs and Trade) and other international organizations before eventual approval by the Council. A further subject studied by this Committee was the Customs treatment of goods imported for display and use at exhibitions and a Convention dealing with this question as well was drawn up and adopted by the Council. All three Conventions were signed by the United Kingdom. This Committee also considered postal traffic, the simplification and harmonization of Customs documents, warehousing, drawbacks and temporary admission, the Customs treatment of registered baggage carried by rail, current clearance procedures for air cargo, and a glossary of international Customs terms. In addition, a series of 'International Customs Norms' were prepared to encourage the development and improvement of procedures in member countries over the whole field of Customs techniques.

One of the principal subjects of international discussion during the fifties was the abolition of tariff barriers in Europe. The decision to form the European Economic Community was taken at Messina in 1955, and the Community was finally established by the Treaty of Rome in 1957. As Britain was not one of the six member countries of this organization, she proceeded energetically with the discussions towards the formation of a wider European Free Trade Area. From the Customs point of view the principal difference between the two concepts was that the EEC was to become a trading area with no internal tariffs or quotas, and a single external tariff and quota structure, leading eventually to the complete harmonization of the members' external commercial policies (including tariffs); the EFTA system, on the other hand, involved only the abolition of tariffs on trade between its members but no harmonization of their tariffs on imports from outside countries.

The European Free Trade Association was finally established at Stockholm in November 1959, the member countries being Austria, Denmark, Norway, Portugal, Sweden, Switzerland, the United Kingdom, and later Finland. Following the Stockholm Convention, many further meetings took place in Vienna, London, Paris and Geneva, as a great deal of preparatory work had to be done to implement the Agreement. Among other things, existing legislation governing the treatment of goods for the purpose of import duties had to be adapted to the new circumstances, and it was necessary to make provision for the verification of the origin of goods traded between the United Kingdom and other EFTA countries, in order to ensure that non-EFTA goods were not receiving favourable Customs treatment in the guise of EFTA goods. Penalties also had to be established to deal with cases where untrue documents were produced. The EFTA Council set up a number of subsidiary committees, including a Customs Committee which was required to enforce co-operative and effective administration of those provisions of the Convention affecting duties and taxes. This Committee, including representatives from the United Kingdom, has met regularly in Geneva in order to fulfil this task.

The separate establishment of these two economic communities did not mean the withdrawal of the United Kingdom from active co-operation with members of the EEC, for this country continued to work with those organizations on which both groups were represented, such as the OEEC, UNESCO, the CCC, the Economic Commission for Europe (ECE), and the International Civil Aviation Organization (ICAO). In October 1961, however, the government of the United Kingdom made a formal approach to the EEC with a view to becoming a member of the Community, but although the negotiations for admission were suspended in 1963, the department continued to maintain close contact with the Customs services of the EEC, and the progress of Customs changes in the Community were carefully observed.

The department was represented on a panel of experts which met under the auspices of GATT to consider the question of simplifying and eventually abolishing consular formalities in connection with imported goods. An ECE Working Party discussed the simplification and standardization of export documents, while at the fourth session of the European Civil Aviation Conference, various aspects of Customs procedures and documentation were discussed in relation to their effect on air traffic.

Other international meetings with which the department was concerned included the Facilitation Division of ICAO which held its sixth session in Mexico City in 1963, the Inter-governmental Marine Consultative Organization (IMCO) which studied the question of maritime travel and transport, the Inland Transport Committee of the ECE, the Council of Europe Committee of Experts on the production and marketing of wine products and spirits, the United Nations Conference on international travel and tourism, a working party of the Conference Europeenne des Administrations de Postes et des Telecommunications (CEPT), the Tourism Committee of the Organization for Economic Co-operation and Development (OECD), and the fifth session of the European Civil Aviation Conference at Strasbourg in 1964.

Negotiations over the establishment of a Free Trade Area between the United Kingdom and the Republic of Ireland resulted in the Anglo-Irish Trade Agreement which came into force in July 1966. The Customs department was mainly affected by the provision in the Agreement that goods originating in and consigned from the Republic of Ireland should be admitted free of protective duties. Goods affected included clocks and watches, musical instruments, and motor vehicles and parts.

Commonwealth relations were not neglected, and the department was represented at the meetings of a Working Party of the Commonwealth Economic Committee, to study ways in which the Certificates of Origin and Value used in trade between Commonwealth countries might be simplified and standardized. It was also represented in a working party of the Council of OECD which studied the economic, fiscal and trade aspects of present practices for the adjustment of internal taxation with regard to goods traded across international frontiers, and in a GATT working party on related questions in the field of border tax adjustments.

Members of the department have always given close study to the Customs practices of other countries. In 1966, for example, there were visits to nine countries, on which studies were made of the procedures used for controlling passenger traffic and mechanical freight handling in the United States and Denmark, mechanized accounting in the Customs clearance of imported goods in Germany and Switzerland, and the compilation of trade statistics in France. Through these and similar studies, and through work in the CCC, it has been possible for the Customs administrations of the United Kingdom and of other countries to profit from each others' experiences and to establish mutual assistance in resolving common problems.

On 31st December 1966 the final reduction in protective duties under the EFTA Convention was made, and from that date no United Kingdom Customs duty was chargeable under the Import Duties Act of 1958 on goods (other than certain agricultural and fishery products) provided they were of EFTA origin, were consigned from EFTA countries, and had not benefited from drawback or similar duty relief from protective duties in the EFTA country of production. In recent years the CCC has dealt with a great variety of matters, including improved Customs treatment of postal traffic (in co-operation with the International Postal Union), a study of the comparative procedure for allowing draw-back on exported goods, an International Customs Norm on the right of appeal in Customs matters and recommendations on the treatment of re-imported goods.

The Council has also occupied itself with the problems arising from the development of international containerized traffic, and in this connection the Permanent Technical Committee was in-structed to draft a Convention for the international through Customs-transit procedure for all kinds of unit loads. Continuing its co-operation with UNESCO, the Committee also prepared a Convention on the temporary importation of scientific equipment for research or educational purposes, and made recommendations on Customs sealing systems used in connection with international traffic. The CCC, which began purely as a European organization, has since acquired members in all five continents, and at the time of writing there are sixty member states.

PAST, PRESENT AND FUTURE

When one examines the development of the Customs and Excise system of taxation a clear pattern emerges. In Saxon and Norman times a system of tolls in kind had grown up, and 'prisage' seems to have been the first attempt of the Norman kings to obtain their perquisites of office. As trade developed, it was to the advantage of the king to accept money payments in lieu of payments in kind, particularly in the case of exports of wool, woolfells and hides, on which a monetary tax appears to have been imposed from the beginning. Local tolls also proliferated, and no real attempt was made to centralize taxation until the time of King John. Early kings always seemed to be short of ready money for the up-keep of their establishments and for the financing of their wars, and it became normal for them to farm their taxes to merchants or syndicates of merchants in return for advance payments. In the Middle Ages, financing of this kind was carried on principally by the merchants of Northern Italy, many of whom found the business of farming the Customs so profitable that they settled in London and established a financial community there. This system was not peculiar to Britain but existed in most European countries at this time. In England, the king from time to time resorted to methods of direct collection, but farming continued to be the normal system of collection of revenues until 1671. It probably reached its height in the days of Elizabeth I when trade was increasing rapidly, and when Sir Thomas Smythe was able to make a substantial fortune out of his operations. On the outbreak of the Civil War, the Long Parliament decided to appoint Commissioners of Customs to organize the direct collection of duties, and likewise the newly instituted Excise. Later, however, both these revenues were put out to 'farm' and it was only when Charles II appointed new Commissioners of Customs in 1671, and of Excise in 1683, that the farming of the revenue finally ceased in this country.

No doubt there had been a great deal of revenue evasion during the farming period as most people did not consider it a crime to defraud the farmers, and the numerous prohibitions, particularly on the export of wool, led to regular attempts at evasion. In general, however, duties were not sufficiently high to make the smuggling of most goods financially attractive. After the Glorious Revolution, and the involvement of this country in the War of the Spanish Succession, however, the duties on tea and brandy were raised enormously to provide money for the war, and large scale evasion on an unprecedented scale took place, continuing during the whole of the eighteenth century and early nineteenth century.

The general attitude of the population towards both Customs and Excise was one of defiance, and all sections of the community, including the magistrates and clergy, conspired to defraud the revenue. There is no doubt that the aristocracy and well-to-do merchants were able to avoid much of this taxation on account of their privileged position, and the enormous scale of evasion in the eighteenth century would suggest that many merchants were behind the smuggling organizations. Many lives were lost in the violent encounters between smugglers and Custom officers.

After the Napoleonic Wars, the arguments of Adam Smith prevailed, and English statesmen became accustomed to the idea of reducing duties. As they were made lighter or were repealed altogether, the incentive for smuggling most goods obviously disappeared. By 1860, when the United Kingdom adopted a policy of free trade, smuggling was virtually confined to tobacco goods and spirits. Violence was almost entirely a thing of the past.

From this time onwards, the tobacco duty became the principal source of Customs revenue in this country, and was closely followed by the revenue from beer and spirits. The Excise duty on home-produced beer and spirits had also grown enormously. Certain ad valorem duties were introduced during the first world war, but these did not have a great deal of impact on revenue and revenue evasion. After the war, however, there were signs of an upsurge in smuggling. But the Import Duties Act of 1932 was the most decisive factor determining a change in the pattern, since Customs control had now to be exercised over an enormous variety of goods.

Methods of enforcement altered as well, physical control of all articles liable to tax becoming virtually impossible. Many articles had to be scientifically analysed before rates of duty could be determined and methods of checking valuations had to be evolved. Detailed investigations were frequently made into firms' accounts and the investigating officers had to be acquainted with methods of accountancy. The introduction of hydrocarbon oil duties after the war, and gradual increases in the rate during the inter-war years, led to the need for a stricter control of the oil used in road transport. Oil employed in other ways was exempted or allowed at a reduced rate, and it was very difficult to prevent the frauds which resulted.

The next measure which made a great impact on development of the Customs and Excise Service was the imposition of purchase tax in 1940. Originally introduced as a temporary wartime measure it has proved to be a most successful method of revenue collection as it is imposed at the wholesale level and is, therefore, easier to collect than if imposed at retail level. But the problems involved in preventing fraud are nevertheless great. The department relies largely on the principal of self-assessment by registered traders, who make returns of goods which become liable to the tax when they sell them to retailers or non-registered traders. Officers supervise the registered traders in their district, and where fraud is suspected, carry out detailed investigations.

After the second world war the Customs and Excise department was stretched to the limit in attempting to check evasion of revenue. Shortages and restrictions brought smuggling to an unprecedented level. Seizures of all types of goods were made, and it was obvious that a good deal of successful evasion must have been carried out in the first few years after the war. Numerous prosecutions for purchase tax frauds and for illicit use of hydrocarbon oils in road vehicles were also brought to the courts.

By degrees, however, as the Customs and Excise department was brought up to strength, and goods in general became more readily available, the incidence of evasion decreased. There were, however, many problems still to be dealt with. The growth of international civil aviation led to the setting up of large airports adequately staffed by Customs and Excise personnel to deal with both passengers and cargo, and arrangements had to be made to prevent illegal landings. One feature of the post-war years was the great increase in the smuggling of dangerous drugs, particularly of cannabis (hashish). Watches also were smuggled on a commercial scale, by making 'runs' to smaller ports on the coast, by ships' crews, by passengers concealing large quantities on their persons, or in the upholstery or special compartments in their cars.

International co-operation in Customs matters is now most extensive and is constantly increasing, every effort being made to remove unnecessary trade barriers. Great emphasis today is laid on facilitating the movement of trade in every possible way. In other fields the department is also rapidly adapting itself to changing circumstances. The extensive growth in the tourist trade, and its importance to our invisible earnings, have led to great relaxations in procedures at the baggage ports and airports. The increasing use of aircraft for freight has meant that simplified and mechanized procedures have been adopted to accelerate the flow of traffic. Developments in the use of containers has caused the establishment of inland container depots and the relaxation of port procedures. Every effort is made to reduce delay to a minimum. Mechanization has been introduced into Custom Houses, and computers produce the trade returns which are eagerly awaited each month. A scheme for carrying out the documentation and control of imports at Heathrow London Airport by the most modern computer techniques is being developed jointly by the Customs department and the airlines, and will be the first system of this kind to be used anywhere in the world.

In the foregoing pages an attempt has been made to tell the history of the oldest part of the machinery of government administration in this country, a story which stretches over a thousand years. During the centuries Customs and Excise activities have penetrated the life of the community in countless ways, and events both great and small have played their part in the development of the Service. On the foundation of long experience the department is now moving towards a future which promises to be as eventful as its past.

Appendix A

CUSTOMS AND EXCISE RECORDS

In general, the records of H.M. Customs and Excise date from 1671. It was then that Charles II appointed Commissioners to manage the Customs and so ended the 'farming' system which, with breaks, had existed since medieval times.

The Customs Outport Records are sometimes confused with the 'Exchequer Port Books', often called 'Port Books', which, although they originated with the Customs Service and were in fact returns of Customs duty collected, were sent to the Exchequer and were therefore regarded as Exchequer records. They are a most valuable source of information about trade and shipping from 1565 to about 1700.

Under the Public Records Act of 1958, the records of H.M. Customs and Excise became public records within the meaning of the Act and it became the responsibility of the Lord Chancellor to see that the provisions of the Act were complied with.

In the course of the implementation of the Act, all the Customs and Excise records of England and Wales have been centralized in London and are being sorted, weeded out, listed and indexed. Classes 1 to 27 are held in the Public Record Office and the remainder, consisting of classes 28 to 103, are for the time being held at the Customs and Excise Headquarters' Repository at the Custom House, London. All these records are under the jurisdiction of the Public Record Office but the Lord Chancellor has, by virtue of the powers conferred on him by the Act, ordered that the Scottish records should remain in Scotland under the Scottish

Record Office. Likewise the records of Northern Ireland remain under the control of the Record Office of Northern Ireland and the records of the Isle of Man also remain in situ.

The process of selection and cataloguing is being carried out in close collaboration with the Public Record Office and the other Public Record Offices involved.

The following telescoped lists of the records of the Department are included here for the benefit of would-be researchers, but it must be borne in mind that all series are not complete and that there are many gaps between the commencing and terminal dates shown. More detailed lists are available in the Record Office in the Headquarters Repository of the Department.

H.M. CUSTOMS & EXCISE DEPARTMENTAL RECORDS
A. AT THE PUBLIC RECORD OFFICE

Class		Description	Dates
CUSTOMS 1	428 vols.	Minutes of Irish Revenue Board Some volumes missing, Indexed from 1720	1716–1829
CUSTOMS 2	10 vols.	Inspector General's Accounts of Imports and Exports	1696–1702
CUSTOMS 3	80 vols.	Ledgers of Imports and Exports	1697–1780
CUSTOMS 4	94 vols.	Ledgers of Imports (Under Countries)	1792–1899
CUSTOMS 5	162 vols.	Ledgers of Imports (Under Articles)	1792–1899
CUSTOMS 6	22 vols.	Ledgers of Imports into Colonies (Under Countries)	1832–1853
CUSTOMS 7	22 vols.	Ledgers of Imports into Colonies (Under Articles)	1832–1852
CUSTOMS 8	140 vols.	Ledgers of Exports of British Merchandise (Under Countries)	1812–1899
CUSTOMS 9	109 vols.	Ledgers of Exports of British Merchandise (Under Articles)	1812–1899
CUSTOMS 10	97 vols.	Ledgers of Exports of Foreign and Colonial Merchandise (Under Countries)	1809–1899
CUSTOMS 11	127 vols.	Ledgers of Exports of Foreign and Colonial Merchandise (Under Articles)	1809–1899
CUSTOMS 12	22 vols.	Ledgers of Exports from Colonies (Under Countries)	1832–1853
CUSTOMS 13	22 vols.	Ledgers of Exports from Colonies (Under Articles)	1832–1853
CUSTOMS 14	39 vols.	Ledgers of Imports & Exports (Scotland)	1755–1827
CUSTOMS 15	140 vols.	Ledgers of Imports & Exports (Ireland)	1698–1829

Class		Description	Dates
CUSTOMS 16	1 vol.	Ledger of Imports & Exports (America)	1768–1773
CUSTOMS 17	30 vols.	States of Navigation, Commerce & Revenue	1772–1808
CUSTOMS 18	491 vols.	Establishment Series I (Quarterly Bills & Salaries)	1675–1813
CUSTOMS 19	63 vols. & 1 bundle	Establishment Series II	1814–1829
CUSTOMS 20	55 vols.	Salary Books & Establishments (Ireland)	1764–1826
CUSTOMS 21	92 vols.	Miscellaneous Books	1715–1857
CUSTOMS 22	31 vols.	Abstracts of Imports (Dutiable) (Under Articles)	1872–1899
CUSTOMS 23	94 vols.	Abstracts of Imports (Under Ports)	1873–1899
CUSTOMS 24	18 vols.	Abstracts of Exports (Under Ports)	1882–1899
CUSTOMS 25	21 vols.	Port Abstract Summaries of Imports (Under Articles)	1873–1899
CUSTOMS 26	21 vols.	Port Abstract Summaries of Exports (Under Articles)	1877–1899
CUSTOMS 27	16 vols.	Transhipments, Imports and Exports (Dutiable)	1884–1899

H.M. CUSTOMS & EXCISE HEADQUARTERS RECORDS

B. AT THE CUSTOM HOUSE, LONDON

Class		Description	Dates
CUSTOMS 28		BOARD AND SECRETARIAT: MINUTE BOOKS	
	1–335		1734–188
CUSTOMS 29		BOARD AND SECRETARIAT: MINUTE ENTRY BOOKS	
	1–15	Musgrave's Notes and Extracts from the Board's Minutes	1696–186
	18–31	Principal Clerk's Minute Books	1814–184

Class	Description	Dates
32– 35	Northern Clerk's Minute Books	1814–1849
36– 39	Western Clerk's Minute Books	1814–1849
40– 42	Coast Guard Minute Books	1833–1849
43– 46	Assistant Secretary's Minute Books	1836–1867
50– 53	Long Room Branch Minute Books	1849–1901
16– 17 47– 49 54– 55	Miscellaneous Minute Books	1732–1904

CUSTOMS 30	**BOARD AND SECRETARIAT: OUT-LETTER ENTRY BOOKS; EXTRA-DEPARTMENTAL**	
1– 8	Private Office Correspondence	1845–1900
	Board to Privy Council & Treasury:	
9– 14	General	1812–1814
15–194	Report Books	1812–1869
195–224	Treasury Letter Books	1814–1882
225–258	Memorial Books	1826–1869
259–274	Irish Affairs	1824–1848
275–282	Scottish Affairs	1824–1848
283–395	Board to Public Offices	1814–1882
396–588	Miscellaneous Letter Books	1868–1910

CUSTOMS 31	**BOARD AND SECRETARIAT: OUT-LETTER ENTRY BOOKS; INTRA-DEPARTMENTAL**	
1	Abstract of Customs General Orders	1700–1776
	Board to:	
2–270	Collectors: Western Ports	1787–1909
271–495	Collectors: Northern Ports	1812–1910
496–504	Outport Officials and Others	1814–1882
505–512	Assistant Commissioners: Ireland	1822–1830
513–571	Assistant Commissioners: Scotland	1823–1872
572–628	Collectors: Ireland	1830–1872
629–669	Collectors: Scotland and Ireland	1869–1910

Class	Description	Dates
CUSTOMS 32	BOARD AND SECRETARIAT: IN-LETTER ENTRY BOOKS: EXTRA- AND INTRA-DEPARTMENTAL	
	Privy Council & Treasury to Board:	
1– 2	Orders and Warrants	1707–1813
3– 75	Registers of Cases Referred	1811–1882
	Irish Affairs:	
76– 80	Registers of Papers received	1823–1830
81– 92	Dublin Docks & Warehouses	1823–1839
93– 97	North West Store, Dublin. Destruction by fire	1833–1836
98	Applications from Port Officials	1844
99–103	Scottish Affairs: Registers of Papers received	1823–1849
	Reports about the Inspection of Ports:	
104–124	Western Ports	1828–1875
125–127	Irish Ports	1830–185?
128–144	Scottish & Irish Ports	1831–185?
145–159	Northern Ports	1831–187?
160–162	Scottish Ports	1847–186?
163	Irish & Western Ports	1849
164–165	United Kingdom Ports	1849–185?
166	Scottish, Irish & Northern Ports	1850
167	Scottish & Northern Ports	1850
168	Northern & Western Ports	1853
169–170	Scottish & Western Ports	1854–185?
171–199	Registers of Papers from Northern Ports	1833–184?
200–201	Registers of Confidential Papers Received	1845–188?
202	Miscellaneous (Spring–Rice papers)	1851–185?
CUSTOMS 33	BOARD AND SECRETARIAT: WORKING PAPERS (Under review)	

Class	Description	Dates
CUSTOMS 34	**BOARD AND SECRETARIAT: PAPERS RELATING TO PLANTATIONS**	
1	Minute Entry Book: Plantation Clerk	1828–1858
	Out-letter entry books: Extra-Departmental:	
2– 19	Reports to Treasury	1819–1855
20– 30	Letters to Public Offices & Private Individuals	1816–1855
31– 73	Out-letter entry books: Intra-Departmental: Board to Collectors	1814–1890
74– 78	In-letter entry books: Extra- and Intra-Departmental	1811–1879
79–115	Plantation Receipts and Disbursements	1767–1851
116–149	Ages, Capacities, Revenue & Trade	1828–1853
150	Index to Plantation Correspondence Establishment	1846–1855
151–153	American Colonies: Customs Establishment	1767–1776
154–158	Plantation Establishment	1805–1851
159–160	Plantation Salaries and Incidents	1812–1826
161–162	Plantation Vacancies	1816–1851
163–166	Plantation Officers: Pensions	1857–1877
167–168	4½ per cent Duties	1776–1840
169–171	Seizures	1828–1853
172	Stores Supplied	1814–1854
173	Particulars of reports to Treasury & Council	1830–1845
	Bundles:	
174–207 (*See* also ustoms 34/862)	Antigua	1777–1854
208–232	Bahamas	1792–1881
233–258 (*See* also ustoms 34/862)	Barbados	1797–1854
259–263 (*See* also ustoms 34/362 and /394)	Berbice	1815–1851

Class	Description	Dates
264–278	Bermuda	1811–1855
279–283	British North American Colonies	1814–1852
284–290	Canada	1832–1851
291–295	Cape Breton	1791–1847
296–322	Cape of Good Hope	1808–1854
323–347	Ceylon	1827–1856
348–350	Curacao	1807–1816
351–366 (*See* also Customs 34/260 and 34/862)	Demerara	1807–1852
367–381 (*See* also Customs 34/862)	Dominica	1813–1852
382–390 (*See* also Customs 34/479 and 34/777)	Gambia	1826–1853
391–405 (*See* also Customs 34/862)	Grenada	1808–1853
406–407 (*See* also Customs 34/497)	Guadeloupe	1812–182
408–478	Jamaica	1803–185
(*See* Customs 34/349 and 34/767)	Martinique	1809–181
479–494	Mauritius	1813–185
495–499 (*See* also Customs 34/688 and 34/702)	Montreal	1819–185
500–507 (*See* also Customs 34/862)	Montserrat	1748–185
508–518 (*See* also Customs 34/862)	Nevis	1804–18
519–588 (*See* also Customs 34/676)	New Brunswick	1786–18
589–612 (*See* also Customs 34/280)	Newfoundland	1809–18

Class	Description	Dates
613–635 (See also Customs 34/787)	New South Wales	1823–1860
636–643 (See also Customs 34/848)	New Zealand	1833–1855
644–677	Nova Scotia	1785–1857
678–681	Prince Edward Island	1814–1835
682–715	Quebec	1762–1856
(See Customs 34/497 and 34/793)	St. Croix	1808–1818
716–719 (See also Customs 34/479 and 34/500)	St. Helena	1835–1852
720–751 (See also Customs 34/862)	St. Kitts	1793–1853
752–766 (See also Customs 34/862)	St. Lucia	1808–1847
(See Customs 34/349 and 34/767)	St. Martin's	1813–1816
767	St. Thomas	1807–1819
768–773 (See also Customs 34/265 and 34/862)	St. Vincent	1811–1846
774–786 (See also Customs 34/479)	Sierra Leone	1813–1855
787–792	South Australia	1832–1854
793 (See also Customs 34/497)	Surinam	1804–182–
794–801 (See also Customs 34/856)	Tasmania	1813–1856
802–811 (See also Customs 34/862)	Tobago	1803–1859
812–827 (See also Customs 34/862)	Tortola	1811–1857
828–847 (See also Customs 34/862)	Trinidad	1802–1852

Class	Description	Dates
848	Van Diemen's Land	1834–1852
849–861	Victoria	1833–1857
862	West Indian	1839
863–916	Promiscuous	1769–1855

CUSTOMS	35	BOARD AND SECRETARIAT: MISCELLANEA (Under review)	

CUSTOMS	36	STATISTICS: TRADE AND SHIPPING	
1– 5			1699–1828

CUSTOMS	37	STATISTICS: REVENUE	
1		Customs: duty yield	1679–1735
2		Seizures: accounts of King's share	1764–176?
3– 49		Receiver General's Accounts	1785–1829
50– 61		Miscellaneous	1787–1905

CUSTOMS	38	STATISTICS: ESTABLISHMENTS	
1– 6		Miscellaneous	1782–189
7– 24		Salaries and Incidents at Outports	1812–185?
25– 31		Incidents at Outports	1830–188
		Coast Guard:	
32– 52		Coast Guard Annual Abstract	1828–185
53– 54		Expenses of the Coast Guard	1855–185
55– 56		Expenses of Revenue Cruisers & Compensation for loss of half pay	1855–185
57– 58		Coast Guard Superannuations	1857–185
59– 60		Revenue Cruiser *Vigilant*. Victualling Accounts	1857–19?

CUSTOMS	39	ESTABLISHMENT: STAFF LISTS	
		United Kingdom:	
1		Customs establishment	1834
2– 9		Customs establishment at Outports	1850–18

Class	Description	Dates
	England and Wales: Customs:	
10– 21	London Headquarters, London Port and Outports	1671–1824
22– 44	Outport establishment	1851–1894
45– 49	Northern Outports	1823–1836
	London establishment: Customs:	
50– 77	Headquarters and Outdoor Departments	1871–1892
78A–79	Headquarters Department	1879–1894
80– 85	Outdoor Department	1871–1892
86–103	Liverpool Establishment: Customs	1864–1894
104–121	Scotland: Customs Establishment at Outports	1860–1885
122	Ireland: Customs	1840
123–140	Customs Establishment at Outports	1860–1885
141–144	Scotland & Ireland: Customs Establishment at Outports	1885–1894
	Superannuations:	
145–159	United Kingdom	1803–1922
160	Scotland	1814–1899
161–162	Ireland	1785–1898
163	United Kingdom: Copyists' and Writers' List Registers of Writers' Pay:	1882–1894
164–167	London	1877–1889
168–172	United Kingdom Outports	1874–1888
173	Thames Coastguard: Salaries and Incidents	1828–1832
174	United Kingdom Outports: Glut pay	1883–1885
175–178	Staff Making Declarations on Admission to Office	1814–1906
179–180	Ages and Capacities	1799–1837
181	Officials charged with disciplinary offences	1850–1874
182	Commissions issued, England and Wales	1814–1822
183–187	Copies of Patents	1671–1856

Class	Description	Dates
CUSTOMS 46	CUSTOMS: REGISTERED PAPERS	1833–1909
CUSTOMS 47 1–749	EXCISE BOARD AND SECRETARIAT: MINUTE BOOKS	1695–1867
CUSTOMS 48 1–142	EXCISE BOARD & SECRETARIAT: ENTRY BOOKS OF CORRESPONDENCE WITH TREASURY	1668–1839
CUSTOMS 49	CUSTOMS & EXCISE: REGISTERED PAPERS POST–1 APRIL, 1909	1909–

OUTPORT RECORDS
ENGLAND AND WALES

Class	Port	Dates
CUSTOMS 50 1–113	ROCHESTER	1820–1917
CUSTOMS 51 1– 32	FAVERSHAM, WHITSTABLE, MARGATE, SANDWICH	1743–1872
CUSTOMS 52 1–111	RAMSGATE	1823–1920
CUSTOMS 53 1– 60	DEAL	1811–1884
CUSTOMS 54 1–365	DOVER	1741–1932
CUSTOMS 55 1– 50	FOLKESTONE	1840–1882

Class	Port	Dates
CUSTOMS 56 1– 85	NEWHAVEN	1889–1883
CUSTOMS 57 1– 26	ARUNDEL	1826–1930
CUSTOMS 58 1–348	PORTSMOUTH	1726–1900
CUSTOMS 59 1–182	WEYMOUTH, BRIDPORT	1694–1892
CUSTOMS 60 1–115	POOLE	1758–1900
CUSTOMS 61 1–175	COWES	1703–1909
CUSTOMS 62 1–243	SOUTHAMPTON	1714–1900
CUSTOMS 63 1– 55	LYME REGIS	1807–1889
CUSTOMS 64 1–178	EXETER, TEIGNMOUTH, BRIXHAM, SALCOMBE	1676–1905
CUSTOMS 65 1–172	DARTMOUTH	1675–1906
CUSTOMS 66 1–215	PLYMOUTH	1775–1895
CUSTOMS 67 1– 70	FALMOUTH	1820–1887
CUSTOMS 68 1–181	PENZANCE, SCILLY ISLES	1722–1927

Class	Port	Dates
CUSTOMS 69	BRISTOL CHANNEL PORTS: PADSTOW, APPLEDORE, BIDEFORD, BARNSTAPLE, ILFRACOMBE, BRIDGWATER	
1–220		1717–1934
CUSTOMS 70	BRISTOL	
1–166		1816–1920
CUSTOMS 71	NEWPORT	
1–127		1705–1899
CUSTOMS 72	CARDIFF	
1–225		1589–1917
CUSTOMS 73	SWANSEA, NEATH	
1–259		1709–1919
CUSTOMS 74	LLANELLY	
1–116		1735–1918
CUSTOMS 75	MILFORD HAVEN, NEYLAND	
1–44		1729–1938
CUSTOMS 76	ABERYSTWYTH, CARDIGAN, PORTMADOC	
1–135		1820–1935
CUSTOMS 77	CARNARVON	
1–103		1779–1921
CUSTOMS 78	BEAUMARIS, PWLLHELI, HOLYHEAD, BANGOR, CONWAY, COLWYN BAY	
1–200		1714–1935
CUSTOMS 79	CHESTER	
1– 76		1816–1938
CUSTOMS 80	LIVERPOOL	
1– 62		1895–1936
CUSTOMS 81	PRESTON, HEYSHAM, LANCASTER	
1– 71		1715–1925

Class		Port	Date
CUSTOMS 82 1–181		WHITEHAVEN	1703–1902
CUSTOMS 83 1–121		WORKINGTON, MILLOM, MARYPORT, SILLOTH, CARLISLE	1820–1929
CUSTOMS 84 1–420		NEWCASTLE	1707–1913
CUSTOMS 85 1–196		SUNDERLAND	1676–1921
CUSTOMS 86		WEST HARTLEPOOL	1819–1927
CUSTOMS 87 1–118		NORTH SHIELDS, SOUTH SHIELDS	1817–1926
CUSTOMS 88 1– 67		MIDDLESBROUGH	1865–1934
CUSTOMS 89 1–159		STOCKTON	1709–1925
CUSTOMS 90 1– 78		WHITBY	1721–1920
CUSTOMS 91 1–121		SCARBOROUGH	1747–1927
CUSTOMS 92 1–388		HULL, GAINSBOROUGH	1722–1921
CUSTOMS 93 1– 90		GOOLE	1828–1914
CUSTOMS 94 1–142		GRIMSBY	1801–1916
CUSTOMS 95 1–133		BOSTON	1732–1920

Class	Port	Date
CUSTOMS 96 1–175	KINGS LYNN, WELLS, BLAKENEY AND CLEY	1660–1953
CUSTOMS 97 1–367	YARMOUTH, LOWESTOFT, SOUTHWOLD	1662–1914
CUSTOMS 98 1–166	IPSWICH, ALDBOROUGH, WOODBRIDGE	1695–1935
CUSTOMS 99 1–211	HARWICH, ALDBOROUGH, MISTLEY	1699–1932
CUSTOMS 100 1–103	COLCHESTER	1700–1918
CUSTOMS 101 1–102	MALDON, BRADWELL, BURNHAM	1700–1924
CUSTOMS 102	LONDON (from 1875 under review)	1714–1874
CUSTOMS 103 1–170 171–186	EXCISE TRIALS Excise Trials Excise Trials: Ireland	 1778–1885 1830–1847

Appendix B

THE REGISTRY OF BRITISH SHIPS

The registration of British ships has always been a responsibility of the Customs Service. It really began as a result of the various Navigation Acts, the object of which was to ensure that the Plantation Trade was confined to vessels which were British owned, built and manned. An Act of 1660 (12 Car. II, c. 18) enacted that 'no goods or commodities whatever of the growth, production or manufacture of Africa, Asia, or America, or any part thereof, or which are described or laid down in the usual maps or cards of those places, be imported into England, Ireland or Wales, Islands of Guernsey or Jersey, or town of Berwick-upon-Tweed, or of the lands, islands, plantations or territories in Asia, Africa or America to His Majesty belonging, as the proprietors and right owners thereof, and whereof the Master and three fourths at least of the mariners are English, under the penalty of the forfeiture of all such goods and commodities, and of the ship or vessel in which they were imported, with all her guns, tackle, furniture, ammunition and apparel . . . and for the prevention of all frauds which may be used in colouring or buying of forain ships, be it enacted by the authority aforesaid, and it is hereby enacted, that from and after the first day of April, which shall be in the year of our Lord one thousand six hundred and sixty one no forain built ship or vessel whatsoever shall be deemed or pass as a ship to England, Ireland, Wales, or town of Berwick, or any of them belonging, or enjoy the benefit or priviledge of such a ship or vessel, until such time that he or they claiming the said ship or vessel to be theirs, shall make appear to the Chief Officer or Officers of the Customs in the port next to the place of his or their aboad, that he or they are not aliens, and shall have taken an oath before such Chief Officer or Officers, who are hereby authorized to administer the same, that such ship or vessel was bona fide and without fraud by him or them bought for a valuable consideration, expressing the sum, as also the time, place and persons from whom it was bought, and who are his part owners (if he have any) all which part-owners shall be liable to take the said oath before the Chief Officer or Officers of the Custom House of the Port next to the place of their aboad, and that no forainer directly or indirectly hath any part, interest, or share therein, and that upon such Oath he or they shall receive a Certificate under the hand or seal of the Chief Officer or Officers of the Port where such person or persons making Oath to reside, whereby such ship or vessel may for the future pass and be deemed as a ship belonging to the said Port, and enjoy the privilege of such a ship or vessel. And the said Officer or Officers shall keep a Register of all such Certificates as he or they shall give and return a Duplicat thereof to the Chief Officers of the Customs at London for such as shall be granted in England, Wales and Berwick and to the Chief Officers of the Customs at Dublin for such as shall be given in Ireland . . .'

The preamble of the Navigation Act of 1695 (7/8 Wm. III, c. 22) stated that, 'great abuses are daily committed to the prejudice of the English navigation, and the loss of a great part of the plantation trade to this kingdom, by the artifice and cunning of ill-disposed persons.' Section 2 of this Act enacted that no goods should be imported or exported to or from the plantations except in ships built in England, Ireland or the plantations, and Section 17 further enacted that English built ships be registered and proof made on oath before the Collector and Comptroller of Customs or in America before the governor or and officers of customs. Section 18 stated that the oath, attested by the governor or customs officer, should after being registered, be delivered to the master of the ship for the security of her navigation and a duplicate immediately transmitted to the Commissioners of Customs in London.

In 1697 the Commissioners of Customs warned the officers, 'to take special care that for every ship or vessel belonging to your port and trading to or from any of His Majesty's plantations, due proof be made upon oath by one or more of the owners before yourselves in the Forms prescribed.' (Customs 97/74a.)

In the reign of George II in an effort to protect the wool trade further legislation was passed and vessels could not qualify to load wool from Ireland for Great Britain until an Oath had been sworn before the Collector that 'no foreigner has directly or indirectly any share, property or interest therein, to his knowledge or belief'. In another Act (15 Geo. II, c. 31) many more directions were given regarding the registration of ships and it was enacted that no ship's name registered could be afterwards changed without registering de novo.

After the American War of Independence many American ships were still trying to claim the privileges of British ownership and in order to tie up any loopholes an Act was passed in 1786 (26 Geo. III, c. 60) which provided for the full registry of all British ships afloat of 15 tons or upwards.

The Registers now contained a very complete description of the vessels showing, apart from the name, number and date of registry, the names of all owners and part-owners and their places of residence. Many other details were given, such as the rig, the number of masts and decks, the dimensions, including the depth of hold and the tonnage. They now became a title-deed to property and shares in British ships and no subject residing outside His Majesty's Dominions was deemed or entitled to be the owner of any ship authorized to be registered under the Act unless he was a member of some British factory, or agent for, or partner in, any house or co-partnership, actually carrying on trade in Great Britain or Ireland. In 1824 a new Act (4 Geo. IV, c. 41) was passed consolidating the law relating to registry and making provision for an account of the subscribing owners and the number of sixty-fourth shares held by each owner to be entered on the back of each Certificate of Registry. Under this Act foreign repairs to a British ship were restricted to 20s. per ton of the burthen of the ship and in the case of a vessel having had such repairs carried out in a foreign country, the Master was required to report upon Oath that the vessel was seaworthy at the time of departure from a port in His Majesty's dominions and that no greater quantity of repairs was carried out than necessary. Ships had to be registered at the ports to which they properly belonged and the ports to which they were deemed to belong were those at or near to which some, or one, of the owners taking the oath under the Act resided. It was also enacted that at every port where registry was made a Book of Registers should be kept by the Collector and Comptroller, in which all the particulars contained in the Form of the Certificate of Registry should be entered and every Register numbered in progression, beginning each progressive numeration at the commencement of each and every year.

There was an element of relaxation inasmuch as provision was made for ships built in 'foreign possessions' for United Kingdom owners to import a cargo before Registry on receipt of a Certificate from the Collector and Comptroller, and that such a Certificate would have, for the voyage, all the force and virtue of a Certificate of Registry under the Act.

Section 14 of the Act enacted that vessels should be surveyed prior to registration, and that a person, or persons, appointed by the Commissioners of Customs, with the assistance of a person, or persons, skilled in the building and admeasurement of ships if considered necessary, should strictly and accurately examine and admeasure such vessels. The formula for working out the tonnage from the measurements was given in Section 15. It was made unlawful for a vessel to be given any other name than that by which she was first registered and it was enacted that the name of a vessel should be painted on her stern in white or yellow letters of a length not less than four inches.

Two years were allowed for the registration of all vessels and shares and after that no earlier Certificate would have any force unless the Collector or Comptroller certified that further time had been granted by the Commissioners of Customs.

In order to avoid the inconvenience involved in Registering

Officers being served with subpoenas requiring them to produce Oaths, Affidavits and Registers in a Court of Law, it was enacted that the Collector and Comptroller and the person or persons acting for them should, upon 'every reasonable request by any person or persons whomsoever' produce for their inspection and examination any Oath, Affidavit, Registry or Entry and permit copies or extracts to be taken and that the copies, upon being proved to be true copies, be allowed and received as evidence without production of the original.

A new Act concerning the measurement of ships was passed in 1835 (5 & 6 Wm. IV, c. 56) and this was obviously brought about by the need to take steam vessels into account. Provision was made for the deduction of the cubical content of the engine room and it was also enacted that the amount of the registered tonnage should be carved or cut on the main beam. There was also a slight change in the formula for converting the cubical contents into tons. Whereas the 1824 Act had laid down that the cubic contents should be divided by 94, the new Act substituted the figure 92·4.

An Act to amend and consolidate the Acts relating to Merchant Shipping was passed in 1854 (17 & 18 Vic., c. 104) and this Act set up the Board of Trade as the Department to undertake the general superintendence of matters relating to Merchant Ships and Seamen. The rules given in this Act for the measurement of ships were more detailed and complicated but at least the figure for dividing the cubical contents in order to ascertain the register tonnage now became 100. This was a great relief to the staff responsible for making the calculations and also to the Officers in the ports who were required to make similar calculations in respect of cargo carried in unregistered spaces and on deck. Section 30 defined the persons authorized to act as Registrars and a list of ports in the British Isles approved for registry was issued (Customs General Order 56/1855). Each vessel registered was required to have an official number; a block of numbers was allocated to each port of Registry as required and these numbers were entered in and issued from an Appropriations Book.

Following upon the Act a large number of General Orders were issued by the Commissioners of Customs and as by this time the Registration of ships had become a complicated procedure arrangements were made for instructions to be issued to Registrars (Customs General Order 50/1855).

Another order made provision for the charge of one shilling for a Certificate of Registry (Customs General Order 69/1855) and it was conceded that vessels registered prior to the 1st May 1855 might retain their old registries but ordered that vessels requiring registry anew or transfer of registry would have to be re-measured under the new law. Since then, despite the change in the value of money, the charge for a certificate is still one shilling although there have been many increases in Registry fees.

Another result of the 1854 Act was that the office of Registrar General of Shipping and Seamen was set up and the existing transcripts of registers were transferred to that Office.

On the 4th January 1855 the first Chief Registrar was appointed (Customs Minute Seat. 4. Jan. 1855) to take over the task of keeping the central record of shipping of the British Empire from another Customs official styled the 'Registrar General of Shipping', who was also responsible for some statistical work. The statistical work of that Office was transferred to a Board of Trade Official, the 'Registrar of Merchant Seamen' who was then given a new title 'Registrar General of Seamen' (17/18 Vic. c. 104. s. 271) and the existing transcripts of registers were transferred to that office.

The Chief Registrar had the important duty of advising Registrars throughout the United Kingdom and the colonies on the details of the new Regulations and of ensuring uniformity of practice (Customs Board to Treasury 19 July 1855). All Registrars in the United Kingdom had to forward to him from time to time full particulars of the registration of vessels. These details were recorded in his Central Register and he then allotted the 'official numbers' which were to be appropriated to ships registered at all ports of the Empire.

In August 1855 it was enacted that the 'copy or transcript of the Register of any British ship which is kept by the Chief Registrar of Shipping in the Custom House in London, or by the

Registrar General of Seamen, under the direction of H.M. Commissioners of Customs or of the Board of Trade, shall have the same effect to all intents and purposes as the original register of which the same is a copy or transcript (18/19 Vic. c. 91. s. 15).

In 1856 the Office of Collector of Customs, London Port and Chief Registrar were united and there were some changes of procedure as a result of the Merchant Shipping Act 1871 (34/5 Vic. c. 110). As a consequence of the Merchant Shipping Act 1872 (35/36 Vic. c. 73) the Central Register kept by the Chief Registrar was discontinued and the sole responsibility for keeping such a register remained with the Registrar General of Seamen who, by a provision in the same Act, was henceforth called 'The Registrar General of Shipping and Seamen'. From the 1st January 1873 the business of allotting ships' official numbers was transferred from the Chief Registrar to the Registrar General of Shipping and Seamen.

The Merchant Shipping Act of 1894 (57/58 Vic. c. 60) is the Act which still governs procedure today and it legislated, as did its predecessor, for the registry of ships at ports throughout what now is the Commonwealth. In recent years, however, many countries of the Commonwealth have passed their own laws relating to shipping, and although in many respects the laws of those countries follow the pattern of the 1894 Act, it is becoming outdated as an Act applying to Her Majesty's Dominions as a whole.

A particular development of recent years is the great increase in the number of private yachts and very many of these are being registered and both the Registrars and the Board of Trade Surveyors are finding that a great deal of their time is spent in applying the rigid procedure of the 1894 Act to these vessels.

SHIP'S REGISTERS

Where the Registers are no longer held in the Port of Registry,
the location is shown in brackets.

Port	Date	Port	Date
Aberystwyth	1824 to date	Colchester	1786 to date
Aldeburgh (Ipswich)	1824 to 1845	Cowes	1786 to date
Arundel (Littlehampton)	1824 to 1855	Dartmouth	1824 to date
Barnstaple	1824 to date	Dover	1824 to date
Barrow	1868 to date	Deal (Dover)	1829 to 1878
Beaumaris (Holyhead)	1786 to date	Exeter	1786 to date
Berwick	1824 to date	Falmouth	1842 to date
Bideford (Bristol)	1786 to 1831	Faversham (Whitstable)	1824 to date
Bideford (Appledore)	1831 to date	Fleetwood	1897 to date
Blyth	1897 to date	Folkestone	1855 to date
Boston	1827 to date	Fowey	1786 to date
Bridgwater (Bristol)	1786 to 1841	Gloucester	1824 to date
Bridgwater	1841 to date	Goole	1828 to date
Bristol	1824 to date	Grimsby	1824 to date
Brixham	1864 to date	Hartlepool	*1845 to date
Cardiff	1838 to date	Hartlepool West	*1860 to date
Cardigan (Fishguard)	1824 to date	Harwich	1824 to date
Caernarvon	1840 to date	Hull	1804 to date
Carlisle (Silloth)	1786 to 1886	Ilfracombe (Barnstaple)	1824 to 1837
Carmarthen (Llanelly)	1839 to 1849	Ipswich	1824 to date
Chepstow (Gloucester)	1786 to 1881	King's Lynn	1836 to date
Chester (Connah's Quay)	1836 to date	Lancaster (Heysham)	1786 to date
Chichester (Littlehampton)	1837 to 1852	Littlehampton	1855 to date

*From 1st April 1967 these two towns were merged. Hartlepool register to be used for all future registrations. West Hartlepool register to die out.

Port	Date	Port	Date
Liverpool*	1786 to date	Rye (Dover)	1855 to 1894
Llanelly	1824 to date	Rye	1893 to date
London Port	1786 to date	St. Ives	1786 to date
Lowestoft	1852 to date	Salcombe	1863 to date
Lyme Regis (Exeter)	1786 to 1880	Sandwich (Ramsgate)	1786 to 1849
Maldon	1786 to date	Scarborough	1786 to date
Manchester (Salford)	1894 to date	Scilly	1786 to date
Maryport (Silloth)	1838 to date	Shields, North	1848 to date
Middlesbrough	1861 to date	Shields, South	1859 to date
Milford	1827 to date	Shoreham	1821 to date
Newcastle	1786 to date	Southampton	1855 to date
Newhaven	1856 to date	Stockton	1838 to date
Newport	1824 to date	Sunderland	1786 to date
Padstow	1824 to date	Swansea	1824 to date
Penzance	1786 to date	Teignmouth	1853 to date
Plymouth	1824 to date	Truro	1824 to date
Poole	1855 to date	Wells & Cley (King's Lynn)	1832 to 1859
Portsmouth	1824 to date	Weymouth	1786 to date
Port Talbot	1917 to date	Whitby	1786 to date
Preston	1786 to date	Whitehaven	1786 to date
Pwllheli (Caernarvon)	1840 to 1851	Wisbech (King's Lynn)	1836 to 185.
Ramsgate	1850 to date	Woodbridge (Ipswich)	1786 to 188
Rochester	1824 to date	Workington	1839 to date
Runcorn	1862 to date	Yarmouth	1886 to date

*Some earlier 'wool' registers are held at Liverpool

Appendix C

WRECK

In medieval times all Wreck of the Sea was considered to belong
to the sovereign of a state and an early statute (3 Edw. I, c. 4) de-
fines wreck as follows:

'What shall be adjudged Wreck of the Sea, and what not.
Concerning Wrecks of the Sea, it is agreed, that where a Man,
a Dog or a Cat escape quick out of the Ship, that Such Ship nor
Barge, not any Thing within them, shall be adjudged Wreck:
but the Goods shall be saved and kept by View of the Sheriff,
Coroner, or the King's Bailiff, and delivered into the Hands of
such as are of the Towns where the Goods were found; so that
if any sue for those Goods, and after prove that they were his,
or perished in his Keeping, within a Year and a Day, they shall
be restored to without Delay; and if not, they shall remain to
the King, and be seised by the Sheriffs, Coroners, and Bailiffs,
and shall be delivered to them of the Town, which shall answer
before the Justices of the Wreck belonging to the King. And
where Wreck belongeth to another than to the King, he shall
have it in like manner, And he that otherwise doth, and thereof
be attainted, shall be awarded to Prison, and make Fine at the
King's Will, and shall yield Damages also. And if a Bailiff do it
and it be disallowed by the Lord, and the Lord will not pretend
any Title thereunto, the Bailiff shall answer, if he have whereof,
and if he have not whereof, the Lord shall deliver his Bailiff's
Body to the King.'

It appears that the intention of the Act was to prevent the destruction or pilfering of the property of persons who had been shipwrecked, provision being made for the owner of wreck to claim it, if he were able to prove his ownership within a year and a day.

Another Act in the reign of Edward I (4 Edw. I, St. 2) enacted that 'Wreck of the Sea', wherever it was found, should be valued and delivered to the Town and under Edward II provision was made for Royal Fish, when it was enacted (17 Edw. II, c. 11) that 'Also the King shall have Wreck of the Sea throughout the Realm, Whales and great Sturgeons taken in the Sea or elsewhere within the Realm, except in certain places privileged by the King'.

Later it was customary for 'wreck of the sea' to be granted to the lord-admiral and in the time of Henry VIII this right was delegated to the vice-admiral of the coast who also had to perform certain duties in connection with wreck and hand over part of the proceeds to the lord-admiral. It is evident that this arrangement was not very satisfactory for in the preamble of an Act in the reign of Queen Anne (12 Anne St. 2. c. 18) it is stated that, 'Owing to many complaints by Merchants both English and Foreign that when there ships ran on shore or were stranded, they were barbarously plundered by Her Majesty's subjects, and their cargoes embezelled'. It was complained that even when cargo had been saved, it was 'swallowed up by exorbitant demands for salvage, to the great loss of Her Majesty's Revenue, and to the much greater damage of Her Majesty's trading subjects'. It was therefore enacted that Sheriffs, Justices of the Peace, Mayors, Bailiffs, Constables, etc. and Officers of the Customs were empowered to demand the Constables of the Ports to summon and call together 'as many Men as shall be thought necessary to the Assistance and for the Preservation of ships in distress' and their cargoes. Officers of the Customs and Constables were also empowered to demand the assistance of Men of War or Merchant Ships belonging to Her Majesty or her subjects which were in the vicinity. If they neglected to comply, the Superior Officer was liable to a fine of £100.

Provision was also made for the Merchants, owners or officers of ships or goods saved to reward those helping to preserve vessels in distress. Goods not claimed within twelve months were to be sold.

Penalties were laid down for those who impeded the saving of a ship or who defaced marks on goods, and Officers of Customs and Constables were empowered 'to repell by Force any such Person or Persons as shall, without such Leave or Consent from the said Commander or Superior Officer, or the said Officer of Customs, or his Deputy, etc. . . . press on board the said ship . . . and molest them in the preservation of the said ship'.

Persons making or assisting in making any hole in a vessel in distress or stealing any Pump or wilfully doing anything 'tending to the immediate loss or Destruction' of a ship were made guilty of Felony, without Benefit of Clergy'.

It was also enacted that the Act should be read 'four times in the Year in all the Parish Churches and Chapels of every Sea-Port Town'.

There was no important change in wreck legislation until 1846 when an Act (9 & 10 Vic. c. 99) appointed 'Receivers of Admiralty Droits' and enacted that every Lord and every Lady of any Manor, or Patentee or Grantee of the Crown, or any other person or Body Corporate who may claim to be entitled to claim Wreck of the Sea, or to any goods found jetsam, flotsam, lagan or derelict should give notice to the Receiver in writing.

All persons finding wreck were obliged to report and deliver it forthwith to a Receiver or Officer of Customs and the latter officials were empowered to seize by Warrant any goods not reported or delivered. The Receiver had to send a report of goods seized to the Principal Officer of Customs at the nearest Port when the value of the goods exceeded £20. Wrecked goods were to be delivered up to the owners provided they made good their claim thereto within twelve months. Wreck not claimed by the owner of the Lord of the Manor was to be sold as Droits of Admiralty and vice-Admirals of Counties were warned not to interfere with wreck.

Under this Act the persons empowered to give orders to save vessels in distress included the master, owner, ships' officers, Receivers, Officers of Customs or Coastguard, Excise Officers and Sheriffs. Such officers were also empowered to use force to suppress plunder and disorder.

The salving of anchors had become something of a business in certain areas, such as the Downs, and to prevent this traffic penalties were imposed on persons purchasing anchors who were to be treated as Receivers of stolen goods.

The legislation at present in force was included in the Merchant Shipping Act of 1894 (57 & 58 Vic. c. 60) as Part IX. Most of the existing provisions were re-enacted; 'wreck' was defined as including jetsam, flotsam, lagan and derelict found in or on the shores of the sea or any tidal water and 'salvage' as including all expenses properly incurred by the salvor in the performance of the salvage services. The duties and the powers of the receiver were defined; he was empowered to pass over adjoining lands in going to aid ships in distress and any damage sustained by an owner of land as a consequence of these rights was made a charge on the vessel, cargo, etc. Penalties were imposed on any such owner who impeded or hindered the receiver in the exercising of his rights.

The power of the receiver to suppress plunder and disorder by force was more clearly defined and it was enacted that if any person was killed, maimed or hurt in resisting the receiver in the execution of his duties, neither the receiver nor person acting under his orders was liable to any punishment or damages. Persons plundering, damaging or destroying wreck were made punishable under the Riot Acts (49 & 50 Vic. c. 38; 1 Geo. I, St. 2. c. 5) and persons finding wreck were required to notify the receiver and, if not the owner, deliver same to the receiver as soon as possible.

Unclaimed wreck, the removal of wreck and offences in respect of wreck, were covered by the Act and regulations laid down for marine store dealers, penalties being imposed for non-compliance. Manufacturers of anchors were required to mark anchors with legible characters, together with the weight and a progressive number. The treatment of salvage was dealt with in detail and it was enacted that all wreck being foreign goods should be subject to the same duties as if imported.

The enactments of the 1894 Act were adapted to new developments by the Merchant Shipping (Salvage) Act of 1916 (6 & 7 Geo. 5, c. 41), which stated the right of the Admiralty to claim salvage for services to certain ships. Furthermore, the Air Navigation Act of 1920 (10 & 11 Geo. 5, c. 41) applied to aircraft the law relating to wreck and salvage of life and property and to the duty of rendering assistance to vessels in distress, including the provisions of the Merchant Shipping Acts 1894 to 1916 any other Act relating to those subjects.

Until the development of steamships in the last century, the sea took great toll of shipping and in certain areas, such as the Cornish Coast, the Bristol Channel, Liverpool Bay, the Pentland Firth and the Goodwin Sands, Customs Officers, in their capacity as Receivers of Wreck, had to spend a great deal of their time dealing with the wrecked ships and their cargoes.

Even in the steamship days, many vessels have fallen victim to the elements and there have been some tragic episodes. One of these, which was described by Charles Dickens in 'The Uncommercial Traveller', was the loss of 'The Royal Charter', which was wrecked at Red Wharf Bay, Anglesey, on the 20th October 1859. In this catastrophe, 446 people who were emigrating to Australia were drowned, and nearly one million pounds in gold went down with the ship. Dickens paid tribute to the good work of the rector of Llanallgo in taking the bodies of the unfortunate victims from Moelfre beach and burying them in Llanallgo churchyard.

During the two world wars, enemy raiders and submarines sank many merchant ships in territorial waters and at certain periods of both wars Receivers of Wreck were kept very busy.

The great increase in the ownership of yachts and pleasure boats since the second world war has had its effect upon the Receiver of Wreck, as in rough weather it is common for small boats and dinghies to be broken away from their moorings and thrown up on a beach.

A change in the definition of wreck in 1963, however, caused such small boats to be regarded as 'lost property' and therefore to become a police responsibility. In order to be regarded as wreck, property had to be a ship, her cargo or a portion thereof but by virtue of the Sea Fisheries Act 1883 and the Civil Aviation Act 1949, the definition of wreck included all fishing boats and any aircraft or part of aircraft found derelict at sea etc. Henceforth, deck cargo washed overboard from a ship in heavy weather or in other circumstances was not to be treated as deck cargo.

Appendix D

THE CUSTOMS AND EXCISE
LABORATORIES

The story of the Excise Laboratory begins with George Philips, who entered the Service as an 'Expectant' on the 17th April 1826. In September 1826 he was appointed an 'Assistant' in the 8th London District and in 1828 he became an Officer in the 89th Division. Two years later he was transferred to the 29th which was abolished in 1833 and he became, in Excise parlance, a 'Dropped' officer. In August 1833 he joined the 7th Division as a Principal Officer and the next year, at his own request, was appointed Officer at Ipswich (7th) Station, and in 1839 he was transferred to Woodbridge 2nd Station.

For some years there had been a great deal of concern about the extent to which adulteration was practised in the tobacco trade. A General Order in 1835 (E GO 8.4.1835) had instructed officers to forward to the Board samples of tobacco which was suspected of being adulterated and five years later an Act was passed forbidding the use of the leaves of certain trees and shrubs in the manufacture of tobacco (3/4 Vic. c. 18).

Surveys had been found of little avail and so were discontinued and it was estimated that in some cases there was as much as 70 per cent adulteration. As a result there was a considerable reduction in importation and a corresponding reduction in revenue.

George Philips had taken a great deal of interest in this problem and had spent a large part of his spare time in the pursuit of scientific studies and the use of the microscope and feeling that he had the answer to the problem of adulteration he offered his services to the Board.

His offer was accepted and in 1842 he was successfully applying his methods in the laboratory which was set up in the Excise Office at Broad Street. As it was now felt that adulterants in manufactured tobacco could now be detected by these methods of analysis, a Tobacco Act was passed in the same year (5/6 Vic. c. 93) which prohibited the admixture of all substances other than those universally recognized as necessary for the preparation of the tobacco leaf.

For two years Philips worked alone on this project and in 1844 was called upon to give evidence as to his methods of analysis before a Select Committee on the Tobacco. After this he was joined by Thomas Dobson, also a chemist of considerable attainments who later became Secretary to the Board of Inland Revenue.

The Excise Board decided to make the laboratory a permanent institution and directed that Philips and seven other officers should matriculate at London University and attend certain classes in chemistry at the University, the Receiver General being ordered to pay the fees for these courses (EBM 2 Oct. 1845). One of these officers, Adam Young, Officer at Thetford, eventually became Deputy Chairman of the Board of Inland Revenue in 1881.

The next important assignment for Philips and Dobson was research into the comparative values of barley, malt, sugar and molasses as materials for brewing and distillation. The results of these experiments were confirmed by the subsequent investigation of Professor Fownes and were eventually published as a Parliamentary Paper (PP 26/1847). Consequent upon this, distillers were allowed to use duty-free sugar in 1847 and duty-free molasses in 1848 and also to use a mixture of any permitted materials (11/12 Vic. c. 100).

Their next principal experiment was an investigation with a view to discovering a method of checking the frauds and misstatements in claims for drawback on exported beer. Up to this time the method which had been used for determining the 'original gravity' of the beer was the rather primitive one of tasting it. As a result of their experiments Phillips and Dobson invented the distillation method which the Excise Board adopted. In later years the accuracy of this method was challenged and the tables which had been produced were submitted to scientific experts who virtually endorsed them and they were finally legalized in 1856 (19/20 Vic. c. 34). The accurate calculation of the original gravity of beer resulted in a great gain to the revenue and the Treasury recognized this by presenting Phillips and Dobson with £1,000 between them (Johnstone's Manual).

When the Excise was united with the Stamps and Taxes to form the Inland Revenue in 1849, Thomas Dobson left the laboratory to become the First Assistant Secretary to the new Board. The Headquarters of the new Department were to be at Somerset House, but on account of lack of space the Laboratory was housed at 30 Arundel Street and remained there until 1859 when it was moved to specially constructed laboratories in Somerset House.

In 1853 a manufacturer applied to the Board for permission to use duty-free spirits in the manufacture of a substitute for sperm oil and the Board directed Phillips, who by this time had been promoted to Surveying General Examiner, to carry out experiments. His experiments showed that the addition of wood Naphtha to ordinary spirits would prevent any abuse by making the mixture so unpalatable that it would repel ordinary drinkers if the spirit in the mixture were exempted from duty (PP 201/1855). These findings were referred to Professors Graham, Hofman and Redwood who supported them and it resulted in an Act being passed in 1855 authorizing the manufacture and use of methylated spirits, under such conditions as would guard against its possible perversion to purposes for which it was not intended (I.R. First Report 1857).

From 1852 from four to six assistants were attached to the Laboratory and when in 1856 the Examiners made a request to the Board to be enlightened in the mysteries of chemical science, it was ordered that every Examiner should spend one month in the Laboratory to acquire at least an elementary knowledge of the detection of fraud by chemical methods.

The laboratory was moved to Somerset House in 1858 and in the same year George Phillips became the Principal. The Board now decided to give the officers the chemical training in their own laboratory rather than at the University College, London, as had previously been the case. At this time Phillips had six permanent assistants, and the work had considerably extended in quantity and scope and it was not long before other government departments obtained permission to use the services of the laboratory.

In 1863 there were investigations to be carried out in connection with the Tobacco Manufacturing Act (26 Vic. c. 7) and in the following year in connection with the possibility of duty-free malt for cattle feeding. In 1865 the hop planters of Kent requested an investigation into the possibility of using tobacco extract as an insecticide and in the next year, at the request of the Board of Trade, the Laboratory analysed lime and lime juice used on merchant ships.

George Phillips retired in 1874 and was succeeded by James Bell who had been the Deputy Principal. At this time the laboratory had a staff of 1 Principal, 1 Deputy Principal, 3 Upper Class Assistants, 2 Lower Class Assistants, 1 Book-keeper, 1 Keeper of Chemicals, 1 Assistant Keeper of Chemicals and 5 temporary assistants.

James Bell had entered the Excise in 1846 and eventually became a Doctor of Science, Doctor of Philosophy and Fellow of the Royal Society. In 1865 he produced a revised edition of Bateman's 'Excise Officers Manual', and in 1873 an edition of Bateman's 'Excise Laws'.

Under Bell's leadership the Laboratory went on from strength to strength and took on more and more commitments unconnected with Excise or Inland Revenue work. They assisted the Customs in connection with the testing of wine and the examination of imported tea. Gradually, for the purpose of checking the drawbacks of Malt and Beer, Inland Revenue Laboratories had been set up in Belfast, Bristol, Cork, Dublin, Glasgow, Hull, Leith, Liverpool, Newcastle, Newhaven and Southampton, and more and more work was being done for other government departments.

THE CUSTOMS LABORATORY

In the meantime, as a result of a change in the method of charging duty on imported wine and the need to test alcoholic strength, the Customs had set up laboratories in 1861 in the London Custom House and at the London, Victoria and St. Katherine's Docks. Later, testing stations were also set up at the outports approved for the importation of wine (23 Vic. c. 23). These testing stations were known as the Customs Wine Laboratories.

In 1875 the Sale of Food and Drugs Act (38/39 Vic. c. 63) imposed on the Customs Service the responsibility for ascertaining the purity of imported tea. This led to the appointment of a tea analyst, James B. Keene, and to the reorganization of the Wine Laboratories and they were formed into Customs Laboratory units each in charge of an Analyst and under the overall supervision of the Principal Chemist at the Central Laboratory in the Custom House, London. Eventually such laboratories were set up in London, Belfast, Bristol, Cork, Dublin, Glasgow, Hull, Leith, Liverpool, Newcastle, Newhaven and Southampton.

The Customs laboratories were involved in further work in 1881 when an Act was passed (C & IRA 1881) which made provision for a distillation test in any case where, by reason of the presence of sweetening or other matter, the correct strength of imported spirits was obscured and could not be ascertained by the use of the Sikes' hydrometer. In 1887 they were assigned the task of testing samples of imported butter and other foodstuffs under the Margarine Act.

1894 GOVERNMENT LABORATORY

In 1887 the Royal Commission on Civil Establishments had considered the possibility of the amalgamation of the two revenue services and had decided against it, but in 1894 the laboratories of the two departments were united to form a Government Laboratory under the control of a Principal Chemist and in 1897 a new Laboratory was built in Clements Inn Passage. A sign of the change in the type of assignment is shown in 1901 when as a result of a number of deaths due to arsenic in beer a 'Water Inspector' was attached to the Laboratory to guard the purity of the London Water supply.

In 1911 the Laboratory was completely divorced from the revenue departments and was made a separate department called the 'Department of the Government Chemist'. In spite of this separation the system of allocating Officers of Customs and Excise to serve in the Laboratory continued until 1933.

SOURCES

Charters of Aethelbald of Mercia. Early Charter of St. Pauls Cathedral (Camden Soc., Vol. 58, p. 6. MS. James 23, p. 35 (Bodleian)

Quindecima of John (Madox, 'History and Antiquities of the Exchequer' Vol. 1, p. 772)

Bernard Achard Pipe Rolls. N.S. 24. 11 John, Rot. 11 d., p. 126

New Custom Stubbs, 'Select Charters', p. 451

Appointment of Collectors and Controllers Cal. Fine Rolls. 27th May 1275. Membm. 23

Maletote of 1297 25 Edw. I, c. 7

Appointment of Searchers Statutes of the Realm, i, p. 132

Carta Mercatoria 31 Edw. I, Memb. 16

Appointment of Ports Fine Rolls. 1303. 31 Edw. I & 1306 34 Edw. I

Farm assigned to Italian Merchants Cal. Pat. Rolls. Ed. I, Mem. 26 ay 15

Order for Direct Payments Cal. Fine Rolls. Apr. 12th and May 13th 1316

Export duty on aliens wool Fine Rolls. 24 June 1317

Wool to Staple port Pat. Rolls. 13 Edw. II, mem. 8

List of ports 1323 Cal. Fine Rolls. 16 Edw. II, Vol. III, p. 145

Taxes on foreign merchants 1328 2 Edw. III, c. 9

Order to Collector, Ipswich Cal. Close Rolls. I Edw. III, May 2nd

The Cocket Seal A. Anderson, 'On Commerce' (London 1821), Vol. 1, p. 299

Prisage of Wool Rot. Parl. Vol. II, p. 105

Abolition of above Hall I. p. 215. Rt. Pl. II, 149, No. 2

Statute of Staple 1353 27 Edw. III, Sess. 2, c. 1 and 3

Appointment of Chaucer Pat. Rolls. June 8th 1374, Mem. 13

Churchman's Custom House Cal. Pat. R. 6 Rich. II, Pt. I, Mem. 36

Mercantilism 5 Rich. II, c. 3

Customer, Controller, Searcher, etc. 14 Rich. II, c. 10

Customers and Controllers not to act by Deputy I Henry IV, c. 13

Searchers not to let offices 4 Hen. IV, c. 21

Export of gunpowder prohibited A. Anderson, op. cit., Vol. I, p. 422

Revenue statistics 1400 Hall, Vol. II, pp. 203 and 212

Revenue statistics 1421 A. Anderson, op. cit., I, p. 434

Penalties on Customers, etc. 3 Hen. VI, c. 3

Defaulting officials 1424 11 Hen. VI, c. 15

Penalties on Customers, etc. 1442 20 Hen. VI, c. 5

Import prohibitions 1463 3 Edw. IV, c. 4

Limitation on vessels 4 Edw. IV, c. 2

Sealing of cloths Macpherson, 'Annals of Commerce', I (London, 1805), p. 688. 12 Edw. IV, c. 3 (not printed)

Tudor Period Bindoff, S. T., 'Tudor England' (1950)

Retaliation against Venetians 1490 7 Henry VII, c. 8

Aliens Rates of Tax II Henry VII, c. 14

Treaty of Commerce 1496 D. Macpherson, op. cit., V. II, p. 9

Grant of Custom to Calais 19 Henry VII, c. 27

Treaty of Commerce 1506 D. Macpherson, op. cit., V. II, p. 28

Rate Book 1507 N. S. B. Gras, 'The Early English Customs System', p. 694 et seq.

Entering of aliens goods 1 Henry VIII, c. 5

Proclamation to King's Officers Letter and Papers, Henry VIII, V. 1, p. 7, No. 11 (1)

Beer barrels 35 Henry VIII, VIII, c. 8

Sale of Public Offices 5/6 Edw. VI, c. 16, s. 2

Vigilatores ad Ripam MSS., British Museum. Add. 30198

Murder of Customer of Faversham Diary of Henry Machyn, Camden Soc., V. 42, 1848

Prohibition of Exportation I & II P & M, c. 5, s. 3

Assessment of Rates Maitland V, II, p. 1034

New Custom House Cal. S. P. (Dom) 1547–80, p. 105, No. 46

Coronation of Elizabeth I Acts P. C. 1558/15/1558, p. 10

Appointment of wharves, etc. 1 Eliz., I, c. 11

Legal quays Maitland II, pp. 1033/4

Prohibition of export of bullion Acts P. C., 8th April 1559

Mercantilism in 1562 5 Eliz. I, c. 5, s. 8

Great Farm of Customs Cal. S. P. (Dom) 1566–79, p. 438

Export prohibitions 8 Eliz. I, c. 3

Comptroller imprisoned Acts P. C., 16th Sept. 1564

Exchequer Port Books 'Modern Practice of the Court of Exchequer' (1730),
    pp. 431ff.

Wine concessions 1571 S. P. (Dom) 1566–79

Dover Harbour levy 23 Eliz. I, c. 6

Walsingham farms Customs S. P. (Dom) 186, 76

Orders to Officers S. P. (Dom) 248, 89

Non-revenue tasks Acts P. C., 9th Oct. 1587

Armada preparations Acts P. C., 22/23rd Aug. 1588

Convoy Duty 1590 Acts P. C., 26th Nov. 1591

Direct Collection of Customs Hist. Mss. Com. Mss of Marquis of Salisbury,
    Pt. IV, C. 6823

Appointment of Surveyors 'Modern Practice of the Court of Exchequer',
    p. 447

Instructions to Customers, etc. ibid., p. 452

Report on Book of Rates Hist. Mss. Com., Pt. IV, p. 613, C. 6823

Cecil's farm 1602 Hist. Mss. Com. Salisbury MSS, Pt. XII, Cd. 5291

Proposal for new Book of Rates Hist. MSS. Com. Hatfield Papers, Pt. XII,
    p. 565

Tonnage and Poundage to James I 2 James I, c. 33

Rex v. Bates Reports in the Court of Exchequer (Lane) 1657

Book of Rates 1611 In Customs and Excise library

Export smuggling of wool Acts P. C., 6th Sept. 1614

Collection of Light Dues Cal. S. P. (Dom) 81, No. 69

Wool smuggling Cal. S. P. (Dom) 171, No. 17

Committee for Trade 1625 'Growth of English Industry and Commerce' (Cunningham), V. II, pp. 175 and 289

Imposition of the Excise Ordinances of the Interregnum

Board of Customs appointed Ordinances of the Interregnum, V. I, pp. 163/4

Plantations Preference Ordinances of the Interregnum, V. I, p. 912

Book of Rates Acts and Ordinances V. I, pp. 1032/8, 16th Dec. 1647

Provision for 'farming' of Customs & Excise Ibid., V. II, p. 1268

Tonnage and Poundage Act 1660 12 Car. 2, c. 4

New Excise duties imposed 1660 Ibid.

Hearth Tax imposed 13 & 14 Car. II, c. 10

Hearth Tax repealed 1 & 2 W & M, c. 10

Coal Tax imposed 18 & 19 Car. 2, c. 13, 8

Navigation Act 1661 12 Car. 2, c. 18

East India Company Charter Macpherson, op. cit., II, pp. 494/5

Quarantine precautions 1663 Remembrancia, 'City of London' 1579/674, p. 349

Wren Custom House Cal Treasury Books 1669, III (I), p. 74

Wren Custom House Ibid., 1671 and (II), p. 796

Customs Board appointed 1671 Cal. Treasury Books III (2), p. 935

Excise Payments (Mistress Nellie) Customs library, Acc. No. 1742

Protections against Jury service, etc. Cal. Treasury Books III (2), p. 1034

Glorious Revolution Remembrancia, City of London, p. 349. Cal. Treasury Books 1669, III

New Board of Customs 1689 Pat. Roll 1 W & M, p. 36. No. 1, Dorsa, 20 Apr. 1689

Sufferance Wharves 6/7 Wm. III, c. 7, s. 14

Tonnage Measurement 6/7 Wm. III, c. 12, s. 10

Naval co-operation with Customs 7/8 Wm. III, c. 28

Customs Officers in Colonies 7/8 Wm. III, c. 22

First Trade Statistics Customs 2/1

Wool Act 1698 9/10 Wm. III, c. 40, s. 3

Poor Law apprentices 2/3 Anne, c. 6. Customs 96/127

Courtesy of Nations 7 Anne, c. 12

Appointment of Congreve as Under Searcher Customs 39/183, p. 57

Tobacco Warehouses 12 Anne, sess. 2, c. 8, s. 5

Wreck 1713 12 Anne, c. 18

Old Pretender collects Excise Customs 48/11, p. 255

Eighteenth Century Background Customs Letter Books. See App. A

Eighteenth Century Smuggling Ibid. and Collier Papers Customs
   Repository

Scotland Customs Letter Books (Dumfries, Perth, Dundee, Montrose)

Quarantine Act 1800 39/40 Geo. III, c. 80

Letters of Marque 41 Geo. III, c. 76

Consolidation of Customs Laws 43 Geo. III, c. 68

Warehousing Act 1803 43 Geo. III, c. 132

Fees and Holidays exhibited 46 Geo. III, c. 82

Copyright Works 1814 54 Geo. III, c. 15, 6

Arrival of Emperor of Russia 1815 Customs Board's Minutes

Sikes Hydrometer legally sanctioned 1816 56 Geo. III, c. 140

Customs Consolidation Act 1819 59 Geo. III, c. 52

Shipwreck Stations Customs Board's Minutes. 16th Jan. 1819

Formation of Coastguard, Commission of Inquiry, 12th Report, 31st Jul.
   1821

Excise duties transferred Customs Board's Minutes, 19 Jul. 1820

Plantations Customs Customs Board's Minutes, 28 Oct. 1825

Repeal of salt duties 5 Geo. IV, c. 65

Female searchers appointed Customs Board's Minutes, 8 Jul. 1826

Prohibitions 1825 6 Geo. IV, c. 107 and c. 109, c. 111, c. 114

Duty free stores for ships 2 Wm. IV, c. 51

Customs Laws consolidated 3 & 4 Wm. IV, c. 51 and c. 52

Cholera epidemic 1832/3 Customs Board's Minutes, 14 Feb. 1832, 26 Aug. 1833, and 11 Sept. 1833

East India Company's Tea monopoly ended Treasury Minute, 1st Jul. 1834

First Revenue steamer Customs Board's Minutes, 1st Sept. 1834

Books for Coastguard Customs Board's Minutes, 18 April 1835, 16 May and 22 Oct. 1836

Customs Moral Welfare Customs Board's Minutes 1840/1

Tobacco Trade Inquiry 1844 Sessional Paper 565/1844

Obscene prints, etc. 1846 9/10 Vic. 102, s. 19

Repeal of Navigation Laws 1849 12/13 Vic., c. 29

London Docks' Dispute Sess. Papers 209/1851, 604/1851, 494/1852

Merchant Shipping Act, 1854 17/18 Vic., c. 104

Light dues – Board of Trade Customs Board's Minutes, 10 July, 1855

Jerquer abolished, Customs Board's Minutes, 3 March 1859

Integration of Landing and Waterguard Departments Sess. Papers, 257–1/1860

Wine Laboratories established Customs Board's Minutes, 1 May 1861

'Alabama' affair Customs Library Acc. No. 490

Charing Cross Station baggage Customs Board's Reports 9/10

Statistical Office established, Customs Board's Report 16th

Customs Building Act 48/3 Vic., c. 36

Beer Duty 43/4 Vic., c. 20

Sea Fisheries 1883 46/7 Vic., c. 22

Repeal of Plate Duty 1890 53 Vic., c. 8

Outdoor staff pay, Hansard, Vol. CCCXLIII, Cols. 308/25

Goschen Minute Sess. p. 161

Repeal of Quarantine Laws 59/60 Vic., c. 19

Dogs Order 1897 S. R. & O. 221/1897

Revenue Statistics 1857–1900 Customs Board's Reports

Nineteenth Century smuggling Customs Outdoor Letter Books and Customs Board's Reports and Papers

Bleriot flight 1909 Customs Registered file 11820/1909

Twentieth Century Inland Revenue Board's Reports Customs and Excise Board's Reports Miscellaneous Papers

BIBLIOGRAPHY

Anderson, Adam   *Origin of Commerce*, London, 1801

Atton, H. &
Holland, H. H.   *The King's Customs* (2 vols.), London, 1908, reprinted London, 1967

Bowen, Frank   *His Majesty's Coastguard*, London, 1928

Carson, E. A.   'The Customs Records of the Kent Ports – A Survey', *Journal of the Society of Archivists*, Vol. 4, no. 1

Carson, E. A.   'The Customs Plantation Records', *Journal of the Society of Archivists*, vol. 3, no. 4

Carson, E. A.   'Customs Bills of Entry', *Maritime History*, vol. 1, no. 2

Chester, W. D.   *Chronicles of the Customs Department*, London, 1885 (privately printed)

Clark, G. N.   *Guide to English Commercial Statistics 1696–1782*, London, 1938

Cobb, H. S. (Ed.)   *The Local Port Books of Southampton*, Southampton University, 1961

Crombie, Sir James   *Her Majesty's Customs and Excise*, London, 1962

Cunningham, T.   *The History of Taxes etc.*, 2nd edit., London, 1773

Dawson, J. W.   *Commerce and Customs, Newport and Caerleon*, Newport, 1932

Dowell, S.   *A History of Taxation & Taxes in England* (4 vols.), London, 1884, reprinted London 1965

East, R.   *Choice chips – Excise*, London, 1877

Farr, G. E.   *Chepstow Ships*, Chepstow Society, 1954

Gras, N. S. B   *The Early English Customs Systems*, Harvard, 1918

Hall, H.   *A History of the Customs Revenue in England* (2 vols.), London, 1885

Hoon, Elizabeth E.   *The Organisation of the English Customs Systems 1696–1786,*
U.S.A., 1938, reprinted Newton Abbot, 1968. (With a critical
historical introduction by R. C. Jarvis)

Hughes, E.   *Studies in Administration and Finance,* London, 1934

Jarvis, R. C.   'Appointment of Ports', Offprint *The Economic History Review,*
2nd Series, Vol. MI, no. 3, 1959

Jarvis, R. C.   *Customs Letter-books of the Port of Liverpool, 1711–1813,*
Manchester, 1954

Jarvis, R. C.   'Sources for the History of Ports', *The Journal of Transport
History,* vol. III, no. 2, November, 1957

Jarvis, R. C.   'Sources for the History of Ships and Shipping', *The Journal of
Transport History,* vol. III, no. 4, November 1958

Larn, R. & Carter, C.   *Cornish Shipwrecks,* Newton Abbot, 1969

Leftwich, B. R.   *History of the Excise,* London, 1908

McCulloch, J. R.   *A Dictionary of Commerce and Commercial Navigation,* London,
1834

McGuire, E. B.   *The British Tariff System,* London, 1951

Macpherson, David   *Annals of Commerce,* London, 1805

Madox, T.   *History and Antiquities of the Exchequer* (2 vols.), London, 1769

Maitland, W.   *History and Survey of London* (2 vols.), London, 1756

Minchinton, W. E.   'The Trade of Bristol in the Eighteenth Century', *Bristol
Record Society,* xx, 1957

Owens, John   *Plain Papers – A History of the Excise,* Linlithgow, 1879

Pittar, T. J. (Ed.)   *Customs Tariffs of the United Kingdom from 1800–1897 with some
Notes upon the more important branches of Receipt from the year
1660,* Command Paper (C8706)

Smith, Adam   *The Wealth of Nations,* 6th edit., London, 1950

Stubbs, William   *Select Charters,* Oxford, 1876; Newton Abbot, 1969

Willan, T. S.   *A Tudor Book of Rates,* Manchester, 1962

Williams, D. M.   'The Liverpool Timber Trade', *Business History,* 8, 1966

Williams, D. M.   'Liverpool Merchants and the Cotton Trade', *Liverpool and
Merseyside,* ed., J. R. Harris

Williams, N. J.   Elizabethan Port Books, Kings Lynn, *English Historical
Review,* vol. LXVI, no. 260, July, 1951

Williams, W. M. J.   *The King's Revenue,* London, 1908

BIBLIOGRAPHY (SMUGGLING)

Browning, H. J.	*They Didn't Declare It*	London; 1967
Chatterton, E. Keble	*King's Cutters and Smugglers*	London; 1912
Farjeon, J. Jefferson	*The Compleat Smuggler*	London; 1938
Forster, D. Arnold	*At War With The Smugglers*	London; 1936
Harper, Charles G.	(See Lord Teignmouth)	
Herrington, B.	*Smugglers Ahoy*	London; 1957
Shore, Lt. Henry N.	*Smuggling Days & Smuggling Ways*	London; 1892
Teignmouth, Lord & Harper, Charles	*The Smugglers* (2 vols.)	London; 1923
Verrill, A. H.	*Smugglers and Smuggling*	London; 1924
Walker, David E.	*The Modern Smuggler*	London; 1960
Williams, Neville	*Contraband Cargoes*	London; 1959
Wood, G. Bernard	*Smugglers Britain*	London; 1966

CUSTOMS AND EXCISE
SIGNIFICANT DATES

743 A.D.	Ethelbald, King of Mercia granted exemption from Customs duties on certain goods imported by the Bishop of London for religious houses.
979	Reference to the Billingsgate tolls.
1204	Quindecima of King John (first attempt at centralization of Customs).
1215	Magna Carta ('ancient and rightful customs').
1275	Nova custuma of Edward I (Collectors appointed by patent, Controllers appointed).
1303	Carta Mercatoria (King's Beam instituted, tronagers (weighers) appointed.
1335	Chercheurs (Searchers) appointed.
1374	Geoffrey Chaucer appointed Controller of Customs London.
1496/9	Cabot Roll. Payments to Cabot by Collector, Bristol on behalf of Henry VII.
1507	First known tariff (Book of rates). Earliest in Customs Library is 1550.
1643/4	Boards of Customs and Excise appointed. Excise introduced.
1662	Customs and Excise back into farm.
1671	Board of Customs restored (Sir George Downing a member).
1683	Board of Excise restored.
1686	English Board of Customs took over administration of Customs in Plantations.
1707	Act of Union. Boards of Customs and of Excise set up in Scotland.
1723	English and Scottish Customs placed under one Board.
1742	Separate Scottish Board restored.

1765	English Board of Customs assumes control in Isle of Man.
1767	Management of American Customs transferred to a Board of Plantation Commissioners in Boston, Massachusetts.
1778	Adam Smith appointed Commissioner, Scottish Board.
1783	Independence of United States recognized and management of Plantation Customs of British North America re-transferred to the English Board.
1789	Burns enters Excise. Died 1796.
1809	Formation of Preventive Waterguard.
1822	Formation of Coastguard.
1823	Scottish and Irish Boards abolished and instead of two Boards, one instituted for the United Kingdom, i.e. Customs Board and Excise Board.
1849	Formation of Inland Revenue (Amalgamation of Excise, Stamps and Assessed Taxes).
1856	Transfer of Coastguard to Admiralty.
1860	Free Trade – Integration of Customs Landing and Waterguard Departments.
1891	Constitution of separate Waterguard and Landing staffs.
1909	Amalgamation of Customs and Excise under one Board.
1932	Import Duties Act.
1940	Introduction of Purchase Tax.
1952	Customs and Excise Act.
1959	Establishment of the European Free Trade Area.

GLOSSARY

Ad Valorem Duty – a duty payable on goods as a percentage of their value.

Ale – a term originally applied to beer brewed without hops but now included in the legal definition of beer.

Alien – a person who is not a British subject.

Ammbe (ame, ohm, amis) – a Cologne wine measure=one-twelfth of a fass.

Anchor (anker) (of brandy) – measure of wine and spirits ($8\frac{1}{2}$ Imp. gallons), cask holding that quantity.

Anchorage – a toll or charge for anchoring.

Appraiser – a person who exercises the calling or occupation of an appraiser or makes any appraisement or valuation chargeable by law with any stamp duty.

Aqua Vitae – the original description of unenumerated, unsweetened foreign spirits (43 Geo. III, c. 69).

Arrack – a spirit distilled from toddy, rice or palm pulp.

Assay – a test to which gold and silver plate imported for sale in the United Kingdom is subjected at an Assay Office to ensure that it is up to the standard prescribed for British plate made for sale.

Aubyage (ambiage) – measure of wine.

Aulnager – an officer appointed in 1328 to measure imported cloth.

Awm (aume) of Wine – 42 gallons (Index Vectigalium).

Baggage Sufferance – a Customs authority to land baggage reported on a ship's report.

Bait – halt for food and rest.

Ballastage – payment of ballast.

Balliage – dues paid to the Corporation of London on all goods and merchandise brought into or carried out of the City and port of London by aliens (12 C. 2, c. 4).

Barrel of Ale or Beer – fixed in 1531 at 32 gallons of ale and 36 gallons of beer (23 H. 8, c. 4); altered in 1803 to 36 gallons of ale or beer made by a common brewer in Great Britain (43 G. 3, c. 69).

Baven (bavin) – brushwood, such as was used in bakers' ovens.

Bill of Sight – a provisional entry enabling an importer to land and examine in the presence of the proper Officer goods in respect of which he has not sufficient information to enable him to pass a perfect entry in in the first instance.

Bill of Store – an entry for the re-importation into the United Kingdom of goods exported therefrom as merchandise.

Black Tea – Bohea, Congou, Souchong and Pekoe teas (7 G. 3, c. 56).

Boarding Station – a place appointed by the Commissioners of Customs and Excise at which a ship arriving from or departing from foreign countries is required to bring to for the boarding and landing of Customs Officers.

Bond – a Customs certificate that bond has been given for the exportation or shipment as stores of bonded, drawback or transhipment goods.

Bonded Warehouse – a warehouse or other place in which dutiable goods are stored pending the payment of duty. The goods are covered by the warehouse owner's bond and secured under the joint locks of the Crown and the warehouse proprietor.

Border Service – an Excise staff stationed in England along the Border between England and Scotland to collect the difference between the rate of spirit duty charged in Scotland and the higher rate payable in England and to examine the baggage of passengers entering England by road from Scotland; discontinued in 1855 when the rates of spirit duty were equalized.

Boundary Post – the Customs post on an approved route across the Land Boundary in Northern Ireland.

Breaking Bulk – the act of beginning to unlade a ship.

Brig (brigantine) – two-masted, square-rigged vessel with additional lower fore-and-aft sail.

Bumboat – a boat plying with fresh provisions for ships; scavenger ships.

Bushel (of British corn) – wheat 60, barley 50, oats 39 imperial pounds weight per bushel.

Bushel (of coal) – one Winchester bushel plus one quart of water.

Bushel (of malt) – 42 lbs. weight of malt or corn of any description or 28 lbs. of sugar.

Buss – a vessel employed in the herring industry.

Busselage – duty paid by bushel or measure.

Butt of Wine – 126 gallons (18 H. 6, c. 17).

Calling Aircraft – aircraft bound from one foreign place to another which calls at an aerodrome in the United Kingdom for any reason such as stress of weather or for stores, without loading or unloading goods or landing or embarking passengers.

Calling Ship – a ship from a foreign place which calls at a port in the United Kingdom merely for the purpose of shipping bunkers or stores and does not remain in port for more than 24 hours.

Cannabis – the dried flowering or fruiting tops of the pistillate plant known as cannabis sativa, from which the resin has not been extracted. Sometimes known as Indian Hemp, Marijuana, Ganja, etc.

Capias – writ of arrest.

Cargo Book – a book containing particulars of the cargo which the master of a coasting ship is required to keep on board for production to the Customs on request.

Carrack – a large cargo ship, a galleon.

Carving Note – a certificate used in Ships Registry stating that the tonnage and official number of a ship have been permanently and conspicuously cut in on the main beam of a ship, that the name is marked on each of the bows and that the name and port of registry are marked on the stern in the prescribed manner.

Cavendish tobacco – sweetened or flavoured tobacco.

Certificate of origin – a certificate attesting the country in which imported goods were grown, produced or manufactured.

Chaldron of Coal – 36 coal bushels (12 Anne, c. 17).

Chocolate – cocoa powder ready for use (6 & 7 W. 3, c. 7).

Coal Meter – a Customs Officer employed in measuring and weighing coal, culm and cinders and certifying the types and quantities for the imposition of the Customs duty.

Coal, Newcastle-upon-Tyne, Duty – a toll of one shilling a chaldron granted by Charles II in 1677 to the Duke of Richmond on coals shipped from Newcastle. It was known as the Richmond shilling and was purchased from the Duke of Richmond by Parliament in 1799.

Coast-bond – a bond entered into by the master of a vessel carrying cargo coastwise to ensure that the goods were not taken abroad to evade the export duties thereon.

Coasting Trade – trade by sea from one port in the United Kingdom to another (C. & E. A.).

Cocket (coquet) – an entry outwards signifying that all Customs requirements had been met by an exporter. A corruption of the Latin term *quo quietus est*.

Cocoa nuts – cocoa beans (10 G. I, c. 10).

Coffey's Still – an apparatus patented in 1832 by Aeneas Coffey, Inspector of Excise, by which spirit is produced from wash in one continuous operation instead of by successive operations in pot stills.

Colorado beetle – an insect resembling a large ladybird which feeds on the leaves and haulms of growing potatoes, completely destroying the crop.

Constructively warehoused – a Customs term to describe the technical warehousing of goods.

Contraband – prohibited traffic, smuggled goods.

Convoy Duty – a Customs Duty imposed in 1798 to cover the cost of the convoying of British ships during the war with France. It was levied on imports and exports and on ships' tonnage. It was repealed in 1801.

Cooper – a vessel or boat licensed by the Board of Trade to supply provisions and other goods, except spirits, to fishing boats in the North Sea.

Corn Bounty, Export – a Customs bounty on the exportation of corn. It was introduced in 1689 and finally ceased in 1814 (54 G. 3, c. 69).

Import – a Customs bounty on the importation of corn or flour from certain countries. It was introduced in 1795 for one year, and renewed in 1799 for two years (41 G. III, c. 10).

Cranage – payment for use of crane.

Crayer – a small vessel employed in the coasting trade (1 Eliz. I, c. 11).

Creek – a tidal inlet which is not a lawful place of importation or exportation without particular licence or sufferance from the port under which it is placed (Index Vectigalium).

Culm – anthracite coal (9 Anne, c. 6).

Custom House Agent – a person licensed by the Commissioners of Customs under bond to act as agent for the entry and clearance of ships, goods and baggage. Abolished in 1862.

Cutter – a term used to describe the eighteenth-century revenue vessels which were provided with a long bowsprit to enable them to out-sail smuggling vessels.

Dandy Note – a Customs document used in the Port of London to advise the officer at the exporting ship's side of the delivery of goods from warehouse for shipment. Derived from the Latin *dando*. Discontinued in 1876.

Debenture – a certificate for drawing back duties on goods exported.

Delle (deal) – a part or portion.

Dogger – two-masted bluff-bowed Dutch fishing boat.

Drawback – repayment of duty paid on certain goods on exportation.

Droit – a piece of wreck taken into custody by a Receiver of Wreck and the record of the receipt and disposal of such goods.

Entry, Customs – a document presented to the Customs before foreign goods are landed or discharged containing details of the goods.

Entry, Excise – a written notice by a trader of his intention to carry on a trade or business subject to Excise control.

Entry, Post – an entry supplementary to a prime entry in order to adjust an undercharge of duty.

Entry, Prime – entry for imported goods subject to Customs duty.

Farthen delles (farthing-deal) – fourth part.

Felony without clergy – sometimes expressed as 'felony without the benefit of clergy'. From early times the clergy and others were entitled to certain privileges, including exclusion from capital punishment. Offences were described as 'with clergy' or 'without clergy' and in the latter case offenders were subject to the full rigour of the law. (v. Blackstone, Comm. 4, p. 365 et seq., 6th ed., London 1774.)

Fish Duty – a Customs Duty imposed in 1660 on imported fish other than fish taken and brought in British ships. Finally repealed in 1853.

Fisheries Bounty, Herring – a Customs bounty granted in 1808 and paid to the curer on herrings caught in British fisheries and landed, cured and packed in Great Britain. Ended in 1829.

Fishes Royal – sturgeon, whales and any other large fish thrown up on the shore or caught near the coast of the United Kingdom. In practice only sturgeon, porpoises, whales and dolphin are recognized as coming within this category and are regarded as belonging to the Crown and dealt with by Receivers of Wreck.

Flatt – a shallow boat used mainly in esturial waters.

Forestalling – the payment of duty on goods in a bonded warehouse at the rate in force on the date of payment in the expectation of an increase of duty before the goods could be delivered.

4½ per cent Duty – a grant in 1663 by Barbados to Charles II in kind on the exportation of all dead commodities grown or produced in the island; repealed in 1838.

Fusee (ffusee) – obsolete light musket (Fr. *fusil*).

Gabelle – a French tax (e.g. on salt) f. med. Latin *gabella*, a tribute

Galley – a large open row-boat.

Gawger – see guager.

Gawner – possibly a person who measured liquids, from obs. gawn – gallon.

Glutman – a Customs Extraman who was employed at times of pressure of work.

Grain – corn, rice, paddy, pulse, seeds, nuts and nut kernels.

Grape Must – unfermented grape juice.

Grogging – the extraction of spirit absorbed in the wood of a cask.

Guager (gauger) – a Customs or Excise Officer engaged in measuring containers and their contents, e.g. spirits, wine and beer.

Home-made – goods manufactured or produced in the United Kingdom.

Home-trade Ship – a ship employed in trading between the United Kingdom, Channel Islands or Isle of Man and the Continent of Europe between the River Elbe and Brest.

Housellage – perhaps from housage, a fee paid for housing or storing goods.

Huffler (hufler) – person who carries provisions and refreshments to ships, a pilot.

Huss – the dogfish, the skin of which was used by fletchers. 'Husse – skynnes for fletchers . . . y dossen IVs' (Customs Book of Rates 1550 – Customs Library).

Immature Spirits – British or imported spirits which have not been warehoused for a period of at least three years.

Inch of Candle – a method of ascertaining by auction the value of goods chargeable with Customs ad valorem duty imported by the East India Company and not shown in the Book of Rates. A candle was lighted at the opening of a sale and the goods sold to the highest offer made while an inch of the candle was burning (7 G. 1, c. 21).

Inward Clearing Bill – a certificate furnished to the Master that all Customs requirements have been complied with by a vessel arriving from foreign in cargo or in ballast. The Master must present this document at the Custom House on entering a vessel outwards.

Jerque Note – in Customs' parlance, an Inward Clearing Bill.

Jerquer – a Custom official who checked the inward file of a vessel arriving from foreign with cargo. Office abolished in 1862.

Jetsam – goods thrown overboard by the owner into the sea where they sink and remain under water.

Keelage (killagium) – a toll or due payable by a ship on entering a harbour.

Kilderkin – a cask for liquids, etc.; capacity varied according to commodity.

King's Pipe – the furnace in a King's Warehouse where tobacco refuse was destroyed. Later used for the destruction of forfeited and prohibited goods such as obscene literature.

King's Warehouse – a place in a Custom House for the storage of goods.

Landing Account – a Customs account of imported goods taken at time of landing.

Lazaret – a place provided for quarantine purposes (6 G. 4, c. 78).

Legal Packages – the minimum legal size of packages in which spirits, saccharin and tobacco may be imported. These have varied but are now: spirits in cask, etc. 9 gallons, saccharin 11 lbs. tobacco (gross) 15 lbs.

Legal Quay – originally appointed by the Court of Exchequer for the landing and shipping of goods in the foreign trade. Now no longer appointed as sufferance wharves are now appointed by the Commissioners of Customs and Excise in lieu (CEA 1952).

Lestage (lastage, lastagium) – toll payable by traders attending fairs, ship's ballast.

Light Dues (or lights) – dues collected from the masters of ships by the Customs on behalf of the Board of Trade for the upkeep of lights and lighthouses.

Long Room – the public office in a Custom House. Named after the Long Room in the London Custom House built by Wren in 1671.

Mainprize – suretyship, form of bail.

Malmsey – strong sweet wine from Greece, Spain, etc.

Mediterranean Pass – a pass issued by the Customs on behalf of the Admiralty to protect British ships from attack by corsairs of the Barbary States. Discontinued in 1853 (4 G. 2, c. 18).

Merchant Stranger – a foreign or alien merchant.

Moreage (moorage) – payment for use of moorings.

Negrohead – a variety of Cavendish tobacco made in the form of a twist and packed in rolls of 6 to 8 lbs. each (26 & 27 V, c. 7).

Noon-tender – a Customs watcher employed to prevent the landing or removal of imported goods while the proper Officer was absent during the midday break or for refreshments. Abolished 1804.

Obscuration – the degree to which the hydrometer strength of spirits is reduced by the presence of colouring or sweetening matter.

Opium, prepared – opium prepared for smoking; includes dross and any other residues remaining after opium has been smoked.

Out-of-Charge Note – a Customs notice cancelling a stop-note when goods under detention are released.

Over-Entry Certificate – a certificate for repayment of duty overpaid on a prime entry.

Pavage – tolls charged on goods brought into a town for sale and applied towards the maintenance of the roads of the town.

Permit – a certificate that duty has been secured by bond or paid on dutiable goods which are being removed. It is also a request to any Officer to permit them to proceed to their destination.

Pesage – dues for weighing.

Peseur (poiseur) – a Customs weigher (derived from Anglo-Norman).

Piazzaman – a Tidesman stationed on Custom House Quay, London.

Pipe of Wine – 126 gallons (18 H. 6, c. 17).

Plantation Certificate – a certificate required under the Navigation Acts that the vessel was built and owned in the plantations and that the goods were of plantation origin.

Pontage – tolls charged on goods carried across a bridge.

Port – a harbour, space of water or coastal area in the United Kingdom appointed by Treasury Warrant as a Customs port.

Portage Allowance – a bounty paid by the Customs to masters of ships from abroad to encourage them to make a true report of their ships and cargoes (27 G. 3, c. 13).

Portage Dues – the right of the Corporation of London to levy dues and carry all merchandise between the Thames and the premises of Merchant Strangers in London (12 C. 2, c. 4).

Post Entry – a Customs entry on which an importer remedies short payments of duty on a prime entry (CEA 1952).

Poundage – Customs ad valorem duties. Term discontinued in 1707 (6 Anne, c. 48).

Pratique – a Customs pass which allows a ship arriving from abroad at a port in the United Kingdom to proceed to her berth in the port when the Officer is satisfied with the state of health on board.

Pre-Entry – procedure under which goods exported duty-free from warehouse or on drawback must be entered at the Custom House before shipment and must be produced to the Officer at the ship's side for examination and clearance before shipment.

Preference – favouring a country by admitting its products at a lower import duty, e.g. Imperial, Commonwealth Preference.

Pricking Note – a Customs form used in the Port of London in connection with the exportation of bonded and drawback goods. The note was pricked as the goods were tallied into the ship. Discontinued 1898.

Prisage – an early form of Customs toll in kind on wine imported. The wine was taken by the King's Butler according to the quantity imported. Eventually prisage was commuted into money payments called Butlerage.

Process Goods – foreign goods imported for repair or process in this country and subsequent re-exportation, and British goods exported for process abroad and subsequent re-importation.

Proof Spirits – spirit which at a temperature of 51° Fahrenheit weighs exactly twelve-thirteenths of an equal measure of distilled water.

Quarantine – the isolation of a ship, persons and goods on arrival in a port in the United Kingdom in an 'infected' state in order to prevent the introduction of plague and infectious disease. Quarantine Stations were appointed where such vessels had to remain for the quarantine period (originally forty days) and until prescribed measures had been taken.

Queen's Warehouse – see King's Warehouse.

Racking – the operation of drawing off wines and spirits from one cask or vessel into another.

Receiver of Wreck – the Collector or principal Officer of Customs of a port, who has been deputed to act as Receiver of Wreck and who is required to conduct enquiries into wreck and salvage and take into custody and dispose of all goods salved or washed ashore.

Registrar of Shipping – the Collector or principal Officer of Customs and Excise of a port which is also a registry port.

Registry Port – a port approved by the Commissioners of Customs and Excise for the registry of British ships under the Merchant Shipping Acts.

Report, Ship's – a report on a prescribed form, which the master, responsible officer or agent of a ship arriving from parts beyond the sea must make at the Custom House within 24 hours of arrival and before bulk is broken.

Riding Officers – a force of armed and mounted Customs Officers established in 1688 and stationed round the coast to prevent the outward smuggling of wool and the inward smuggling of goods which had escaped detection by Waterguard Service afloat.

Rode – wine measure of 24 aumes.

Rummage – the search of a ship by Customs and Excise Officers for dutiable or prohibited goods concealed on board.

Sailcloth Bounty – a Customs bounty of 1d. per ell granted in 1713 on the exportation of British-made sailcloth (12 Anne, c. 16).

Scavage – dues charged by the Corporation of London on merchandise brought by aliens within the precincts of the City and shown for sale. Ended in 1833.

Search Warrant – an authority to search premises granted by a Justice of the Peace on an Officer's sworn information when he knows or has reasonable grounds for suspecting that dutiable or prohibited goods are being harboured, kept or concealed.

Searcher – a Customs Officer appointed by Letters Patent in 1299, originally to control the import and export of currency and later to prevent the importation or exportation of dutiable goods without payment of duty. His duties were afterwards confined to exported goods and eventually to export documentation (12 R. 2, c. 2).

Sestornne (sestorne) – measure of 4 gallons of oil or wine.

Shallop – light open boat (Fr. *chaloupe* = sloop).

Shebeen – a house, shop, room, premises, etc. where excisable liquors are trafficked in by retail without a Justice's certificate of Excise licence.

Shipping Bill – an account on a prescribed form which an exporter of goods or stores is required to make before shipment.

Silk Bounty – a Customs bounty granted in 1722 on the exportation of British manufactures of silk; finally ceased in 1825.

Skipped on the Quay – the temporary transfer on imported goods from one package to another for the purpose of taking the tare of the import cask or package or for the purpose of repairing it.

Sloop – small one-masted fore-and-aft rigged vessel.

Smack – sloop (esp. for fishing).

Snow – a small sailing vessel resembling a brig.

Specific Duty – a Customs or Excise duty charged by reference to weight or any other measure of quantity as distinct from an ad valorem duty (q.v.).

Specification – the document prescribed as the Shipping Bill for the exportation of free goods.

Spirits Bounty – a bounty of 30s. per ton of 252 gallons granted in 1733 on the exportation of British spirits distilled from malt, barley or corn. Discontinued in 1826.

Spirits, Enumerated – brandy, rum, imitation rum and Geneva.

Stairs (stayers) – a landing stage (partic. on River Thames).

Stiffening Order – a Customs authority to load heavy goods as ballast on a vessel before the discharge of the whole of the inward cargo and before entry outwards of the ship.

Stop Note – a notice issued to an importer when goods are placed under detention by the Customs.

Stores Authority – a Customs form on which the master or owner of a foreign-bound vessel authorizes the person named to ship bonded or drawback goods for consumption on the voyage.

Stores Content – a statement signed by the master of a foreign-bound vessel or his agent, containing particulars of the bonded stores shipped or remaining on board, together with a declaration that all requirements of the Merchant Shipping Acts have been complied with.

Subsidy – a term formerly applied to Customs duties on the importation or exportation of goods.

Succades – imported confectionery and fruits preserved by sugar not otherwise distinguished by name and not related separately. The term was discontinued in 1874.

Sufferance Wharf – a place in a Customs port approved by the Commissioners of Customs and Excise for the landing and shipping of goods in the foreign trade. Abolished by Customs and Excise Act 1952 and replaced by Approved Wharfs.

Sweets – any liquor made from fruit and sugar or from fruit and sugar mixed with other material and which has undergone a process of fermentation. It includes British wines, mead etc. (FA 1901/10).

Tawer – maker of white leather.

Teller – the cashier in the Long Room of a Custom House.

Tennage – payment for use of ground.

Ton (tun) **of wine** – a cask of 252 gallons (12 C. 2, c. 4).

Tonnage Duty – a Customs duty imposed in 1694 on the tons burthen of all ships, except those in ballast, arriving in the United Kingdom from or departing to foreign parts (5 & 6 W & M, c. 20). It was varied by later Acts and finally repealed in 1825.

Towage – charge for towing a vessel.

Town Customs – dues taken on goods by a city or corporate town for the maintenance of bridges, quays, harbours etc. (12 C. 2, c. 4).

Transire – a Customs document required to be furnished to the Customs by the master of a vessel loading coastwise cargo. It contains an account of the cargo and a declaration that the Merchant Shipping Acts have been complied with. When signed by the Customs it constitutes a permit or let-pass for the cargo to go to its destination, where the transire must be produced to the Customs within 24 hours of arrival and before any cargo is unloaded.

Transit Shed – a shed in a Customs port approved by the Commissioners of Customs and Excise where foreign cargo may be landed prior to report and entry (CEA 1952).

Trinity House – the principal Lighthouse and Pilotage Authority in the United Kingdom. Dues are collected for this body by the Customs by arrangement with the Board of Trade (see Light Dues).

Tronage – a charge on goods weighed at the tron.

Tronour (troneur) – originally an official who weighed wool on the scales known as the 'tron'.

Tronum (tron) – beam for weighing.

Tuck (tuck-stick) – a rounded, pointed type of sword or spit, formerly used as a weapon and sheathed in a cane-stick, now used for spitting certain cargoes by way of examination.

Verjuice – juice drawn from sour grapes or apples unfit for wine or cider, or from sweet grapes or apples while still acid or unripe (8 Anne, c. 7).

Victualling Bill – a Customs bond which the master of an emigrant ship was required to give before clearance. One of the conditions of the bond required the master to provide each steerage passenger with a daily supply of pure water (MSA 1894). (Now obs.)

Waterside Officers – Customs Officers employed on landing, shipping and warehousing duties.

Weigher – a Customs Officer who weighed goods. In 1882 weighing was discontinued and reliance placed on Master Porters' returns.

Whale Fishery Bounty, Southern – a Customs bounty allowed in 1819 for five years on British ships equipped and clearing from a port in Great Britain for the Southern Whale Fishery (59 G. 3, c. 113).

Wherry – light shallow rowing boat.

Winchester Bushel – a round bushel with a plain and even bottom being $18\frac{1}{2}$ inches wide throughout and 8 inches deep (8 & 9 W. 3, c. 74).

Woolfells – sheepskin with the wool attached.

Wort – the liquid obtained by dissolving sugar or molasses in water or by extracting the soluble portion of malt or corn in the process of brewing (Inland Revenue Act 1880).

Writ of Assistance – a writ issued by the Court of Exchequer under which an Officer of Customs and Excise may enter and search premises for uncustomed and prohibited goods.

Yacht (yatch) – light, fast sailing ship.

INDEX